PARTY RULES?

Dilemmas of political party regulation in Australia

PARTY RULES?

Dilemmas of political party regulation in Australia

Edited by Anika Gauja
and Marian Sawer

Australian
National
University

PRESS

ANU PRESS

Published by ANU Press
The Australian National University
Acton ACT 2601, Australia
Email: anupress@anu.edu.au
This title is also available online at press.anu.edu.au

National Library of Australia Cataloguing-in-Publication entry

Title: Party rules? : dilemmas of political party regulation in
                  Australia / editors: Anika Gauja, Marian Sawer.

ISBN: 9781760460761 (paperback) 9781760460778 (ebook)

Subjects: Political parties--Australia.
                  Political parties--Law and legislation--Australia.
                  Political participation--Australia.
                  Australia--Politics and government.

Other Creators/Contributors:
                  Gauja, Anika, editor.
                  Sawer, Marian, 1946- editor.

Dewey Number: 324.2994

Contents

Figures

Tables

Abbreviations

ABC	Australian Broadcasting Corporation
ACT	Australian Capital Territory
ADI	Australian Defence Industries
AEC	Australian Electoral Commission
ALP	Australian Labor Party
AMEP	Australian Motoring Enthusiast Party
ANAO	Australian National Audit Office
APA	Australian Progressive Alliance
APPDP	Australian Political Parties for Democracy Program
AusAID	Australian Agency for International Development
CDP	Christian Democratic Party
CEDAW	Convention on the Elimination of All Forms of Discrimination against Women
COAG	Council of Australian Governments
DLP	Democratic Labor Party
FOI	freedom of information
GVTs	group voting tickets
HEMP	Help End Marijuana Prohibition Party
ICAC	Independent Commission Against Corruption
ICT	information and communication technology
IDEA	Institute for Democracy and Electoral Assistance
IDU	International Democratic Union
IFES	International Foundation for Electoral Systems
JLN	Jacqui Lambie Network
JSCEM	Joint Standing Committee on Electoral Matters

JSCER	Joint Select Committee on Electoral Reform
LC	Legislative Council
LDP	Liberal Democratic Party
LFF	Liberals for Forests
LNP	Liberal National Party
MP	Member of Parliament
NAA	National Archives of Australia
NLA	National Library of Australia
NSW	New South Wales
NT	Northern Territory
NXT	Nick Xenophon Team
OECD	Organisation for Economic Co-operation and Development
OPV	optional preferential voting
OSCE	Organization for Security and Co-operation in Europe
PAA	Parliamentary Activities Allowance
POP	partial optional preferential
PUP	Palmer United Party
SA	South Australia
SASP	Save the ADI Site Party
SBS	Special Broadcasting Service
STV	single transferable vote
TAA	Travel and Accommodation Allowance
UK	United Kingdom
UN	United Nations
US	United States

Acknowledgements

This book arose from a workshop entitled 'The Legal Regulation of Political Parties in Australia' held at the University of Sydney in June 2014. We are grateful to the Academy of the Social Sciences in Australia for funding this workshop and to all those who contributed to the discussion and presented stimulating papers. In addition to the authors in this volume, the paper-givers included Brian Costar, Stewart Jackson, Ron Levy, Narelle Miragliotta, Zim Nwokora and Nicholas Reece. One feature of the workshop was a roundtable on party law in practice, cosponsored by the Electoral Regulation Research Network. The roundtable had the following participants: Colin Barry (former NSW Electoral Commissioner), Gareth Ward MLA (Chair, Joint Standing Committee on Electoral Matters, NSW Parliament), Luke Foley (then Leader of the Opposition in the NSW Legislative Council) and Geoff Ash (Registered Officer, Greens NSW).

The book has benefited significantly from the attention of the Social Sciences Editorial Board of the ANU Press and the excellent reviewer reports it commissioned. It has also benefited from numerous helpful suggestions by Graeme Orr and from the work of Emily Tinker at ANU Press.

Contributors

Anika Gauja

Anika Gauja is an Associate Professor in the Department of Government and International Relations, University of Sydney. Her research focuses on party regulation, reform and partisan engagement. She is the author of *Political Parties and Elections* (2010), *The Politics of Party Policy* (2013) and *Party Reform* (2017).

Sarah John

Sarah John is the Research Director at FairVote, a non-partisan non-profit organisation based in Washington, DC, that researches the impact of electoral systems in the United States. She received her PhD and LL.B at Flinders University and has published on electoral reform and electoral systems.

Norm Kelly

Norm Kelly is author of *Directions in Australian Electoral Reform* (2012) and has published articles and book chapters on electoral law. He has worked in the international democracy development field for the past decade, including in party development, candidate training, election observing, research and writing, working throughout Melanesia, Australia and Afghanistan. Previously, Norm was a Member of Parliament in Western Australia. He is now based in Wellington, New Zealand.

Yvonne Murphy

Yvonne Murphy is a PhD candidate and part-time lecturer in the Department of Government at University College Cork. Her research interests lie in parliamentary and electoral politics, with particular emphasis on institutional design and influences on the decision-making of politicians. Prior to her career in academic research, Yvonne worked as a political advisor and researcher in the Irish Parliament. She is currently co-editor of the *Irish Political Studies: Data Yearbook*.

Graeme Orr

Graeme Orr is Professor of Law at the University of Queensland, specialising in the law of politics and, until recently, was the international editor of the *Election Law Journal*. His books include *The Law of Politics: Elections, Parties and Money in Australia* (2010), *Ritual and Rhythm in Electoral Systems* (2015) and *The Law of Deliberative Democracy* (with Ron Levy, 2016).

Jennifer Rayner

Jennifer Rayner received her PhD in Political Science from The Australian National University in 2015. She is the author of *Generation Less: How Australia is Cheating the Young* (2016) and currently serves as an adviser to the Australian Labor Party in the Federal Parliament.

Marian Sawer

Marian Sawer, AO, FASSA, is ANU Public Policy Fellow and Emeritus Professor in the School of Politics and International Relations at The Australian National University. She led the Democratic Audit of Australia 2002–2008 and was responsible for a wide range of audit publications, including the co-authored *Australia: The State of Democracy* (2009). She is co-editor of the *International Political Science Review*.

1

Party rules: Promises and pitfalls

Marian Sawer and Anika Gauja

Australian politics has been synonymous with party politics for much of its history. Today the strong party identifications of the past have been breaking down and a multiplicity of minor parties and microparties has been winning seats in our parliaments, from the Australian Sex Party to the Motoring Enthusiast Party. For some commentators, this represents a welcome injection of diversity into the Australian political system. For others, however, these parties create confusion among voters and frustrate the mandates of 'democratically' elected legislators. Is this a problem and, if so, what should be done about it? What is or what should be the role of political parties in representative democracy and do we need stronger party regulation to underpin it? Why is there always a gap between what we seek from regulation and what is actually achieved?

In this introduction, we set out the main regulatory challenges concerning the place and function of political parties in Australian representative democracy. We begin by examining the constitutional recognition of political parties in a comparative context and trace the increasing international trend to legislative regulation associated with the role of political parties as 'public utilities'. We then turn to recent developments in party regulation in Australia and the existing literature, highlighting the most significant aspects of the debate over party regulation. We see this as occurring in four main areas: the provision of public funding, the regulation and restriction of private funding, limits on expenditure and the extent to which the law should regulate the 'internal' activities of political parties—most notably, candidate selection.

Political parties and recognition of their place in democracy

While political parties have played a central role in our political system since the late nineteenth century, legal recognition was slow to emerge. Parties were absent from the Australian Constitution, as they were from other written constitutions of the time. When the American Constitution was drafted, for example, the influence of 'faction' was seen as distorting the formation of the popular will or the disinterested judgement that legislators should bring to issues. Later, many women's suffrage activists were highly critical of the 'corrupt system of party politics', while others despaired of an 'iron law of oligarchy', which meant that imperatives of organisational survival inevitably took priority over the original goals of social democratic parties.[1]

After World War II, much of this original suspicion of political parties began to evaporate. In the wake of fascism and again in the Cold War context, the existence of effective party competition became central to the very definition of democracy, at least in the West. The term 'democracy' was to be reserved for political systems where a plurality of political parties was able to contest elections. The freedom to join (or form) a political party of choice became emblematic of the freedom of association.

It might seem odd, then, that political parties were not mentioned in either the Universal Declaration of Human Rights (1948) or the International Covenant on Civil and Political Rights (1966), which eventually flowed from it. This silence most likely stems from the impossibility of reaching consensus on the relationship between democracy and party pluralism at a time when there were many

---

1   Leading Australian suffragists like Rose Scott urged enfranchised women not to become 'camp followers to a corrupt system of party politics'. Betty Searle (1988) *Silk and Calico: Class, Gender and the Vote*, Sydney: Hale & Iremonger, p. 29. The concept of the iron law of oligarchy was put forward by Robert Michels, based on observation of the German Social Democratic Party. Robert Michels (1911) *Political Parties: A Sociological Study of the Oligarchical Tendencies of Modern Democracy*, Leiden: Klinkhardt.

'people's democracies' that were both one-party states and members of the United Nations (UN).[2] Nonetheless, by 1996, the Human Rights Committee, the treaty body for the covenant, issued General Comment 25, which concluded that the freedom to join or form political parties was an essential adjunct to the right to participate in periodic elections, something covered by the covenant.[3] In the twenty-first century, guarantees of party pluralism have been included in a number of regional treaties and charters on democratic governance.

Ideally, in addition to being a vehicle for electoral competition, political parties also provide a meaningful space for political engagement and democratic deliberation and for policy development and agenda setting. These are all crucial democratic functions and, hence, we might expect parties to receive some recognition in democratic constitutions. However, while elections have been subject to detailed regulation, this has not generally been true of political parties until recent decades. Political parties began receiving constitutional recognition in postwar Europe, first in Iceland, Austria, Italy and Germany, but then more generally and in countries emerging from authoritarian and communist rule (see Table 1.1).

For example, in Germany, the 1949 Basic Law speaks of the role of political parties in 'the formation of the political will of the people'.

The constitutions of a number of European countries, including Germany, Spain and Portugal, go beyond recognition of the external role of political parties and also require parties to be democratic in their internal structure and operation. In Australia, however, political parties were generally regarded as private entities until the 1980s. They are still mentioned in the Australian Constitution only in relation to the filling of casual Senate vacancies (a successful amendment in 1977), rather than in relation to their broader democratic functions, in contrast with many European constitutions.

---

2   Gregory H. Fox (1992) 'The Right to Political Participation in International Law', *Yale Journal of International Law* 17: 556–8.

3   Human Rights Committee (HRC) (1996) 'General Comment 25(57)', General Comments under article 40, paragraph 4, of the International Covenant on Civil and Political Rights, Adopted by the Committee at its 1510th meeting, UN Doc. CCPR/C/21/Rev.1/Add.7, available at: www1.umn.edu/humanrts/gencomm/hrcom25.htm.

Table 1.1 Date of first acknowledgement of political parties in national constitutions: Europe

Country	Year
Iceland	1944
Austria	1945
Italy	1947
Germany	1949
France	1958
Cyprus	1960
Malta	1964
Sweden	1974
Greece	1975
Portugal	1976
Spain	1978
Norway	1984
Hungary	1989
Croatia, Serbia, Bulgaria	1990
Latvia, Romania, Slovenia	1991
Czech Republic, Estonia, Lithuania, Poland	1992
Ukraine	1996
Finland, Switzerland	1999
Luxembourg	2008

Source: Party Law in Postwar Europe, available at: partylaw.leidenuniv.nl.

Nonetheless, Australia has not been immune to the global trend towards increased regulation of political parties in the late twentieth and early twenty-first centuries. As Ingrid van Biezen notes, parties have increasingly been treated as public utilities to be regulated for the achievement of public purposes rather than as private associations based on voluntary principles.[4] These public purposes include legislative recruitment, electoral competition and the formation of government and opposition, as well as developing policy agendas and mobilising the vote.

---

4   Ingrid van Biezen (2004) 'Political Parties as Public Utilities', *Party Politics* 10: 701–22.

It is notable that this increased regulation and the treatment of parties as public utilities have coincided with changes in the relationship between parties and democracy throughout the world, including decreases in strong party identification and increases in non-party movements and campaigns as sites of political activity. Throughout the Western world, party membership has been dropping since at least the 1980s and, in Australia in 2006, the Australian Bureau of Statistics estimated the number of those belonging to political parties to be as low as 1 per cent of the adult population. Trust in political parties is also at an all-time low, with a recent survey showing only 3 per cent of Australian respondents had a lot of trust in political parties.[5] The general disaffection with political parties is reflected in the way those registering new ones sometimes try to avoid the word—for example, the Nick Xenophon Team, the Jacqui Lambie Network or the longer-established Australian Greens or Pauline Hanson's One Nation.

Australians are much more likely to engage in other forms of political participation such as attending a protest march, meeting or rally (5.2 per cent), signing a petition (22.5 per cent) or engaging in political consumerism (24.6 per cent).[6] In 2016, the campaigning organisation GetUp! claimed membership of over 1 million—far more than all the political parties combined.[7] It should be noted, however, that its definition of membership is less rigorous than that of Australian political parties, which in turn are notoriously secretive about their membership numbers.

Not only has the role of political parties as a venue for political participation been shrinking, it also has been problematised by influential strands of democratic theory: rational choice and deliberative democracy theory. Rational choice or the economic theory of democracy suggests that what is central to democracy is party competition in the electoral marketplace. Internal party democracy gets in the way of efficient competition for votes as it gives too great

---

5   Andrew Markus (2014) *Mapping Social Cohesion: The Scanlon Foundation Surveys 2014*, Melbourne: Monash University, p. 32, available at: scanlonfoundation.org.au/wp-content/uploads/2014/10/2014-Mapping-Social-Cohesion-Report.pdf.
6   Australian Bureau of Statistics (ABS) (2007) *General Social Survey: Summary Results Australia 2006*, ABS Cat. No. 4159.0, Canberra: ABS. In contrast with the 2006 party membership figure, in the 1960s some 4 per cent of the adult population were estimated to be party members.
7   See getup.org.au/about.

a role to party members in the selection of candidates and development of policy.[8] As part of the case for the 'inefficiency' of internal party democracy, it is also suggested that the preferences of party activists are likely to be more 'extreme' than those of party voters.[9]

In contrast, deliberative democracy theorists argue that it is the quality of public debate rather than the efficiency of party competition that is the central democratic value. They argue that political parties may detract from rather than contribute to deliberative quality, which includes respectful consideration of evidence and argument and a consequent readiness to change position. This quality may be absent from the way in which parties contribute to parliamentary debate, which may be highly adversarial and disrespectful. It may also be absent from the way in which policy is made inside parties, which may marginalise party members and owe more to leadership decisions informed by non-deliberative market research. While advocates of deliberative democracy often seem to give up on political parties or parliaments as venues for democratic deliberation, it has been argued that political parties could beneficially conduct internal deliberative polls when developing party manifestos.[10]

Expanding party regulation: Public funding and candidate selection

Regardless of these competing democratic arguments, if parties are becoming less central to the political life of ordinary citizens, why has this coincided with their increased regulation? Some would argue that this is not a coincidence.[11] Political parties have falling memberships but election campaigning has become increasingly expensive, particularly when it involves paid advertising in the electronic media. In many democracies, political parties now receive public subsidies to assist them in their campaigning and this funding requires regulation.

---

8   Joseph Schumpeter (1943) *Capitalism, Socialism and Democracy*, London: Allen & Unwin.
9   John May (1973) 'Opinion Structure of Political Parties: The Special Law of Curvilinearity', *Political Studies* 21: 135–51.
10   Jan Teorell (1999) 'A Deliberative Defence of Intra-party Democracy', *Party Politics* 5 (3): 373.
11   Richard Katz and Peter Mair (1995) 'Changing Models of Party Organization and Party Democracy: The Emergence of the Cartel Party', *Party Politics* 1(1): 5–28; Ingrid van Biezen and Peter Kopecky (2007) 'The State and the Parties: Public Funding, Public Regulation and Rent-seeking in Contemporary Democracies', *Party Politics* 13(2): 235–54.

While such public funding is a relatively recent phenomenon, beginning with countries such as Costa Rica, Uruguay and Germany in the 1950s, today public funding exists in three-quarters of liberal democracies.[12] Public funding is seen as important in enabling political pluralism, on the one hand, and in shielding parties from private interests, on the other; so important that it is now enshrined in the constitutions of a number of developing democracies. It also reflects the understanding that while many people now prefer to engage in political activity outside the party system, political parties are still central to the operation of representative democracy.

Public funding is usually distributed by criteria such as votes at the previous election or, for new parties, community support reflected in opinion polls or the size of party membership. It is intended to ensure that all parties have the means to communicate their message, regardless of how deep the pockets of their supporters are. A less sympathetic viewpoint would be that incumbent political parties shore up their advantage through the appropriation of state resources of various kinds, even including, in Australia, the use of parliamentary allowances for party databases, including annual amounts for software and training. For some, the rent-seeking relationship of political parties with the state is of greater concern than the reliance of political parties on private money, although both might be detrimental to the public good. There is now a large literature developing the concept of the 'cartel party'—addressed by several authors in this book—which compensates for a declining membership by drawing increasingly on state resources, in collusion with other parties that form part of the cartel.[13] Others have contested the explanatory power of the cartel thesis, at least in relation to Australia, suggesting that the major parties simply act as rational utility maximisers rather than actively colluding against those outside the cartel.[14]

With public funding comes increased regulation of political finance, intended to make more transparent or decrease reliance on private sources of funding and to ensure a more level playing field for electoral competition. As Graeme Orr nicely puts it in this volume,

---

12   Van Biezen and Kopecky, 'The State and the Parties'.

13   See Richard Katz and Peter Mair (2009) 'The Cartel Party Thesis: A Restatement', *Perspectives on Politics* 7(4): 753–66.

14   Murray Goot (2006) 'The Party System, One Nation and the Cartelisation Thesis', in Ian Marsh (ed.) *Political Parties in Transition?*, Sydney: The Federation Press.

the three rationales of public funding and political finance regulation are: 'resourcing parties, dampening demand for private money and political equality'. Concern over the playing field for electoral competition also leads to the introduction of party registration, linked to access to the ballot paper. The requirements for party registration (for example, number of members, number of candidates being fielded, ability to pay the registration fee) can effectively control the number of political parties able to contest elections. While political scientists have often explored the relationship between the nature of the electoral system and the nature of the party system (majoritarian systems encouraging two-party systems; proportional representation encouraging multiparty systems), less attention has been given to the effects of party regulation on party systems. One recent exception has looked at the relationship between the nature of party regulation, party formation costs and the number of political parties in Latin America.[15]

As pointed out by Graeme Orr, party registration is not the only limitation on access to the ballot paper; there are also candidate deposits, which may add up to a large amount if the party is running in all seats.[16] They are, however, refundable if the candidate wins more than a certain proportion of the vote—usually 4 per cent in Australia. The combined effects of party registration requirements and nomination deposits may ensure that the ballot paper is not so crowded as to preclude informed and effective choice by voters, but it may also suit the interests of established parties in discouraging challengers.

As political parties are the gatekeepers of political office, the way they select their candidates and leaders has become an issue of public interest. There has been much public dissatisfaction expressed over the fact that a prime minister can be overthrown through a 'palace coup' in his/her parliamentary party without reference to a broader constituency such as the party membership. This has led to reforms in how party leaders

---

15   Gerardo Scherlis (2014) 'Political Legitimacy, Fragmentation and the Rise of Party-formation Costs in Contemporary Latin America', *International Political Science Review* 35(3): 307–23.
16   Graeme Orr (2015) 'The Law Governing Australian Political Parties: Regulating the Golems?', in Narelle Miragliotta, Anika Gauja and Rodney Smith (eds) *Contemporary Australian Political Party Organisations*, Melbourne: Monash University Publishing.

are selected in a number of countries.[17] Increasingly, as the practices of political parties become subject to judicial review, there is a concern that the internal processes of parties should themselves be democratic and that rules be applied fairly and openly.

Another development has been the perception since at least the 1990s that the under-representation of women in legislatures constitutes a democratic deficit. This understanding of political equality has been reinforced by interpretation of the UN Convention on the Elimination of All Forms of Discrimination against Women (CEDAW) and by the Beijing Platform for Action, as well as by the many international organisations providing democracy assistance and assessment. Since political parties are recognised to be the gatekeepers of legislative recruitment, commitments to increase the legislative representation of women (and, in some cases, of ethnic minorities) have brought in their train increased regulation of candidate selection by parties. Since 1991, when Argentina led the way with legislation for electoral gender quotas, some 60 countries have followed suit, including most recently Greece and Ireland.[18] Globally, some 28 countries also have ethnic quotas for elections for their national parliament, which can involve mechanisms such as special districts as well as requiring ethnic quotas to be applied to party lists or reserving seats for ethnic parties.[19] Sanctions applied to political parties for failing to meet the quota may include rejection of the party list or loss of election funding. The introduction of quotas has proved more difficult in countries with single-member electoral systems, where quotas may appear to strengthen the hand of party leaders at the expense of local democracy in parties.

While political science has been enriched by classic studies of political parties for more than a century, party regulation is a much more recent subject of inquiry. It is, however, now attracting the attention of political scientists. They have created cross-national databases on

---

17 William P. Cross and André Blais (2012) *Politics at the Centre: The Selection and Removal of Party Leaders in the Anglo Parliamentary Democracies*, Oxford: Oxford University Press.
18 Another 34 countries have reserved seats and, in an additional 37 countries, at least one parliamentary party has a candidate quota in its rules. See International Institute for Democracy and Electoral Assistance (International IDEA) (2013) *Atlas of Electoral Gender Quotas*, Stockholm: International IDEA.
19 Karen Bird (2014) 'Ethnic Quotas and Ethnic Representation Worldwide', *International Political Science Review* 35 (1): 12–26.

party regulation as well as studies of its character and consequences for the nature of party competition, political legitimacy and parties' relationship with the state.[20] Working with the International Institute for Democracy and Electoral Assistance (IDEA), political scientists have also created a database on electoral quotas worldwide (quotaproject.org), showing whether these are legislated or simply adopted into party rules. A new political science literature examines the effectiveness of different types of quota regulation in ensuring political parties become a more inclusive source of legislative recruitment, whether this involves gender or ethnic quotas.[21] In addition to the massive literature on electoral quotas, there is also an emerging interest in other aspects of party regulation and how it can be used to promote gender equity and inclusiveness.[22] For example, public funding of parties may include fiscal incentives for the promotion of gender equality within the party organisation. In Finland, 12 per cent of the annual subsidy provided to parliamentary parties must be used to fund their women's wings.[23] This interest in party regulation to promote gender equality extends beyond formal regulation to the realm of 'soft regulation'.

In general, 'soft regulation' or standard setting is an increasingly significant aspect of any form of regulation and complements more 'traditional' sources such as constitutions and legislative instruments.[24]

---

20   Ingrid van Biezen (2012) 'State Intervention in Party Politics: The Public Funding and Regulation of Political Parties', in Keith Ewing, Jacob Rowbottom and Joo-Cheong Tham (eds) *The Funding of Political Parties: Where Now?*, Abingdon: Routledge; Ekaterina Rashkova and Ingrid van Biezen (eds) (2014) 'A Contested Legitimacy: The Paradoxes of Legal Regulation of Political Parties, *International Political Science Review* 35(3)(Special Issue).

21   For important examples of the quota literature, see Mona Lena Krook (2009) *Quotas for Women in Politics: Gender and Candidate Selection Reform Worldwide*, New York: Oxford University Press; Susan Franceschet, Mona Lena Krook and Jennifer Piscopo (eds) (2012) *The Impact of Gender Quotas*, New York: Oxford University Press; Mona Lena Krook and Pär Zetterberg (eds) (2014) 'Electoral Quotas and Political Representation: Comparative Perspectives', *International Political Science Review* 35(1)(Special Issue).

22   Sarah Childs (2013) 'In the Absence of Electoral Sex Quotas: Regulating Political Parties for Women's Representation', *Representation* 49(4): 401–23.

23   Mona Lena Krook and Pippa Norris (2014) 'Beyond Quotas: Strategies to Promote Gender Equality in Elected Office', *Political Studies* 62: 16, doi:10.1111/1467-9248.12116; Julie Ballington and Muriel Kahane (2014) 'Women in Politics: Financing for Gender Equality', in *Funding of Political Parties and Election Campaigns: A Handbook on Political Finance*, Stockholm: International IDEA, available at: idea.int/publications/.

24   See Orly Lobel (2004) 'The Renew Deal: The Fall of Regulation and the Rise of Governance in Contemporary Legal Thought', *Minnesota Law Review* 89: 343–470; Bengt Jacobsson and Kerstin Sahlin-Andersson (2006) 'Dynamics of Soft Regulation', in Marie Laure Djelic and Kerstin Sahlin-Andersson (eds) *Transnational Governance: Institutional Dynamics of Regulation*, New York: Cambridge University Press.

While soft regulation can take place at all levels of governance, particularly in relation to environmental issues, the issuing of standards of democratic performance takes place primarily at the international and regional levels. Such soft regulation encompasses the norm-generating activities of transnational bodies, including the international standards, codes of conduct, handbooks and guidelines they produce and disseminate. It does not involve the direct use of sanctions on the part of the norm-generating body. However, it has been described as 'inquisitive regulation', because member states are often required to report to or 'open up' to others so they can examine and critically judge what they are doing.[25] Peer pressure is generated through rankings that are regularly produced and released to the media and through sharing of best practice. Such rankings may also be of considerable interest to international donors.

There are many examples of international bodies developing standards and rankings relating to different areas of democratic governance and election management, including Transparency International, the Inter-Parliamentary Union and the International Foundation for Electoral Systems (IFES). For a good example of such soft regulation in the area of party regulation see the *Guidelines on Political Party Regulation* drawn up by the Venice Commission of the Council of Europe and the Office for Democratic Institutions and Human Rights of the Organization for Security and Co-operation in Europe (OSCE). The 10 underlying principles set out in these guidelines include equal treatment, meaning that party regulation should treat all parties equally and prevent incumbent political parties or candidates from using state resources to obtain unfair advantage. Equal treatment also covers temporary special measures for women and members of minorities subject to past discrimination.[26]

Other international bodies providing support for democracy building also include elements in their standard-setting to promote gender equality. For example, the guidelines on party finance drawn up by the International IDEA include recommendations to close the gender funding gap in elections through conditional public funding, while

---

25   Bengt Jacobsson (2006) 'Regulated Regulators: Global Trends of State Transformation', in Djelic and Sahlin-Andersson, *Transnational Governance*, p. 207.
26   Organization for Security and Co-operation in Europe (OSCE) (2011) *Guidelines on Political Party Regulation*, Warsaw: OSCE Office for Democracy and Human Rights, available at: osce.org/odihr/77812?download=true.

the Organisation for Economic Co-operation and Development (OECD) also cites as good practice that public funding of political parties be conditional on gender ratios.[27] In addition to the international bodies concerned with democratic governance, the international associations of political parties may also engage in soft regulation and the promotion of gender equality norms. For example, the Socialist International, which brings together some 150 social-democratic, socialist and labour parties, has helped promote the use of electoral gender quotas; the adoption of these in party rules is one of the factors taken into consideration when new parties apply to join. Soft regulation is not as highly developed in the field of party regulation, however, as it is in the field of electoral governance.

Party regulation in Australia

As noted above, the first and only reference to political parties in the Australian Constitution—which requires the filling of casual Senate vacancies by a representative of the same party—was inserted in 1977. Although the Labor Party was emerging as Australia's first 'mass' political party in the 1890s, at the time of the Constitutional Conventions, there was (and still is) no mention of the democratic functions of political parties. This silence over the role of political parties in representative democracy is also true of Australia's State constitutions; in 2000, the Queensland Constitutional Review Commission felt the issue of constitutional recognition of political parties was one 'whose time has not yet come in Australia'.[28]

While the time for constitutional recognition has not yet come in Australia, the statutory recognition of political parties was also very slow in coming. A pioneering 1914 analysis of Australian political systems noted the way in which the political centre of gravity was

---

27   Organisation for Economic Co-operation and Development (OECD) (2016) *2015 Recommendation of the Council on Gender Equality in Public Life*, Paris: OECD, available at: oecd.org/gov/2015-oecd-recommendation-of-the-council-on-gender-equality-in-public-life-9789264252820-en.htm.

28   Constitutional Review Commission's 2000 Issues Paper, quoted in Scott Bennett (2002) *Australia's Political Parties: More Regulation?*, Parliamentary Library Research Paper 21, Canberra: Parliament of Australia.

moving from parliament to parties but proved completely faulty in its prediction that regulation could be expected to follow 'at any rate so as to regulate the process of selecting candidates'.[29]

In the 1970s, there was still considerable resistance even to statutory recognition of political parties, let alone regulation of internal processes. The efforts of the Whitlam Government to legislate for party names to appear on ballot papers were rejected in the Senate, leaving it up to the Tasmanian Labor Government to become the first to introduce party registration.[30] Systems of party registration were finally introduced in most jurisdictions in the 1980s, although Queensland and Western Australia waited until 1992 and 2000, respectively, and the Northern Territory until 2004 (see Table 1.2).

While generally the introduction of party registration meant the appearance of party names on ballot papers, this was not the case in New South Wales (NSW). The anomaly occurred because the State Labor Government introduced party registration for the purpose of public funding through a separate Act, with an authority separate from the NSW Electoral Commission. So although parties were registered in NSW from 1981 for the purpose of public funding, their names did not appear on ballot papers even after parties were allowed to lodge group tickets for the Legislative Council. It was not until 1991 that NSW voters were finally allowed to see the party affiliations of the candidates on their ballot papers. Even then it was only because the Australian Democrats held the balance of power in the Legislative Council and the government needed their support for a planned redistribution.[31] While the Australian Democrats were generally at the forefront of electoral reform, small parties with relatively few people to hand out how-to-vote cards outside the polling place also had a natural interest in getting their party's name on to the ballot paper.

29   W. Harrison Moore (1914) 'Political Systems of Australia', in G. H. Knibbs (ed.) *Federal Handbook*, [prepared in connection with the 84th meeting of the British Association for the Advancement of Science, Australia, August 2014], Melbourne: Government Printer, p. 564.

30   At first, the party registration requirements in Tasmania were only a slight expansion of the previous requirements for candidate nominations, requiring statutory declarations from seven members for a party to be registered (Part viiia, *1974 Tasmanian Electoral Act*). Nonetheless, party names did appear on Tasmanian ballot papers in the 1976 and 1979 State elections, contrary to accepted wisdom that they first appeared on Commonwealth ballot papers.

31   Antony Green (2001) 'The 1991 Election', in Michael Hogan and David Clune (eds) *The People's Choice: Electoral Politics in 20th Century NSW. Volume 3*, Sydney: Parliament of New South Wales and University of Sydney, p. 316. Party registration was transferred from the *Election Funding, Expenditure and Disclosures Act* to the *Parliamentary Electorates and Elections Act* ahead of the 1991 election (information from Antony Green, 22 March 2016).

Table 1.2 Date of initial introduction of party regulation by jurisdiction

	C'wealth	NSW	Victoria	Queensland	WA	SA	Tasmania	ACT	NT
Registration	1983	1981	1984	1992	2000	1985	1974	1988	2004
Organisational requirements#	–	–	–	2002	–	–	–	–	–
Public funding	1983	1981	2002	1994	2006	2015##	–	1994	–
Donation disclosure	1983	1981	–‡	1994	1992	2015##	–	1994	2004
Donation caps (beyond caps for anonymous donations)	–	2010##	–	2011–14	–	–	–	2012–15	–
Foreign/interstate or sectoral donation ban	–	2009	2002	2011	–	–	–	2012–15	–
Candidate spending caps	1902–80	2010	1903–2002	2011–14	1907–79	1893–1969; 2015##	1907–85; 1985–(LC only)	2012	–
Party spending caps	–	2010	–	2011–14	–	2015##	–	2012	–

Requirements beyond a written constitution, minimum number of members or sitting Member of Parliament (MP).

Legislated 2013; expenditure caps apply only to those who opt in for public funding.

‡ Political parties registered federally required to lodge copy of federal disclosure returns with Victorian Electoral Commission.

‡‡ A cap on in-kind contributions was introduced in 2008.

Source: Authors' research.

All jurisdictions now require the registration of party names and abbreviations for ballot-labelling purposes, and the registration of party emblems has been introduced in 2016 under changes to the *Commonwealth Electoral Act*.[32] The growth of party regulation was sometimes controversial and was opposed in principle by the conservative parties (see Sarah John, this volume).

The first book on Australian electoral and party regulation did not appear until some 50 years after the first books on the party system.[33] This delayed scholarly interest to some extent reflects the delayed transition of Australian political parties from organisations regarded as essentially private and beyond the purview of the law to organisations from which public accountability was demanded. During this period, scholarship on regulation was blossoming, but regulatory theory was yet to be applied to the regulation of political parties.[34]

This began to change with a major Australian project on electoral and party regulation. Graeme Orr, Bryan Mercurio and George Williams brought together political scientists and legal scholars as well as electoral administrators to work on this project and received funding from both the Australian Research Council (ARC) and the Electoral Council of Australia, the body that represents Commonwealth, State and Territory electoral commissions. This tradition of bringing together different disciplines and linking scholars and practitioners has continued under the auspices of both the Democratic Audit of Australia and the Electoral Regulation and Research Network, and is maintained in the current volume. Research has been published on the impact and politics of electoral and party laws[35] and, in particular, the

---

32   After the 2013 federal election, in which the Liberal Democratic Party won a Senate seat in NSW, the Liberal Party of Australia recommended that party symbols be included on the ballot paper to reduce potential confusion caused by similar party names.

33   Louise Overacker (1952) *The Australian Party System*, New Haven, Conn.: Yale University Press; James Jupp (1964) *Australian Party Politics*, Melbourne: Melbourne University Press. Then, some 50 years later, Graeme Orr, Bryan Mercurio and George Williams (eds) (2003) *Realising Democracy: Electoral Law in Australia*, Sydney: The Federation Press. Two years earlier some material on partisanship and party regulation had appeared in a collection on Australian innovations in electoral governance: Marian Sawer (ed.) (2001) *Elections Full, Free and Fair*, Sydney: The Federation Press.

34   The development of the massive interdisciplinary research program on regulation (RegNet) housed at The Australian National University is best described in Peter Drahos (ed.)(forthcoming) *Regulatory Theory: Foundations and Applications*, Canberra: ANU Press.

35   See, for example, Anika Gauja (2010) *Political Parties and Elections: Legislating for Representative Democracy*, Farnham: Ashgate; Graeme Orr (2010) *The Law of Politics: Elections, Parties and Money in Australia*, Sydney: The Federation Press.

vexed issue of campaign finance regulation.[36] These studies have been complemented by assessments of how well party law and electoral legislation serve Australian democracy,[37] and to what extent they meet international standards of good practice.[38] A central problem in achieving the latter aim is that regulatory reform is dependent on parties in government, which are likely to be more concerned with their own interests than with international best practice. As Anika Gauja argues in this volume, courts have often stepped in to enforce democratic freedoms and protect the rights of party members where legislators are reluctant to do so.

Australia has a long tradition of innovation in the area of electoral administration, but also a tradition of partisan distrust of proposals for change. Since 2013, there has been a plethora of activity at both federal and State levels, and there is more to come. The 2013 federal election provided a vivid example of the unintended consequences for the party system of a previous electoral reform, paving the way for further reforms. In 1983 the single transferable vote (STV) system for the Senate was reformed to minimise the informal vote resulting from the requirement for voters to mark preferences for all candidates on the ballot paper. Instead, voters were now given the choice either to mark their preferences for all candidates 'below the line' or to vote for just one party 'above the line' and have preferences distributed in accordance with registered tickets. Most voters chose the easier above-the-line option; its flaws became highly visible only when, for tactical reasons, parties began distributing preferences to unlike rather than like parties, in ways disapproved of by their voters.[39]

In 2013 there was a surge in the number of parties contesting the election, with 54 different parties registered (see Norm Kelly, this volume). There were so many party and candidate names that font

---

36   See, for example, Sally Young and Joo-Cheong Tham (2006) *Political Finance in Australia: A Skewed and Secret System*, Report No. 7, Melbourne: Democratic Audit of Australia, available at: apo.org.au/research/political-finance-australia-skewed-and-secret-system-0; Joo-Cheong Tham (2010) *Money and Politics: The Democracy We Can't Afford*, Sydney: UNSW Press.

37   Marian Sawer, Norman Abjorensen and Phil Larkin (2009) *Australia: The State of Democracy*, Sydney: The Federation Press.

38   Norm Kelly (2012) *Directions in Australian Electoral Reform: Professionalism and Partisanship in Electoral Management*, Canberra: ANU E Press, available at: press.anu.edu.au/titles/directions-in-australian-electoral-reform/.

39   Marian Sawer (2005) 'Above-the-Line Voting in Australia: How Democratic?', *Representation* 41(4): 286–90.

sizes on Senate ballot papers had to be reduced (to 7.6 points in NSW) and voters in the larger States had to be issued with plastic magnifying sheets with which to read them. Most of these new parties had little community support but had names designed to attract some groups of voters, such as the Smokers Rights Party. Some of these microparties, which crowded the Senate ballot papers for the different States and Territories, were successful in gaining Senate seats thanks to elaborate arrangements for 'preference harvesting', which had been pioneered at the State level. A Victorian candidate of the Motoring Enthusiast Party gained election to the Senate with only 0.5 per cent of first-preference votes, building a quota (14.3 per cent) through deals that gave him preferences from the group voting tickets (GVTs) registered by 23 other parties. Only 3.5 per cent of the votes that elected him were votes for his own party, with the rest coming via the voting tickets of unrelated parties, ranging from the Shooters and Fishers to the Animal Justice Party.

This kind of outcome prompted much adverse comment, and the major parties were particularly critical of the existing regulation that had allowed this proliferation of parties. The regular inquiry into the conduct of the federal election by the Joint Standing Committee on Electoral Matters (JSCEM) recommended that the number of members needed to register a party be increased and that the system of GVTs registered by parties be replaced with an optional preferential system whereby voters could express their preference for one or more parties above the line or for a minimum number of candidates below the line. While these recommendations would clearly reduce the number of parties contesting federal elections, they were justified in terms of the need to redress a system where 'electors felt their votes had been devalued by preference deals and that they had been disenfranchised by being forced to prefer unpreferred candidates'.[40] In the event, group tickets were abolished and voters were instead given the option of listing their own six preferences for parties above the line or for 12 candidates below the line.[41] Nothing was done to tighten up the requirements for party registration and individual parliamentarians could still register a party without any membership

40   Joint Standing Committee on Electoral Matters (JSCEM) (2014) *Interim Report on the Inquiry into the Conduct of the 2013 Federal Election: Senate Voting Practices*, Canberra: Parliament of Australia, p. 2.
41   *Commonwealth Electoral Amendment Act 2016*.

requirement. Others continued to register microparties for advocacy purposes, including the Australian Equality Party (Marriage), the Renewable Energy Party and The Arts Party, needing only to satisfy the requirement for 500 members and a written constitution (and the $500 registration fee).

It should be noted that the proliferation of political parties is an international phenomenon. While lax requirements for party registration are a contributing factor, another is that social media has made party formation much less labour intensive:

> In Spain over 400 parties have been created since 2010. Parties are proliferating. Why? Largely because social media have made it so much easier, less time consuming and less expensive to create them.[42]

Those signing an electronic petition, for example, can be signed up to a related party and this is a common way to build party membership lists.

At the State level, some recent regulatory reforms have had a much shorter lifespan than the Senate GVTs. This is particularly evident in the area of political finance, where partisan differences may mean that reforms enacted by a government of one political persuasion will be changed or undone by a subsequent government. This has recently occurred following the change of government in NSW (2011) and Queensland (2012), while in the Australian Capital Territory (ACT), with a change of heart rather than a change of government, a minority Labor government undid the cap on donations introduced by a previous minority Labor government.

Important debates in Australian party regulation

In general terms, the debate surrounding the legal regulation of political parties has focused on two main areas: political finance and matters of party organisation, such as candidate selection. Political finance in turn involves two interrelated, but distinct, elements: the private funding of political parties and the provision of state

---

42   Simon Tormey (2015) *The End of Representative Politics*, Cambridge: Polity, p. 101.

resources. Each of these elements encompasses a range of regulatory and public policy responses, such as disclosure regimes, restrictions on donations and expenditure and the provision of direct and indirect public subsidies (election funding, tax breaks, free broadcasting time, parliamentary resources and funding of party think tanks or policy development), and sits within a broader debate about the regulation of political finance more generally—including the regulation of lobbying and government advertising. As political parties receive public money and are seen to perform public functions (see the discussion of parties as 'public utilities' earlier in this chapter), regulatory responses creep into the party organisation, touching on functions such as candidate selection.

The public funding of political parties

To begin with the provision of state resources to political parties: in general, there is a hierarchy of enjoyment of such resources. Incumbent governments may benefit from the use of government advertising for partisan purposes and from strategic distribution of discretionary grants programs ('pork-barrelling'), while all incumbent parliamentarians benefit from resources such as electorate staff[43] and parliamentary allowances (see Yvonne Murphy, this volume). Supposedly, such staff and allowances are provided for parliamentary and electorate purposes, with any other effects, such as promoting the re-election of the parliamentarian, only incidental. However, the use of allowances for electoral campaigning purposes has been normalised and has long been recognised as unfairly advantaging incumbents.[44] In 2010 an independent review of parliamentary entitlements, appointed by the Rudd Government, recommended that access to printing and communications entitlements be removed from the date of the announcement of a federal election, along with travelling allowance for parliamentary staff working at party campaign headquarters. The review committee noted the latter created the 'not unreasonable perception that staff were engaged in party political

---

43   In the Federal Parliament, under the *Members of Parliament (Staff) Act 1984*, both Senators and Members of the House of Representatives are provided with four full-time electorate officer positions, supposedly to help them carry out their parliamentary and electorate responsibilities but not party work.

44   Nicole Bolleyer and Anika Gauja (2015) 'The Limits of Regulation: Indirect Party Access to State Resources in Australia and the United Kingdom', *Governance: An International Journal of Policy, Administration and Institutions* 28(3): 321–40.

business at public expense'. An Australian National Audit Office (ANAO) report noted that as of May 2015 no progress had been made in implementing these recommendations.[45]

Because the use of such parliamentary resources for partisan purposes has been normalised, only the most egregious cases receive media headlines. One such case was the expenses claim lodged by the Speaker of the House of Representatives for hiring a helicopter, supposedly for official purposes, but in fact to make a spectacular entrance at a party fundraiser.[46] The helicopter scandal (known colloquially as 'Choppergate') prompted another review of the parliamentary entitlements system. This was more circumspect than the unimplemented 2010 review, recommending that the more publicly acceptable term 'work expenses' be used instead of 'entitlements', but that 'electioneering' should not be explicitly excluded from the definition of 'parliamentary business'. As the review noted, this differed from the practice in New Zealand and other comparable countries, which do not allow parliamentary allowances to be used for electioneering.[47]

In another development, party policy launches are now often delayed because of the convention that parliamentary allowances can continue to cover travel costs and staff overtime until the campaign launch. Because of the introduction of pre-poll voting, this means that voting can begin before the party's election manifesto has been released; access to campaign resources is clearly being prioritised here over the timeliness of the formal policy launch. Candidates of parties not represented in parliament have the least access to public resources. They may be entitled to some free broadcast time on Australian Broadcasting Corporation (ABC) and Special Broadcasting Service

45   See Recommendations 14, 15 and 16 of the Committee for the Review of Parliamentary Entitlements (2010) *Review of Parliamentary Entitlements Committee Report*, Canberra: Department of Finance, available at: finance.gov.au/publications/review-of-parliamentary-entitlements-committee-report/; Australian National Audit Office (ANAO) (2014–15) *Administration of Travel Entitlements Provided to Parliamentarians*, ANAO Report No. 42, Canberra: ANAO, available at: anao.gov.au/~/media/Files/Audit%20Reports/2014%202015/Report%2042/AuditReport_2014-2015_42.pdf.
46   Paul Osborne (2015) 'Speaker Bronwyn Bishop Charters Chopper for Liberal Event', *Sydney Morning Herald*, 15 July, available at: smh.com.au/federal-politics/political-news/speaker-bronwyn-bishop-charters-chopper-for-liberal-event-20150715-gid93n.html.
47   John Conde and David Tune (2016) *An Independent Parliamentary Entitlements System: Review*, Canberra: Department of Finance, pp. 58–60, available at: finance.gov.au/sites/default/files/independent-parliamentary-entitlements-system-review-feb-2016.pdf.

(SBS) radio and television, depending on the number of seats they are contesting and their level of demonstrated public support. After the election, they will be eligible for public funding providing a threshold level of electoral support has been achieved—usually 4 per cent of the vote.

In Australia, as elsewhere, major parties may behave in a cartel-like fashion to deny public resources to minor parties or Independents (see Graeme Orr and Jennifer Rayner, this volume). One interesting example is the exclusion of minor parties from televised leaders' debates during election campaigns. Minor parliamentary parties such as The Greens (or indeed The Nationals) are routinely excluded from such leaders' debates in Australia, unlike in comparable democracies such as the United Kingdom and Canada, and the matter has not been taken to court as it has in New Zealand.

On the other hand, minor parties holding the balance of power have been able to ensure that they share in some of the resources and funding programs introduced to benefit the major parties. One example is the allocation of parliamentary party status and the additional resources and staffing that flow from such status, which is separate from the resources provided to government and the official opposition. Since the 1980s, there has been a threshold of five members or Senators for recognition as a parliamentary party in the Federal Parliament, and there are similar thresholds in other parliaments. At the federal level, The Greens have enjoyed parliamentary party status since 2007. Flowing from this status, The Greens' leader in the Senate has a range of entitlements including, in 2015, some charter air transport and 13 additional staff members above the normal entitlement to electorate staff.

There is as yet no formal regulation in any of the Australian jurisdictions regarding parliamentary party status, which by no means flows automatically from party registration for electoral purposes. So far, minor parties holding the balance of power (or serving as a coalition partner) have been the ones that have helped determine the minimum number of seats required for eligibility.[48] Minor parties and Independents have also helped ensure additional staff for

48   Norm Kelly (2004) *Determining Parliamentary Parties: A Real Status Symbol*, Democratic Audit of Australia Discussion Paper, December, Melbourne: Australian Policy Online, available at: apo.org.au/files/Resource/kellypaper.pdf.

crossbenchers who do not satisfy these requirements. The argument is that additional personal staff are required in the absence of the resources flowing from parliamentary party status (although another way to provide assistance with parliamentary functions such as legislative review would be to ensure adequate resources for the parliamentary library and research service).[49]

Although the rationale for the additional resources may be the need for Independents or parties with only one or two members to cover all portfolio areas, the resources provided are more closely tied to balance-of-power status. For example, when four Independents and the sole Greens member of the House of Representatives held the balance of power after the 2010 federal election, they were allocated two additional staff each, whereas Senator Xenophon (Independent) and Senator Madigan (Democratic Labour Party) were allocated only one additional staff member. After the 2013 federal election, this differential allocation between House of Representatives and Senate crossbenchers was reversed. Independents and members of minor parties in the House of Representatives no longer held the balance of power and their additional staff entitlement was reduced to one. On the other hand, the eight minor party and Independent Senators holding the balance of power from 2014 were allocated two additional staff. In 2016, thanks to the government having only a majority of one, Independents and minor party representatives in the House of Representatives regained a potential balance of power role. As a result, their additional staff entitlements were lifted to three, in line with an increase for the crossbench Senators (see Table 1.3). Questions about the regulation or otherwise of parliamentary party status are explored in this volume by Yvonne Murphy.

Table 1.3 Additional resources allocated for minor parties*
and Independents in the federal parliament

	House of Representatives	Senate
2010	2 additional staff	1 additional staff
2013	1 additional staff	2 additional staff
2016	3 additional staff	3 additional staff

* Parties falling below the threshold for parliamentary party status (five members).

---

49   Sawer et al., *Australia*, p. 131.

Other examples of minor parties joining the cartel include the funding of party think tanks through grants-in-aid administered by the Finance portfolio: first the Australian Democrats and then The Greens succeeded in joining this funding stream. Today the Labor and Liberal parties receive almost $250,000 each year for the Chifley and Menzies research centres, respectively, while The Nationals and The Greens receive around $90,000 each for the Page Research Centre and the Green Institute, respectively. All the think tanks (apart from the Page Research Centre) disclose their grants-in-aid funding on their websites and their deductible gift recipient status is also declared, which makes gifts to the party think tanks tax deductible.

Another example of a funding stream that a minor party sharing the balance of power has been able to join is the Australian Political Parties for Democracy Program (APPDP), introduced by the Howard Government. This provides $1 million each to the Liberal and Labor parties every year and, since 2011, has also provided $200,000 a year to The Greens. This particular program has received headlines from time to time, which may be worth exploring from the point of view of how cartel-like behaviour contributes to the general image of politicians and political parties 'rorting the system'.[50]

The APPDP has the objective of 'strengthening democracy internationally', but only 50 per cent of the funds need to be spent in developing democracies; the rest can be spent on other kinds of international activities. In 2009 the program was subject to an adverse ANAO report that found insufficient accountability in its administration by the Department of Finance, with no requirement that the money be spent on the purposes outlined in funding applications. While, as mentioned, only 50 per cent of the funds are required to be spent as overseas development assistance, the ANAO findings still raised significant questions: only 44 per cent of the funds had been spent on countries targeted for development assistance, while 36 per cent had been spent on activities in countries such as the United

---

50   'Rorting the system' is an Australasian expression particularly applied to the misappropriation of public resources.

Kingdom and the United States or on non–country-specific activities, and 20 per cent had gone to administrative costs and subscriptions to international organisations.[51]

As a result of the damning ANAO report, the program was shifted to the then Australian Agency for International Development (AusAID) in 2009. This shift resulted in more adverse attention when it was noticed in the Australian Electoral Commission's disclosure returns from political parties that money was being spent out of the aid budget to pay party officials to travel business class to meetings of fraternal political parties, particularly in North America and Europe, or to meetings of their corresponding international bodies such as the Socialist International or the International Democratic Union (IDU). The IDU is the international body for over 80 centre-right parties, such as the US Republicans and the British and Canadian conservative parties.[52] It has regular meetings at which member parties can exchange ideas and election-winning techniques and strategies. Australian Prime Minister John Howard was elected IDU chairman in 2002 and served in this capacity for 12 years, making the introduction of the APPDP by his government extremely timely.

On the other side of politics, the disclosure returns revealed that the AusAID funds were being used to pay part of a senior Labor Party official's salary.[53] The ensuing outcry resulted in an announcement that the program had been scrapped, as part of the Abbott Government's cuts to the aid budget.[54] However, interestingly, 'negotiations' led to the program being reinstated, back in the Finance portfolio. It was difficult to locate in the 2015–16 Portfolio Budget Statement, as there was no spending line corresponding to the program and only a reference that key deliverables relating to parliamentary entitlements included 'management and support of the approved Political Party Programmes

---

51   Australian National Audit Office (ANAO) (2009) *The Administration of Grants under the Australian Political Parties for Democracy Program*, ANAO Report No. 18, Canberra: ANAO, available at: anao.gov.au/Publications/Audit-Reports/2008-2009/The-Administration-of-Grants-under-the-Australian-Political-Parties-for-Democracy-Program.
52   The IDU calls itself 'The Freedom International' in an implied contrast with the Socialist International. See idu.org.
53   Pamela Williams (2013) 'How AusAID Pays for Labor Official's Salary', *Australian Financial Review*, 15 November; Michael Smith (2014) 'Australian Political Parties for Democracy Program: Ripe for Rorting', *News.com*, 5 February.
54   Noel Towell (2014) 'Political Parties Stripped of Millions in Junket Cash', *Sydney Morning Herald*, 14 February.

within the entitlement framework' (p. 56). So although the program is a 'key deliverable', expenditure on it is buried under 'administered expenses' and, according to a Department of Finance spokeswoman, '[d]etails about the expenditure under the current APPDP deeds are not available publicly'.[55]

Subsequently, *The Australian* newspaper gained APPDP program plans and acquittals through a freedom of information (FOI) request, finding that the Labor and Liberal parties were still spending the money on maintaining relations with overseas counterparts in the developed world and with the Socialist International and IDU, respectively. The Labor Party spent only about 43 per cent of its funding in developing countries while the Liberal Party did not even specify the proportion spent on this purpose.[56]

Paradoxically, one of the aims of the program is to 'encourage representative, accountable, inclusive and transparent democratic political parties', making the secrecy surrounding its funding and the need to use FOI to find out anything about it particularly reprehensible. Only The Greens admit to its existence on their Global Greens website and outline how it has been used. Clearly, it is not in the interests of the cartel parties to draw attention to misuse of this funding source or indeed to its existence at all, and this contributes to the lack of accountability. Occasional publicity about the program seems entirely accidental, as when an undercover conservative campaign group in the United States caught on camera Young Labor members trying to remove Donald Trump campaign signs. They were recorded boasting about Australian taxpayer funds paying for their work on the Bernie Sanders campaign for the Democratic presidential nomination.[57]

---

55   An inquiry to the officer in the Department of Finance managing the program was passed to the Department's Media Centre, which responded on 7 December 2015 that: 'the budgeted expenses for APPDP fall under administered expenses. It is incorporated in the ordinary annual services (Appropriation Bill No. 1) budget. Details about the expenditure under the current APPDP deeds are not available publicly.'
56   Sean Parnell (2016) 'Labor Envoys Campaigned for Sanders', *The Australian*, 15 April, p. 8.
57   Tom McIlroy (2016), 'ALP Operatives on Taxpayer-Funded US Trip Caught up in Hidden Camera Campaign Sting', *Sydney Morning Herald*, 28 February, available at: smh.com.au/federal-politics/political-news/alp-operatives-on-taxpayerfunded-us-trip-caught-up-in-hidden-camera-campaign-sting-20160227-gn5chk.html.

This secrecy can be compared with the relative transparency of an overseas equivalent, despite some similar issues. In Germany, the Federal Ministry for Economic Cooperation and Development has a webpage about the funding of the German political foundations.[58] There are six of them, and government funding is divided between them in proportion to their affiliated party's representation in the Bundestag. Funded to provide democracy assistance domestically as well as overseas, including promotion of civil society (and trade unions, in the case of the Friedrich Ebert Foundation), they are credited with an important role in the transitions to democracy in Spain and Portugal and later in Chile.[59]

In the 1980s there were scandals over the German foundation funds being used as a source of domestic party finance and there was a Constitutional Court challenge by the Greens. As a result, the system was strengthened and the Greens were incorporated into it. Theoretically, the foundations are not allowed to pass funding on to their affiliated party. In practice, relations between parties and foundations have been labelled 'symbiotic', and both Transparency International and Germany's Taxpayers' Alliance have continued to press for regular governmental reports on the funding of political foundations. A renewed suit challenging the foundations' 'hidden party financing' was filed in 2012 by the small Ecological-Democratic Party (ÖDP), but was rejected in August 2015 by the Constitutional Court.[60]

Regulating the private funding of party politics

Moving on from secretive public funding to the regulation of private funding of political parties: broadly speaking, the regulation of political finance in Australia was extremely laissez faire for about 30 years from 1980, when previous campaign expenditure limits were dropped at the federal level. Public funding was introduced in

---

58   Federal Ministry for Economic Cooperation and Development (2010–16) *Bilateral Development Cooperation: Players—Political Foundations*, Bonn: Ministry for Economic Cooperation and Development, available at: bmz.de/en/what_we_do/approaches/bilateral_development_cooperation/players/political_foundations/index.html.
59   Michael Pinto-Duschinsky (1991) 'Foreign Political Aid: The German Political Foundations and their US Counterparts', *International Affairs* 67(1): 3363; Ann L. Phillips (1999) 'Exporting Democracy: German Political Foundations in Central-East Europe', *Democratization* 6(2): 70–98.
60   Information kindly provided by Rainer Eisfeld.

this period in most jurisdictions but did not (as intended) lessen the reliance of the major political parties on private donations to meet rising campaign costs. There were no controls on the source or size of donations and few limits to expenditure or restrictions on electronic advertising (apart from a three-day ban immediately before and on election day). The only regulatory requirements were for disclosure of donations, but these were very lax, with many loopholes and with scheduled disclosure usually coming long after the electoral event for which the donations were made. A notable example of this was the disclosure some 16 months after the 2004 federal election of a million-dollar campaign donation made to the Liberal Party by Lord Ashcroft, a citizen of the United Kingdom and Belize. This donation also highlighted the lack of restrictions concerning foreign donations despite this being a standard item in international guidelines relating to political finance regulation.[61]

While the level of disclosure thresholds and the timing/frequency of reporting have been the subjects of reform efforts in Australia, other important issues are the types of activities covered (or not) by disclosure provisions. As discussed in the concluding chapter of this volume, there is a highly lucrative source of revenue for the major parties in selling 'access' to senior party figures through charging for places at dinners and receptions that they attend. This source of revenue can be legally hidden; if it involves purchasing access and influence for companies, it can be classified as a legitimate 'business expense' rather than as a donation.[62] Apart from the electoral integrity principles involved, which led the former Queensland Labor Premier Anna Bligh to forbid her ministers attending such events, the selling of access also offends against equality principles by giving those with corporate money at their disposal privileged access to ministers. At the same time, reliance on external sources of funding potentially diminishes the role of party members.

A series of scandals at State and local government levels concerning political donations by property developers led to a tightening of political finance regulation in NSW and Queensland, starting with

---

61   See, for example, Elin Falguera, Samuel Johns and Magnus Ohman (eds) (2014) *Funding of Political Parties and Election Campaigns: A Handbook on Political Finance*, Stockholm: International IDEA, available at: idea.int/publications/funding-of-political-parties-and-election-campaigns/.

62   Sawer et al., *Australia*, p. 141.

a ban on developer donations in NSW in 2009 and leading on to the introduction of caps on donations and expenditure in both States. A new Coalition government in NSW then attempted to go further and copy the Canadian example of banning corporate or union donations and restricting the right to make political donations to individuals on the electoral roll. This legislation was extremely controversial because it prevented the payment of union affiliation fees to the Labor Party, thus interfering with the party's internal structure, which had been in place for more than 100 years. It was subsequently disallowed by the High Court on the grounds that it was in breach of the freedom of political communication.[63] The case illustrated how different democratic principles—including those of a level playing field, electoral integrity, freedom of political expression and freedom of association—may be jostling with each other and with partisan interests in electoral regulation.

Meanwhile, political finance reform at the federal level had stalled, despite commitments by the Rudd Government and by Senator John Faulkner as Special Minister of State. This was not only because of partisan opposition but also because of opposition from State Labor Party branches that had been successful in raising large business donations. Scandals concerning money and politics have been more difficult to keep on the front page at the federal level and less effective in promoting reform. While federalism has lived up to its reputation for nourishing policy experimentation at the subnational level, the 'enervation' at the federal level[64] has ensured the continuation of loopholes in political finance regimes. For example, NSW property developers, who are prohibited from making political donations in that State, were able to make large donations to the federally registered Free Enterprise Foundation, which was then able to pass the money on to the NSW Liberal Party. The NSW Premier, frustrated with the way his relatively tight political finance regime was undermined by the lax federal system, called in 2015 for a national political finance regime to be put on the agenda of the Council of Australian Governments

---

63   *Unions NSW v New South Wales* (2013), HCA 58 (18 December). The subsequent McCloy case and its implications for campaign finance regulation are discussed in Chapter 8.
64   Graeme Orr (2016) 'Party Finance Law in Australia: Innovation and Enervation', *Election Law Journal* 15(1): 58–70.

(COAG).[65] Matters came to a head in 2016 when the NSW Electoral Commission withheld $4.4 million in public funding from the Liberal Party on the grounds of inadequate disclosure of private funding channelled through the Free Enterprise Foundation.[66]

The trade-off for increased regulation of private donations is often increased public funding. Indeed, NSW has even looked at banning all private donations and having full public funding of election campaigns (one of the terms of reference for the inquiry set up by the NSW Premier in 2014). The ACT has introduced relatively strict regulation of expenditure, in effect from the beginning of 2016: $40,000 per candidate, third party or associated entity in the election year. The ACT has also introduced the highest rate of public funding in Australia: $8 per vote in 2016 for parties or a candidate gaining at least 4 per cent of the vote. Both major parties argued this higher rate of funding would help reduce their reliance on donations, but paradoxically at the same time removed the previous cap on such donations.[67] As The Greens commented, '[t]he big parties are taking with one hand, and then taking with the other'.[68]

It is clear that lax regulation and recurrent scandals over both private and public funding have contributed to the low esteem in which Australian political parties are held. Transparency International's 2013 Global Corruption Barometer found that, in Australia, 58 per cent of respondents felt that political parties were corrupt or extremely corrupt. Political parties were seen as more corrupt than any other political institution except the media.[69]

---

65 Sean Nicholls (2015) 'Political Leaders Urged to Unite in Overhaul of Political Donations Law', *Sydney Morning Herald*, 28 July, available at: smh.com.au/nsw/mike-baird-to-take-national-donations-reform-to-coag-20150727-ggvks0.html.
66 Sarah Gerathy (2016) 'Liberal Party used "Charitable" Free Enterprise Foundation to Disguise Donations: NSW Electoral Commission', *ABC News*, 24 March, available at: abc.net.au/news/2016-03-24/nsw-liberal-party-disguised-political-donations-free-enterprise/7272446.
67 For the changes to campaign finance laws in the ACT, see elections.act.gov.au/news/2015/changes_to_act_legislative_assembly_campaign_finance_laws_commence_today_3_march_2015.
68 'Cap on Donations Removed by New ACT Laws', *ABC News*, 20 February 2015, available at: abc.net.au/news/2015-02-20/cap-on-political-donations-removed-by-new-act-laws/6153332.
69 Transparency International (2013) *Global Corruption Barometer*, Berlin: Transparency International, available at: transparency.org/gcb2013/country/?country=Australia.

Regulatory bodies

Australian electoral management bodies have a well-deserved reputation for professionalism and partisan neutrality. However, this creates the paradox that these bodies are usually reluctant to take on the kind of regulatory functions that might mire them in partisan controversy, such as regulation of truth in political advertising or oversight of party preselections. For example, the Australian Electoral Commission (AEC) has stated it wants no role in internal party management matters, preferring that the party or the courts resolve internal conflicts.[70] One recent exception has been the NSW Electoral Commission, which has strongly supported a recommendation that governance and accountability obligations be introduced for political parties and that the Electoral Commission be the regulator of these.[71]

In general, regulatory responsibility for political parties is divided between government departments and bodies with statutory independence, such as electoral commissions. Electoral commissions generally have responsibility for administering election funding of political parties and disclosure regimes relating to gifts and donations. They are also responsible for party registration and auditing compliance with statutory requirements and are, in turn, answerable to a minister and to legislative oversight bodies such as the JSCEM at the federal level. On the other hand, it will be a finance department, directly under the control of the government of the day, that will have responsibility for regulating other forms of party funding such as the incumbency benefits outlined above and, at the federal level, the funding of party think tanks and international activities. Public servants are required to be responsive to the government of the day, and the Opposition and minor parties benefiting from public resources will have little incentive to push too hard on accountability and transparency issues. The Australian regulatory regime governing access to public resources (other than those allocated by electoral

70   Australian Electoral Commission (AEC) (2005) *Funding and Disclosure Report Election 2004*, Canberra: AEC, pp. 40–1.
71   NSW Electoral Commission (2015) 'The Final Report of the Expert Panel: Political Donations and the Government's Response', Submission to the Joint Standing Committee on Electoral Matters, 16 October, p. 14.

commissions) is perhaps at odds with international standards, such as those set out in the Venice *Guidelines on Political Party Regulation*, requiring equal treatment of parties contesting elections.

Expanding regulatory reach: Candidate selection

Periodic media attention to 'branch stacking' and other dubious practices within parties affecting their role in legislative recruitment has led to calls for electoral management bodies such as the AEC to supervise party preselection ballots. However, as we have seen, the AEC is reluctant to take on this regulatory function for fear of being embroiled in partisan controversy.[72] The same reluctance would apply in Queensland, where Electoral Commission Queensland was given audit powers in 2002 in relation to preselection ballots. This occurred under changes to the *Electoral Act*, requiring, for the first time in Australia, that party constitutions contain provision for preselections 'satisfying the general principles of free and democratic elections'. It is notable that as of 2015 no other jurisdiction has followed this path of legislating for internal party democracy.

However, it seems that the political parties have successfully fended off any statutory interference with their internal organisational practices only to find themselves coming under the purview of the courts regarding the extent to which their own rules are followed. In 1999 a South Australian Labor parliamentarian successfully sued his party in the Supreme Court for failing to follow its own rules in relation to membership. This illustrated the extent to which Australian courts had departed from the old view concerning the 'private' nature of political parties and were prepared to enforce party rules. Nonetheless, there remain doubts over the extent to which courts should be involved in the internal affairs of political parties and whether this is the best way to ensure procedural fairness.[73]

The issue of judicial versus legislative regulation is further explored in this volume by Anika Gauja.

---

72 Joint Standing Committee on Electoral Matters (JSCEM) (2001) *User Friendly, Not Abuser Friendly: Report of the Inquiry into the Integrity of the Electoral Roll*, Canberra: Parliament of Australia, available at: aph.gov.au/Parliamentary_Business/Committees/House_of_Representatives_Committees?url=em/elecroll/report.htm.
73 For an overview of cases from 1993 onwards in which courts have accepted jurisdiction over intraparty disputes, see Orr, *The Law of Politics*, Ch. 6.

Apart from concerns over malpractice there are also concerns over how appropriate it is to have legislators effectively selected by a shrinking party membership that is not even seen to be particularly representative of party voters. This has led to various reform proposals for 'community preselections', giving members of the community a role in preselection, and The Nationals and the Labor Party have experimented with these. Yet these participatory reforms raise several important regulatory issues, including how such intraparty contests should be funded, the extent to which they should be subject to external oversight, as well as the rights of non-members to challenge party processes and decisions.[74]

Turning from the question of more open methods of candidate selection to more inclusive candidate selection, it is notable that candidate selection falls outside the protection of antidiscrimination legislation in Australia.[75] Political parties are also exempt from statutory equal opportunity requirements of any kind, unlike in many comparable countries. For example, Ireland, a country from which Australia inherited a number of its political traditions, in 2012 opted to follow other European countries in legislating an electoral gender quota. Under the Irish legislation, political parties would lose 50 per cent of their public funding at the 2016 general election unless women (and men) made up at least 30 per cent of their candidates.

Australia has not followed suit in terms of legislation, although the Australian Labor Party did introduce an effective party quota in 1994. Labor's quota has led to a significant increase in the proportion of women in its parliamentary parties: by May 2015, women had become 43 per cent of Labor parliamentarians around Australia. This has not led, however, to the phenomenon of 'contagion of women candidates' identified in Europe, when adoption of quotas by one party leads to other parties significantly increasing their number of women candidates, whether by quotas or otherwise.[76] On the contrary,

---

74   Graeme Orr (2011) 'Party Primaries for Candidate Selection? Right Question, Wrong Answer', *University of New South Wales Law Journal* 34(3): 964–83.

75   See Graeme Orr (2011) 'Legal Conceptions of Political Parties through the Lens of Anti-Discrimination Law', in Joo-Cheong Tham, Brian Costar and Graeme Orr (eds) *Electoral Democracy: Australian Prospects*, Melbourne: Melbourne University Press.

76   Richard E. Matland and Donley T. Studlar (1996) 'The Contagion of Women Candidates in Single-Member District and Proportional Representation Electoral Systems: Canada and Norway', *Journal of Politics* 58(3): 707–33.

the Liberal Party, for example, has had a falling number of women preselected for winnable federal seats. What follows is that parties of the right have relatively few women in their parliamentary parties on whom to draw for executive office.[77] In turn, this means that, generally, when governments change, so does the gender composition of cabinets, despite Australia's international commitments to achieving gender balance in public decision-making. The soft regulation deriving from these treaty commitments has so far failed to reach across the political spectrum, but is unlikely to be exchanged for hard regulation linking public funding to gender diversity of candidates.

These recent developments illustrate both the opportunities and the potential pitfalls for legislators, who, in adopting regulatory reforms, have to take into account the interests of their own parties, the limits posed by public opinion (for example, concerning the public funding of political parties or gender quotas) as well as the normative objectives sought through party regulation. As we have seen, these objectives include protection against bribery and corruption; support for healthy party competition; reduction in reliance on large private donors, or at least an increase in transparency; encouragement of internal democracy and fair and open processes; and promotion of more inclusive candidate selection. The overall goal has been to ensure that political parties are able to fulfil their democratic functions in a way that sustains public confidence in the political system and results in greater citizen engagement in politics. There is a gap, however, between what we seek from party regulation and what is actually achieved. This volume will investigate why this gap exists in the particular case of Australia, although the findings will have resonance elsewhere.

---

77   In September 2016, women constituted 42 per cent of Labor parliamentarians around Australia but only 23 per cent of Liberal parliamentarians. See 'Composition of Australian Parliaments by Party and Gender, as at 16 September 2016', Canberra: Australian Parliamentary Library, available at: www.aph.gov.au/About_Parliament/Parliamentary_ Departments/Parliamentary_Library/pubs/rp/rp1617/Quick_Guides/PartyGender.

Structure of the book

As noted above, research has begun to be published on party regulation in Australia, particularly relating to campaign finance, but this is the first full-length book to deal with all aspects of party regulation. Chapter 1 has introduced comparative perspectives on the legal and constitutional recognition of political parties and their place in democracy. It covers debates on key issues around party regulation and recent developments in Australia, which illustrate some of the main areas of contention.

The second chapter, by Sarah John, introduces a case study of the failure of the Whitlam Government to achieve party registration in the 1970s. The case study is used to illustrate more general patterns in the progression from party recognition to party regulation and the partisan and other dynamics involved. Of particular interest are the kinds of recompense offered for increased levels of regulation—not only party labels on ballot papers but also tax benefits and public funding.

In the third chapter, Norm Kelly opens up the subject of the effects of party regulation on the party system, including the number and diversity of political parties and the opportunities they provide for political participation. He explores the world of the microparties and finds that many provide little opportunity for members to be involved in party activities and may actually discourage such participation.

Yvonne Murphy (Chapter 4) then introduces a topic that has generally been neglected: the question of the regulation of parliamentary party status and the access to resources brought by such status. She shows how the requirements for such status vary across Australia and how those unable to meet the requirements have to rely on negotiation with government. While microparties argue their need for additional resources to cover all portfolio areas, allocation depends on bargaining power rather than need.

Political finance scholarship has been particularly strong in Australia and the next two chapters provide major new contributions to this scholarship. Graeme Orr (Chapter 5) provides a case study of Queensland to illustrate the political dynamics of regulation in this area and to probe the relevance or otherwise of the cartel thesis. Jennifer

Rayner (Chapter 6) questions whether campaign finance regulation can achieve one of its stated aims: the achievement of a level playing field for electoral competition. Her rich empirical evidence and two case studies, from NSW and Queensland, suggest that donation and spending caps may not achieve this aim, although there are other arguments to support them.

In Chapter 7, Anika Gauja grapples with the puzzle of why political parties have been able to defend their claim to 'autonomy' in relation to their internal organisation so successfully, particularly compared with other voluntary organisations in receipt of public funding. She finds that while the parties of government have had a vested interest in fending off regulation of their internal workings, courts have become more willing to require that principles of natural justice and democratic governance apply in intraparty decision-making.

The conclusion (Chapter 8) to the book summarises the evidence as to why the gap exists between international standards and Australian practice or between the regulatory treatment of political parties as privileged political actors and their failure to attract members or adhere to principles of democratic governance. It recommends that to close the gap between aspirations and achievement, reform of party regulation should be a more inclusive process, involving political actors beyond parties already in parliament. In the end, however, the democratic principles involved remain contested (for example, internal democracy versus effective party competition) and their implementation will always need further scrutiny.

2

Resisting legal recognition and regulation: Australian parties as rational actors?

Sarah John

For at least a century, political parties in the older democracies like Australia, Canada, New Zealand, the United Kingdom and the United States have been at the centre of politics. This centrality is not without its tensions, one of which is that political parties have never fitted neatly into the private/public dichotomy that has so long obsessed Western political and legal thought.[1] Initially, political parties were private associations and were unknown to the law. But, at the same time, they fulfilled very public purposes: organising the legislature and linking citizens and the state. Today, by contrast, political parties are legally recognised and, to varying degrees, regulated, supported and entrenched as quasi-state agencies—even though they retain some of the legal characteristics of private associations.[2] The unusual path parties have taken, transitioning from private organisations with

---

1   Jeff Weintraub and Krishan Kumar (1997) *Public and Private in Thought and Practice: Perspectives on a Grand Dichotomy*, Chicago: University of Chicago Press; Nathaniel Persily and Bruce E. Cain (2000) 'The Legal Status of Political Parties: A Reassessment of Competing Paradigms', *Columbia Law Review* 100(3): 775–812; Anika Gauja (2013) *Political Parties and Elections: Legislating for Representative Democracy*, Farnham: Ashgate, pp. 12–14.
2   Also see Gauja, Chapter 7, this volume.

public functions to 'a special type of public utility'[3] with persistent private rights, raises questions about the role of parties in shaping their own destiny. These questions are especially salient because political parties themselves controlled the very legislatures that effected their transition from private to public.

In the context of Australian efforts to legally recognise political parties in the early 1970s, this chapter presents two competing models of the role that parties might have played in shaping their transition from private to public: one of deliberate, rational choice; and the other of a more bumbling, or 'muddling', character. The chapter explores these two models, focusing on two key areas: 1) the processes of research, learning and reasoning within political parties as they broached electoral innovations that would lead to their recognition or regulation; and 2) the motivations of political parties in promoting and opposing proposals that included legal recognition.

In 1974, the Australian Labor Party (ALP), led by Prime Minister Gough Whitlam, introduced two Bills that, if passed, would have legally recognised Australian political parties for the first time.[4] The first, the Electoral Laws Amendment Bill 1974, would have created a register of political parties enabling the listing of party names on ballot papers next to their nominated candidates; the second, the Electoral (Disclosure of Funds) Bill 1974, would have regulated the finances of political parties without providing any recompense for the restrictions imposed on party fundraising practices. While the 1974 Bills never became law, the internal deliberations of political parties about them are revealing.

Utilising newly available and never before analysed archival documents, this chapter shows that partisan interests were central to the decisions eventually made by political parties regarding the printing of party affiliations on the ballot. However, those interests were not actively pursued on their discovery and, when serious efforts were made to advance those interests, the parties discovered that they were open to multiple, often contradictory, interpretations that evolved during the reform process.

---

3   Ingrid van Biezen (2008) 'State Intervention in Party Politics: The Public Funding and Regulation of Political Parties', *European Review* 16(3): 351.
4   Apart from the brief recognition of parties to assist military voting in World War I, under the *Commonwealth Electoral (War-Time) Act 1917.*

Electoral and financial interests in reform had been tentatively identified in both major Australian political parties—the ALP and the Liberal Party—in the 1950s, decades before any serious efforts were made to fully explore the implications of legislating for the printing of party affiliation on the ballot paper. Once moves were made towards legislating, the Liberal Party discovered its electoral and financial interests clashed and that both were subservient to the goals of control and autonomy. In the ALP, the advancement of party interests was displaced as the primary goal of reform by a desire to modernise Australian electoral law to be more like Canadian law.

Archival documents suggest that partisans desired a rational approach, one in which they could calmly advance their party interests when developing policy on the recognition and regulation of political parties. In both parties, the development of their policy positions on party labels was cautious and intended to be methodical and fully encompassing. However, they fell far short of this goal.

On the ALP side, Cabinet and the minister in charge of electoral regulation initially learned about policy options in secret, with abundant advice from the bureaucracy and extensive and repeated research trips to explore international electoral regimes. The Canadian model was quickly idealised and gained the most attention, ensuring that decisions were made based on a set of limited policy options. Enthusiasm for the Canadian model sidelined a full exploration of all regulatory options, as well as an honest assessment of political realities, ultimately contributing to the defeat of the policy proposal.

In the Liberal Party, the organisation undertook comprehensive research studies and party-wide consultations, while the parliamentary party generated tomes of analysis outlining the pros and cons of different regulatory options. Yet the party's policy goals were unsettled and in conflict, and the party organisation made decisions more by a conservative consensus than by reference to the impact of policy on their goals.

This chapter's chief conclusion is that the policy development process tended to resemble something more akin to the model of administrative decision-making outlined long ago by Charles E. Lindblom than the rational decision-making process that both parties desired. Despite their best intentions, both political parties 'muddled through' the issue of party labels on ballot papers more than they rationally advanced their self-interest.[5] Information was limited. The policy development process took unexpected, 'muddling' courses, which reflected the passions and predispositions of prominent individuals and a compromise between disagreeing elites. This is perhaps surprising, given that the policy development process on party labels was not rushed, was largely outside the public view and was informed by long and resource-intensive research processes, as well as the experience and insight of the bureaucracy. Yet, even in this unusual case, the process fell short of the expectations of rational choice accounts of the role of party in the evolution of the relationship between party and state.[6]

The relationship between political parties and the state

The path taken by political parties from private organisations with public functions to semi-public agencies has been different in each jurisdiction. The journey began in the American States, which first started to recognise and regulate political parties in the second half of the nineteenth century. American party organisations began life as private associations, with association and speech rights protected in the US Constitution (in the First Amendment and, after Reconstruction, the Fourteenth Amendment). As political parties grew in strength and influence throughout the nineteenth century, middle-class distaste

---

5 Charles E. Lindblom (1959) 'The Science of "Muddling Through"', *Public Administration Review* 19(2): 79–88.

6 For example, Richard S. Katz and Peter Mair (1995) 'Changing Models of Party Organization and Party Democracy: The Emergence of the Cartel Party', *Party Politics* 1(1): 5–28. On the topic of the relationship between party and electoral law generally, rational choice accounts include Anthony Downs (1957) *An Economic Theory of Democracy*, New York: Harper; Carles Boix (1999) 'Setting the Rules of the Game: The Choice of Electoral Systems in Advanced Democracies', *American Political Science Review* 93(3): 609–24; Richard S. Katz (1980) *A Theory of Parties and Electoral Systems*, Baltimore: The Johns Hopkins University Press.

for powerful party leaders and machines, and for the working-class immigrant folk they brought into politics, gathered steam. Calls for state intervention to limit the power of party leaders grew loud.[7]

The American judiciary had earlier expressed openness to the regulation of private corporations where they exerted a real or 'virtual' monopoly over the supply of a good or service 'affected with a public interest'.[8] This opened an analogous path to the regulation of *political* monopolies, the Republican and Democratic parties, both of which indisputably performed functions affected with a public interest. In this environment, States and, later, the people (using the initiative process) passed a swathe of laws regulating the behaviour and internal composition of political parties.[9]

The regulation in the late nineteenth and early twentieth centuries legally recognised and entrenched political parties as the units organising politics.[10] The laws conferred benefits on the existing Republican and Democratic parties, but limited their autonomy to conduct their own affairs. On the one hand, the laws raised barriers to the entry of new political parties. On the other, direct primary laws took away the most significant power of the two major political parties:

---

7   Leon D. Epstein (1986) *Parties in the American Mold*, Madison, WI: University of Wisconsin Press; Sarah John and Donald A. DeBats (2014) 'Australia's Adoption of Compulsory Voting: Revising the Narrative—Not Trailblazing, Uncontested or Democratic', *Australian Journal of Politics and History* 60(1): 1–27; Austin Ranney (1975) *Curing the Mischiefs of Faction: Party Reform in America*, Berkeley: University of California Press.

8   In response to legislative attempts to regulate the grain storage industry in the nineteenth century, the American judiciary developed the concept of a 'public utility', which applied to those private companies that provided public services such as water, electricity and grain storage. This concept permitted what would otherwise be unconstitutional rigorous state regulation: *Munn v Illinois* 94 US 113 (1876). In that case, the 'virtual' monopoly was over 14 grain storage warehouses, owned by nine different companies, all charging the same rates for grain storage, at the Port of Chicago.

9   See Epstein, *Parties in the American Mold*; James S. Fay, (1982) 'Legal Regulation of Political Parties', *Journal of Legislation* 9(2): 263–81; Ranney, *Curing the Mischiefs of Faction*; Alan Ware (2000) 'Anti-Partism and Party Control of Political Reform in the United States: The Case of the Australian Ballot', *British Journal of Political Science* 30(1): 1–29.

10   For example, the Porter Law, in which California recognised political parties for the purpose of holding voluntary primary elections, was passed in 1866 (Cal. Stat. 1865–1866, c. 359, §§ 1–7). The California legislature passed a multitude of laws regulating political parties in the 1890s. See Leonard M. Friedman (1956) 'Reflections upon the Law of Political Parties', *California Law Review* 44(3): 65–71. For nationwide overviews, see Adam Winkler (2000) 'Voters' Rights and Parties' Wrongs: Early Political Party Regulation in the State Courts, 1886–1915', *Columbia Law Review* 100(3): 873–99; Joseph R. Starr (1940) 'The Legal Status of American Political Parties, I', *American Political Science Review* 34(3): 439–55; and Joseph R. Starr (1940) 'The Legal Status of American Political Parties, II', *American Political Science Review* 34(4): 685–99.

to choose who could bear the party label (that is, the power over party nominations). While some of the specific details of individual direct primary schemes were struck down as unconstitutionally limiting association rights,[11] most iterations of the direct primary—even those in which the state allows unaffiliated voters to participate in intraparty nomination contests—have been upheld.[12]

In other English-speaking jurisdictions, where constitutional barriers to regulation were less significant,[13] legal regulation of political parties, paradoxically, began much later and remains less intrusive. In these places, recognition and, later, regulation of political parties did not begin until the 1970s, close to a century after American regulation began. In Canada, parties were first legally recognised in 1970 and first regulated in 1974, when the *Election Expenses Act 1974* became law.[14] As noted by Kelly in this volume, in Australia there were only two examples of the legal recognition of political parties before the 1977 amendment to the Constitution concerning the filling of casual Senate vacancies.

In New Zealand, it was 1993 before parties were legally recognised and regulated (and even then only because the party vote, a central part of the mixed-member proportional system adopted in that year, necessitated the registration of political parties).[15] In the United Kingdom, political parties were not formally recognised until 1998, when registration of political parties was introduced to give parties greater control over

---

11   Famously, in *California Democratic Party v Jones* 530 US 567 (2000), the US Supreme Court struck down California's blanket primary regime. In the blanket primary, voters were presented with a single ballot containing all candidates for all offices and they could vote for any candidate, irrespective of party, and the candidate of each party with the most votes proceeded to the general election.

12   For example, *State ex rel. Van Alstine v Frear* 142 Wis. 320, 125 N.W. 961, 966 (1910); *Clingman v Beaver* 544 US 581, 582 (2005); *Miller v Brown* 503 F.3d 360 (4th Cir. 2007). See, generally, Christine M. Collins (2010) *Primary Elections: A Look into Four Primary Election Systems*, Sacramento: McGeorge School of Law, University of the Pacific.

13   Anika Gauja (2013) *Political Parties and Elections: Legislating for Representative Democracy*, Farnham: Ashgate, pp. 2–3. There was no constitutionally entrenched bill of rights in Canada until 1982 (when Canada adopted the Canadian Charter of Rights and Freedoms). Both New Zealand (1993) and the United Kingdom (1998) passed statutory rights Bills, but only in the last decade of the twentieth century. While these documents increased the rights of individuals, they are all less individualistic than the US Bill of Rights and so provide less extensive association rights.

14   *Canada Elections Act 1970* (Can); *Election Expenses Act 1974* (Can); John C. Courtney (1978) 'Recognition of Canadian Political Parties in Parliament and in Law', *Canadian Journal of Political Science* 11(1): 33–60.

15   *Electoral Act 1993* (NZ), Part 4; Gauja, *Political Parties and Elections*, p. 74.

the use of their names.[16] Party-controlled legislatures are not the only ones that have been reluctant to regulate. Courts in common law countries have been less willing than their US counterparts to uphold challenges that might pierce the party veil. They have only tentatively allowed slight interventions in, and regulation of, internal party affairs, citing the rights of private associations to autonomy as the reason for their reluctance.[17] Regulation remains less extensive[18] and, in all of these places, party control over nominations persists— and is absolute in Australia, Canada and the United Kingdom (see also Gauja, this volume).[19]

Comparing regulatory regimes

Despite the different paths taken in individual jurisdictions, general commonalties among countries emerge. A comparison of the evolution of regulatory regimes in different jurisdictions elicits a hierarchy of six different levels of recognition and regulation (summarised in Table 2.1):

1. ignorance
2. recognition without registration
3. recognition with registration
4. regulation without recompense
5. regulation with recompense
6. recognition with registration and reward.

---

16   Association of Electoral Administrators (1998) 'Registration of Political Parties Bill 1998', *Representation* 35(2–3): 114; *Registration of Political Parties Act 1998* (UK).

17   *Cameron v Hogan* (1934) 51 CLR 358; *Young and Rubicam Ltd v Progressive Conservative Party of Canada* Superior Court of Quebec (22 March 1971) 803–933; *Clarke v Australian Labor Party* [1999] SASC 433; *Figueroa v Canada (Attorney General)* 2003 SCC 37 [143]; Anika Gauja (2006) 'From Hogan to Hanson: The Regulation and Changing Legal Status of Australian Political Parties', *Public Law Review* 17(4): 282–99; Graeme Orr, Bryan Mercurio and George Williams (2003) 'Australian Electoral Law: A Stocktake', *Election Law Journal* 2(3): 383–402.

18   Graeme Orr (2014) 'Private Association and Public Brand: The Dualistic Conception of Political Parties in the Common Law World', *Critical Review of International Social and Political Philosophy* 17(3): 332–49.

19   In New Zealand, section 71 of the *Electoral Act 1993* requires political parties to 'ensure that provision is made for participation in the selection of candidates representing the party for election' by current financial members of the party and/or delegates selected by current financial members of the party. See Gauja, *Political Parties and Elections*, Ch. 5.

Table 2.1 Levels of legal intervention in political parties

Level of state interference	Characteristics	Characterisation	Examples	Years present in Australia
Ignorance	No legal recognition of the existence of political parties or their role in politics.	Cherished by political parties but untenable in twenty-first century.	US States until 1860s – 1890s; Canada until 1970; New Zealand until 1993; United Kingdom until 1998.	1901–77
Recognition without registration	Legal recognition of existence and role in politics, *without* legal definition of political party or executive authority to assess whether a party is legally a party.	Superficially appealing to political parties but unstable, as it gives rise to disputes about ownership of party brand without mechanism for resolution.	Australia, 1977–83.	1977–83
Recognition with registration	Legal recognition of the existence of parties and their role in politics, *with* legal definition of political party and/or executive authority to assess whether a party is legally a party.	Balanced, but sets precedent for future regulation.	US States, 1888–1900s.	n/a; proposed in 1973–75
Regulation without recompense	Legal limitation or regimentation of the role of parties in politics *without* the provision of state assistance.	Rare.	New Zealand, 1993 – present.	n/a; proposed in 1973–75
Regulation with recompense	Legal limitation or regimentation of the role of parties in politics *with* the provision of state assistance.	Balanced and stable.	Germany; United States, 1900s – present.	n/a
Recognition with registration and reward	Legal recognition of the existence of parties and their role in politics, *with* executive authority to set criteria of what constitutes a party and the conferral of state assistance.	Asymmetrical* and appears to provide evidence of political parties' use of laws for their own selfish ends.	Australia, 1983 – present.	1983 – present

* Gary Johns (1999) 'Political Parties: From Private to Public', *Commonwealth & Comparative Politics* 37(2): 89–113.

Source: The author.

The common starting point is the legal *ignorance* of political parties, in which the law makes no mention of political parties and neither confers benefits nor imposes limitations on political parties. Parties are in law—as well as in fact—private voluntary associations. This was the relationship between party and state in the American States in most of the nineteenth century. It ended first in California and New York in 1866[20] and latest, among the admitted States, in Louisiana in 1896.[21] Ignorance remained the legal status of political parties in Canadian law until 1970, in Australia until 1977, in New Zealand until 1993 and in the United Kingdom until 1998 (Table 2.1). During this time, only candidates were regulated and electoral law read as though elections were contested entirely by individual candidates conducting their own campaigns, raising their own funds and developing their own policy positions.

Generally, the first forays of the state into the realm of party activity involved the legal *recognition* of political parties. Recognition, in which the state acknowledges the existence of political parties without limiting party behaviour, often precedes the legal *regulation* of political parties, in which party autonomy is limited. There are two categories of relationships between party and state that involve recognition without concomitant regulation: recognition without registration and recognition with registration. Each comes with obvious benefits to political parties, without immediate restrictions on the freedom of the party to do as it pleases.

Recognition without registration is a first level of government recognition of parties in which the state recognises the existence of political parties for the purposes of conferring benefits (such as party labels on ballot papers), but does nothing more. In this stage, the state does not determine any registration criteria or define 'political party'. Instead, political parties self-identify as such and the state obliges by putting their labels on the ballot paper next to their nominated candidates or (in the Australian case) by filling casual vacancies in consultation with the party that previously held the seat.

20   Robert C. Wigton (2013) *The Parties in Court: American Political Parties Under the Constitution*. Plymouth: Lexington Books, p. 4.
21   Spencer D. Albright (1942) *The American Ballot*. Washington DC: American Council on Public Affairs, p. 28.

Recognition without registration tends to be unstable as it gives rise to disputes about the ownership of a given party 'brand' without providing a mechanism to resolve those disputes. In the twentieth century, before registration and regulation of political parties was a well-practised art, recognition without registration was proposed and utilised. For example, Australian political parties were constitutionally recognised for the purpose of casual Senate vacancies from 1977, but no system of party registration was established at the federal level until 1983.[22] In the United Kingdom, a situation of quasi-recognition without registration existed between 1969 and 1998, allowing party candidates to describe their affiliation, in six or fewer words. The parties used this to list their candidates' party affiliation on the ballot paper.[23]

Recognition with registration involves the state legally defining 'political party' and delegating power to the executive and/or judicial branches to determine whether an organisation is, in law, a political party. Legal political parties are formally registered, if they conform to some state-determined criteria, for the purposes of appearing on the ballot, filling vacancies, receiving public financing and/or qualifying for free TV time. New South Wales (NSW) adopted recognition with registration in 1981, when parties were first legally recognised and a register was created for the purposes of receiving public reimbursement of their campaign expenses. Recognition with registration is relatively uncontroversial, and it is beneficial to political parties in the immediate term. However, recognition with registration is not a natural end point as it tends to encourage or set a precedent for two opposing developments: 1) the introduction of limits on party autonomy via the legal regulation of political parties; and 2) the use of the law to achieve party ends, especially to legislate state funds to political parties to support their activities.

The next level of state involvement in parties is the *regulation* of political parties, in which particular behaviours or internal structures are limited or compelled. Regulation necessarily limits party autonomy and control.[24] Legal recognition and registration are

---

22   At the State level, party registration had been established in Tasmania in 1974 and New South Wales in 1981 (see Table 1.2).

23   Association of Electoral Administrators, 'Registration of Political Parties Bill 1998'.

24   Ingrid van Biezen (2008) 'State Intervention in Party Politics: The Public Funding and Regulation of Political Parties', *European Review* 16(3): 337–53.

typically antecedent to or are concomitant with the first attempts to regulate party activity, since the subject of any regulation typically must be legally defined and recognised for regulation to be effective. Regulation may be accompanied by recompense for the imposition of rules and restriction, but that is not always the case.

The state regulates without recompense if it limits party autonomy and control over party internal affairs by prescribing or proscribing behaviour without also providing preferential treatment—such as financial aid in the form of public funds for campaign expenses— to compensate parties for the loss of autonomy and/or control. For example, the state might limit party funding sources (by banning contributions from corporations or foreign sources) but provide no compensatory benefits such as public funding or party labels on ballots.

Regulation without recompense is a relatively unusual state of affairs, though one example is New Zealand, which requires recognised political parties to use democratic selection processes as a condition of registration while providing few benefits to them.[25] Regulation without recompense was also proposed in Australia in 1973–75, when the ALP introduced the Electoral (Disclosure of Funds) Bill 1974 with provisions to register political parties, limit party spending and require disclosure, without any compensatory provisions.[26]

The two most common regulatory regimes that have evolved can be described (Table 2.1) as *regulation with recompense* and *regulation with registration and reward*. In regulation with recompense, the state prescribes and/or proscribes behaviour and also provides generous (but not disproportionate) subventions and privileges to parties. At the most incongruous, the state may provide recognition with registration and reward, which comes with considerable subventions and privileges but without serious state-imposed limits on party autonomy. These two regimes, and their commonness, pique our suspicion that parties take advantage of their monopoly-like position in the legislature. They

---

25 Johns, 'Political Parties', p. 92.
26 The Electoral (Disclosure of Funds) Bill 1974 (Cth) would have regulated parties, limiting their control and autonomy, without offering any recompense. The Bill would have created a register—of political party agents—and opened parties to criminal prosecution for breaches of spending caps and donation disclosure provisions by, in effect, incorporating political parties. *Electoral (Disclosure of Funds) Bill 1974* (Cth) s. 3.

also reflect the fact that, in recent decades, established political parties in many democracies have come to rely on the state for an increasingly large proportion of their resources.[27] Both these regimes, through the conferral of benefits on those parties with official status, typically have the effect of restricting electoral competition. They tend to perpetuate the existence and electoral 'success' of established parties, while controlling the entrance of new actors with, for example, public funding of parties based on prior electoral performance.[28] In effect— and perhaps by intention—existing parties come to exert control over the electoral marketplace. Katz and Mair characterised this emergent relationship between party and state as 'cartelisation'.[29]

The relationship between the cartel party and the state is fraught with tensions. On the one hand, cartel political parties are funded largely by the public purse, have a privileged legal status and serve the most public of functions (governance), so they seem very much like state-provided public agencies. On the other hand, parties seek to maintain considerable autonomy by retreating to their claims of private association rights. This is especially true when we consider the category of *recognition with registration and reward*. In this category, parties are legally recognised, through a party register, and are granted privileges or special treatment (most commonly tax advantages, public financing of campaign expenses, annual organisational support and/or state-funded nomination contests). However, the state refrains from seriously limiting party freedom or setting standards for the conduct of internal affairs, with the justification—and inconsistent logic[30]— that political parties are private associations and so the government should not interfere in their internal affairs.

Gary Johns classifies this type of relationship between a party and the state as 'asymmetrical' because parties reap the advantages that accompany public status and retain most of the freedoms that attach

27   Alan Ware (1987) *Citizens, Parties and the State: A Reappraisal*, Cambridge: Polity Press; Zareh Ghazarian (2006) 'State of Assistance? Political Parties and State Support in Australia', *Australian Review of Public Affairs* 7(1): 61–76.
28   Richard S. Katz and Peter Mair (1996) 'Cadre, Catch-All or Cartel? A Rejoinder', *Party Politics* 2(4): 531. The cartelisation thesis has been contested in the Australian context. See, for example, Murray Goot (2006) 'The Australian Party System, Pauline Hanson's One Nation and the Party Cartelisation Thesis', in Ian Marsh (ed.) *Political Parties in Transition?*, Sydney: The Federation Press, pp. 181–217.
29   Katz and Mair, 'Changing Models of Party Organization and Party Democracy'.
30   Johns, 'Political Parties', p. 94.

to private status.[31] Arguably, recognition with registration and reward best characterises the relationship between political parties and the Federal Government in Australia today. The political parties obtain many benefits conferred by the law, including public financing, party labels on ballot papers and (the recently weakened)[32] party ticket voting in the Senate, with few regulatory strings attached.[33]

Studying the role of party in the transition from private to public

The transition in the legal relationship between party and state, from ignorance to one of the other five categories, is especially interesting because it is largely a result of self-imposed action. Parties dominated the legislature long before the law ever recognised their existence. As such, it is unlikely that the transition in the relationship was entirely (or even largely) the result of change imposed on parties by reformers outside them. Instead, the transition more likely reflects decisions made by political parties.

The prevailing assumption in political science, especially in the United States, is that political parties approach these regulatory decisions from a perspective of fully informed and completely self-aware self-interest. This self-interest is typically understood in terms of maximising the number of legislative seats received from votes won in the next election.[34] Rational choice theory presents a parsimonious model of party action, inferring a singular, unequivocal and known self-interest in the policy from the consequences of its adoption. In the rational choice model, partisans would be expected to start with a clearly defined objective (a single self-interest), attain information on

---

31   ibid.

32   The *Commonwealth Electoral Amendment Act 2016* weakens the power of political parties to determine their voters' preference orders by abolishing group voting tickets. For more, see Kelly Buchanan (2016) 'Australia: Changes to Senate Electoral Law Passed Following Overnight Debate', *Library of Congress Global Monitor*, 28 March.

33   On the lack of balance between regulation and reward in Australian campaign finance law, see Graeme Orr (2007) 'Political Disclosure Regulation in Australia: A Lackadaisical Law', *Election Law Journal* 6(1): 72–88.

34   David M. Farrell (2011) *Electoral Systems: A Comparative Introduction*, 2nd edn, Basingstoke, UK: Palgrave Macmillan; Monique Leyenaar and Reuven Y. Hazan (2011) 'Reconceptualising Electoral Reform', *West European Politics* 34(3): 437–55.

all the possible policy alternatives and decide on the policy that best achieves their electoral objective—and, of course, act to implement that policy (or prevent the implementation of an alternative).

However, it has long been established in the study of policy development and administrative decision-making that rational accounts of policymaking impose impossible standards on policymakers and fail to describe the reality they face.[35] Applying Lindblom's branch model of 'muddling through' to the party policymaking context, we might expect partisans to make policy with incomplete information and poorly defined objectives, to assess the merit of a policy by reference to consensus and to follow idiosyncratic paths to policy development (sometimes going down policy rabbit holes), rather than staying unwaveringly focused on their party's self-interest.

In assessing these competing models, it is difficult to gauge how intentionally political parties have approached regulation since the study of the motivations and behaviour of political actors is inherently difficult.[36] As noted by James E. Anderson, '[s]olid, conclusive evidence, facts, or data, as one prefers, on the motives, values, and behavior of policy-makers ... are often difficult to acquire or simply not available'.[37] There exists suspicion, and legitimate concerns, that the publicly observable behaviour of political parties and politicians is orchestrated for political purposes (or, at a minimum, tempered by the watching electorate), which discourages ascribing much credence to what parties say publicly. Similarly, retired politicians and political operatives in otherwise candid interviews may reflect on their past actions through rose-coloured glasses or suffer from fading recall.

Fortunately, political parties, party organisations and engaged partisans have been avid record keepers, especially since World War II. As sensitivities relax, old wounds heal and access restrictions are loosened (usually 30 years after the records were created, though this time varies significantly), an increasing wealth of unexplored data becomes available. These unexplored data include administrative records, correspondence and reports, many of which reveal intimate

---

35 Lindblom, 'The Science of "Muddling Through"'.
36 See, for example, Anika Gauja (2014) 'Building Competition and Breaking Cartels?', *International Political Science Review* 35(3): 339–54.
37 James E. Anderson (2003) *Public Policymaking: An Introduction*, 5th edn, Boston: Houghton Mifflin, p. 24.

details of the private inner machinations of political parties, their constituency organisations, executive committees, campaign committees, legislative caucuses and Cabinet. They allow insights into the role of party in the transition from private to public that would have otherwise remained internal and private. Using these records to explore an Australian case study from the early 1970s, this chapter turns to assessing the two models of party policy development with particular focus on the process of learning and research in which parties engaged to inform themselves about such proposals and the motivations of political parties in promoting and opposing laws to legally recognise them.

Party labels on the ballot paper: Recognition without regulation resisted

After a near record 23 years in Opposition, the ALP won government in December 1972 and immediately began planning a series of electoral reforms aimed at levelling what it saw as an uneven electoral playing field. These reforms included two key measures relating to political parties: one to list the names of political parties next to their nominated candidates on the ballot paper; the other to regulate the finances of political parties. Together these reforms, if passed, would have inaugurated the legal recognition of Australian political parties. Both initiatives were modelled on recent Canadian reforms. Yet each reform was of a different character: one legally recognising and registering parties; the other regulating political party finances without providing recompense for lost autonomy and funding sources. Neither Bill passed into law; both were defeated by the Liberal Party (in coalition with the Country Party) in the Senate.

These Bills would have been the first to recognise or regulate political parties. From their emergence in the 1890s, Australian political parties had been, in legal terms, unequivocally private associations of which the state was officially ignorant. The reality, of course, was strikingly different. Parties were firmly at the centre of politics in the 1970s.

Most voters identified with a party and consistently voted for that party, irrespective of the particular candidate the party ran in the offices for which they were voting.[38]

Inevitably, as time went on, the discord between legal status and reality had become less and less tenable. The tension was especially great as it related to ballot papers. One of the consequences of being unknown to the law was that ballots made no mention of party. In the House of Representatives, the names of candidates were listed in alphabetical order with no other information or cues provided to voters.[39] The organisation of the Senate ballot paper was especially revealing of the discord between law and fact: candidates on the ballot paper were 'grouped' into columns by party, listed in the order the party chose, but without the name of the party anywhere on the ballot paper. It was the Nationalist Party, an early predecessor of the Liberal Party, that introduced the practice of 'grouping' candidates, in 1922, and the United Australia Party, the immediate predecessor to the Liberal Party, that amended the law to enable candidates within a 'group' to specify the order in which they were listed, in 1940.[40] However, despite this apparent concession to the existence of political parties, party labels did not appear anywhere on the Senate ballot before 1983.

While the absence of party labels seems odd today, it was common around the world through to the 1970s and beyond. Indeed, the US State of Virginia did not include party designations for State races on its ballot paper until the 2000 election,[41] and Ontario legislated to put party labels on ballots only in 2007.[42]

In the latter part of the twentieth century, political parties often expressed the view that party affiliation ought to be printed on the ballot paper and its absence was a problem. In Australia, the method

---

33   Simon Jackman (2003) 'Political Parties and Electoral Behaviour', in Ian McAllister, Steve Dowrick and Riaz Hassan (eds) *The Cambridge Handbook of the Social Sciences in Australia*, Cambridge: Cambridge University Press, pp. 266–86.
39   At the time, candidates on the House of Representatives ballot were ordered alphabetically by surname, with no other identifying information. Address and occupation—two cues to voters that were printed on ballot papers in other nations—were absent, possibly as a consequence of the strong labour movement in Australia.
40   *Commonwealth Electoral Act 1922* (Cth) s. 4; *Commonwealth Electoral Act 1940* (Cth) s. 7.
41   Alex Garlick (2015) 'The Letter after Your Name: Party Labels on Virginia Ballots', *State Politics and Policy Quarterly* 15(2): 147–70.
42   *Statutes of Ontario 2007*, Ch. 15.

devised to guide voters towards the party's nominated candidates in the absence of party labels or perfect political information among their partisans was the 'how-to-vote' card. How-to-vote cards are single sheets printed and distributed by political parties that indicate the party's nominated candidates. They are virtually identical to the party tickets printed by American political parties in the nineteenth century, except that how-to-vote cards cannot be deposited into the ballot box to cast a valid vote. Instead, a voter must transcribe the information on the how-to-vote card to his or her state-printed ballot paper. In the 1970s, most voters used their party's how-to-vote cards to identify their party's candidate.[43]

By the 1960s, both major political parties had come to appreciate that there were benefits to changing the law to recognise political parties so that party affiliations could appear on the ballot paper, though each party stressed different advantages. The ALP emphasised potential electoral gain: the party believed (rightly) that the primary cue to their followers was the party label, not the candidate's name. In the 1950s, the Queensland State ALP Executive reasoned that if 'the Party name [was] inserted alongside that of the Candidate in Ballot Papers', it 'would prevent informal voting'.[44] The party believed that the rate of informal voting was higher among ALP voters, which was likely the case, and any reduction in informal voting would bring more ALP votes than Liberal votes into the count.

For the Liberal Party of Australia, the chief advantages of legal recognition for the purposes of printing party affiliations on ballot papers were savings, in both money and volunteer labour, through the abolition of how-to-vote cards. For example, in a meeting with Senator Alan Missen in May 1974, Victorian Liberal Party officers expressed '[s]trong support for the abolition of How to Vote Cards which are

---

43   Indeed, even after the introduction of party labels on ballot papers, the majority of voters admitted to following how-to-vote cards: per the 1996 Australian Election Study cited in Clive Bean (1997) 'Australia's Experience with the Alternative Vote', *Representation* 34(2): 103–10.
44   Australian Labor Party [hereinafter ALP] (8 November 1957) 'Resolutions from Queensland', in *Australian Labor Party Federal Secretariat Records*, Canberra: National Library of Australia [hereinafter NLA], MS4985, Box 4.

considered a waste of money'.[45] After careful, cautious and deliberate study of the reform, the party leadership summarised the expected advantages of party affiliation on the ballot in these terms:

- it would assist electors, especially those voting by post or absentee voters
- it could save paper on printing how-to-vote cards
- it could reduce the number of party workers needed on polling day.[46]

In this private commentary, the Liberal Party explicitly identified interests in the printing of party affiliation on the ballot paper.

The identification of interests in legal recognition and the printing of party affiliations on the ballot paper came long before the parties adopted policy endorsing the idea. The fear of regulation was strong. Parts of the ALP, concerned about levels of informal voting, had agitated for legal recognition on ballot papers almost since Federation.[47] This early reform energy was satisfied by an amendment to electoral regulations, probably in the 1910s, allowing voters to take printed matter (that is, how-to-vote cards) into the polling place—a practice that was illegal in many other places for fear it would lead to ballot

45   Alan Missen (9 October 1974) 'Proposed Electoral Reforms: Notes of a Discussion Following an Address by Senator Alan Missen to a Conference of Victorian Liaison Officers', in *Alan Missen Papers*, NLA, MS7528, Box 223.

46   Liberal Party of Australia (c. 1975) 'Confidential Attachment A', in ibid., Box 302, Folder 'Commonwealth Electoral Act', p. 29.

47   The 1915 ALP Federal Conference adventurously advocated a single party ticket ballot paper covering both the House and the Senate, resolving: 'That a single ballot paper be used for the Senate and House of Representatives with the names and Party designations of the Parties so arranged that a single vote may be recorded for the whole Party Ticket.' ALP (31 May 1915) 'Official Report of the Sixth Commonwealth Conference of the Australian Labor Party (Opened at the Trades Hall, Adelaide, 31 May 1915)', in Patrick Weller (ed.) (1978) *Federal Executive Minutes 1915–1955: Minutes of the Meetings of the Federal Executive of the Australian Labor Party*, Melbourne: Melbourne University Press, pp. 18–20.

stuffing.[48] However, satisfaction was short lived. Calls for party labels on ballot papers soon re-emerged—first, from the party organisation, then, by 1960, from the parliamentary party.[49] By the late 1960s, the idea of party affiliations on the ballot paper was well-established ALP policy.

Support for the idea of party affiliations on the ballot came from the Liberal parliamentary party as early as the 1950s. In contrast, the papers of the Liberal Party show that the organisational wing opposed legal recognition of political parties and the printing of party labels on the ballot at that time.[50] The parliamentary party sought to convince the organisation to endorse the idea throughout the 1950s and into the 1960s, with little success.[51] For example, in 1968, Reg Withers, then State President of the Western Australian (WA) Liberal Party, urged the organisation to endorse the use of party labels on the Senate ballot paper.[52]

---

48   The actual amendment has not yet been located, however, it is evident that how-to-vote cards were not allowed in 1915, when ALP MPs Dr William R. N. Maloney and William Laird recommended party ballot papers to the Royal Commission into Electoral Laws and Administration, explaining: '[C]onsiderable delay is caused in the polling booths by persons not being clear as to the name of the candidate for whom they desire to vote. To get over this difficulty we suggest that the elector be allowed to take into the booth a list with the names of the candidates he wishes to vote for printed thereon; or, as an alternative, that a party ballot-paper be provided.' Royal Commission upon the Commonwealth Electoral Law and Administration (1914–15) 'Report from the Royal Commission upon the Commonwealth Electoral Law and Administration, 1914–1915', in *Commonwealth Parliamentary Papers 1914–1917. Vol. II (General)*, p. 447.

49   Documents from *Australian Labor Party Federal Secretariat Records*, NLA, MS4985, Box 1: ALP (8 May 1950) 'Meeting of Federal Executive at Masonic Hall. First Session'; ALP (1951) 'Submission by Branches, Committee etc. for Items to be Placed on the Platform etc. for Resolutions to be Passed'; ALP (Federal Executive) (15 July 1953) 'Meeting of the Federal Executive of the Australian Labor Party'; ALP (1957) 'Submission by Branches, Committee etc. for Items to be Placed on the Platform etc. for Resolutions to be Passed (22nd Federal Conference)'. Documents from *Australian Labor Party Federal Secretariat Records*, NLA, MS4985, Box 4: O. J. Washington to J. R. Willoughby (8 November 1957); Federal Labor Women's Conference (10–12 September 1962) 'Minutes of the Australian Labor Party Federal Conference of Labor Women'; ALP (1965) 'Submission by Branches, Committee etc. for Items to be Placed on the Platform etc. for Resolutions to be Passed'.

50   Documents from *Liberal Party of Australia Records*, NLA, MS5000, Box 134, Folder 'Electoral Act': Liberal Party Federal Secretariat (c. 1953) 'Report on Staff Planning Committee Meeting of 21 March 1952'; Electoral Reform Committee (Government Senators) to the Leader of the Government in the Senate and Government Senators (c. January 1954); J. R. Willoughby to Allen Fairhall (22 November 1956).

51   Documents from ibid.: Attachment to a letter from L. W. Hamilton to J. R. Willoughby (November 1956); R. Willoughby to Allen Fairhall (18 January 1954) 'Confidential'.

52   Documents from ibid.: Liberal Party of Australia (Staff Planning Committee), 5–6 March 1968, 'Extract from 68th Meeting of Staff Planning Committee'.

In the 1970s, views were changing and the organisation was divided on the issue. By late 1973, the State Liberal Party organisations in South Australia and Tasmania favoured party labels, while there was considerable disagreement within the Queensland organisation.[53] In 1975, Withers— by now a Senator and Leader of the Opposition in the Senate—summarised the position of the party organisation as 'mixed' regarding party labels (and therefore legal recognition). Importantly, Withers reported, the party was 'generally opposed' to the concept of registration, with concerns raised about its long-term impact on party autonomy.[54]

Although the parliamentary wing of the Liberal Party was in no way bound by the views of the organisation and could have acted to advance its policy preference, it did not introduce a Bill to recognise political parties while in government between 1949 and 1972.

By contrast, when the ALP won government, the parliamentary party began acting on its electoral reform policy preferences, including party affiliation on ballot papers. Fred Daly, Minister for Services and Property (the ministry in charge of the *Commonwealth Electoral Act 1918*), briefed by the Chief Electoral Officer, Frank Ley, furtively developed an electoral reform agenda within his department that included the legal recognition of political parties. In secret, Daly refined and whittled down his reform agenda as more information was collated, the Canadian model was idealised and the decisions of Cabinet were factored in.[55] As the process went on, the electoral interests that initiated the electoral reform process were displaced by Daly's desire to emulate the Canadian system.

After months of studious research and refinement, Daly introduced the Electoral Laws Amendment Bill 1974 into the House of Representatives in November 1974 without first consulting the ALP organisation or discussing the Bill with the Liberal Party Opposition. In clause 21, the Bill provided for the 'Printing of Party Affiliations on Ballot-Papers'.[56]

53   Liberal Party of Australia, Federal Secretariat, Research Department (1973) *Liberal Party Views on Electoral Reform*, Canberra, in ibid., Box 321, pp. 9–10.
54   Liberal Party of Australia (c. 1974) 'Electoral Laws Amendment Act 1974 (clause by clause)', in *Alan Missen Papers*, NLA, MS7528, Box 223, p. 3.
55   Sarah John (2014) Experience and Expectation: Socialization and the Different Motivational Bases of Party Policy on Campaign Finance Reform in Australia, Canada and the United States, PhD dissertation, School of International Studies, Flinders University, Adelaide, Ch. 7.
56   *Electoral Laws Amendment Bill 1974* (Cth) s. 21.

In the hierarchy of regulation (Table 2.1), clause 21 of the Electoral Laws Amendment Bill 1974 would have introduced recognition *with* registration, legally recognising parties and creating a party register for the purposes of printing the party affiliation of an individual candidate next to their name on the ballot paper.

Policy learning and transfer: From Canada to Australia

The party label provisions in the Electoral Laws Amendment Bill 1974 should have been relatively uncontroversial. Daly's reform plans were well researched and grounded in international experience and not overtly in ALP interests. The Liberal Party was open to the idea of registration, at least initially. However, Daly was inexperienced in government, having served since 1943 but only as an Opposition member. Inexperience in the art of advancing Bills in government may have contributed to the poor execution of the political campaign for the passage of the Bill, and its ultimate demise.

Towards the end of the ALP's long years in Opposition, Daly had drafted and introduced a doomed Opposition electoral Bill.[57] His interest in electoral reform continued in government, when he became the minister in charge of the *Electoral Act 1918*. In his new official role, and with the resources of the bureaucracy finally behind him, Daly deliberately sought out an international precedent on which to model his electoral legislation. During his tenure as Minister for Services and Property, Daly took multiple research trips (in 1973, 1974 and 1975) to comparable countries (the United Kingdom, New Zealand, Canada and the United States) to study electoral legislation.[58] Daly travelled with Frank Ley, who, as Chief Electoral Officer, was a nonpartisan bureaucrat, and met with a multitude of electoral administration officials, including Californian county registrars of voters, the New York Board of Elections, the New York Secretary of State and, importantly, the Chief Electoral Officer of Canada and Clerk

---

57   The *Commonwealth Electoral Bill (No. 2) 1971* (Cth), which would have provided for optional preferential voting and stricter one-vote, one-value provisions, was introduced on 1 April 1971 by Daly.
58   Frederick Daly (1980) 'Change the Rules [draft notes for speech]', in *Frederick Daly Papers*, NLA, MS9300, Box 80.

and President of the Canadian House of Commons.[59] All of this research was done in secret, with only occasional rumours circulating about Daly's trips and ideas or the likely contents of an electoral reform Bill.

In an idiosyncratic turn, Daly quickly fixated on the new Canadian system as the solution for Australia: a party registration scheme, introduced in 1970 and tested in the 1972 election, coupled with an expansive campaign finance regime, which commenced in 1974. In part, the Canadian model stood out because it was one of only a few existing models for reform in comparable countries. In the 1970s, the United Kingdom and New Zealand—perhaps more natural models— had not yet legally recognised political parties. (Indeed, parties in the United Kingdom had avoided legal recognition by allowing nominated candidates to describe, ostensibly in their own words, their political affiliation on the ballot.) By contrast, the United States was so far down the path of legal regulation with recompense—with its primaries, statutory party organisations and complex campaign finance regulation—as to be neither particularly applicable to the Australian case nor attractive to Australian party leaders. Canada, like the third bowl of porridge, was just right, with private party organisations and a nascent—but modern, balanced and well-designed—regulatory regime.

Daly spoke gushingly about the Canadian system and the people who introduced it.[60] His infatuation with the new Canadian system did not go unnoticed. In reviewing a draft copy of Daly's second reading speech for the Electoral (Disclosure of Funds) Bill 1974, Liberal Party leader Billy Snedden annotated 'Again!' in big scrawled script next to Daly's effusiveness (across several pages) about the wonder of the proposed campaign finance law in Canada.[61] In that same speech, Daly quoted a Progressive Conservative Party of Canada activist, Flora MacDonald (quite an obscure reference in Australia), on the goals

59   Pauline Larkey [Daly's Private Secretary] to Mr D. Eddowes (12 June 1973), in ibid., Box 132, Folder 'Overseas Visit 13 June to 24 July 1974'; Canadian High Commission to Minister Fred Daly (12 June 1974), in ibid., Box 80; Parliament of Australia, the Parliamentary Library, Legislative Research Service (2 June 1977) 'Public Financing of Political Parties in the Federal Republic of Germany, Scandinavia, Canada, U.S.A., and UK', in ibid., Box 80.
60   See Frederick Daly (11 July 1974), 'Response to Question without Notice', in *House of Representatives Parliamentary Debates (Hansard)*; Frederick Daly (12 February) 'Second Reading Speech, Electoral Bill', in *House of Representatives Parliamentary Debates (Hansard)*.
61   Frederick Daly (1974) 'Second Reading Speech [Draft]', in *Sir Billy Snedden Papers*, NLA, MS6216, Box 204, Folder 21, p. 9.

of the Canadian reform.[62] Daly's speeches on his electoral Bills did not reflect an impartial, objective assessment of the merits of Canadian reforms; rather, they were indicative of a very personal affection for the system.

The mechanism Daly chose for determining the party affiliations of candidates in the Electoral Laws Amendment Bill 1974 was taken from the Canadian reform of 1970.[63] In the registration regime introduced by Pierre Trudeau's Liberal Party, with support from the Conservative Party,[64] a party was entitled to register if it ran candidates in 50 seats across Canada (about 19 per cent of the then 264 seats in the House of Commons).[65] In recognition of the State-based organisation of Australian political parties, Daly's initial scheme would have established registration on a State-by-State basis, requiring a party to nominate candidates in one-quarter of the House of Representatives seats in that State before qualifying for registration.[66] After considering the fate of the Country Party, which tended to nominate candidates only in rural areas, the requirement was lowered to 20 per cent of seats in a State by the time the Bill reached parliament. Cabinet had advice that, under this new lower standard, all the parties that typically won seats in the House would have qualified for registration in all the States based on their 1974 election nominations—*except* for the Country Party in Victoria, which fielded only six candidates out of the nine required.[67] None of these plans or reasoning was conveyed to the Liberal–Country Party Coalition.

---

62 ibid., p. 9.

63 Australian Government (17 September 1974) 'Commonwealth Electoral Act 1918–1973: Proposed Additional Amendments [Cabinet Submission No. 1332]', in *Cabinet Records*, Canberra: National Archives of Australia [hereinafter NAA], A5915, CL21 Part 1, p. 6.

64 *Canada Elections Act 1970* (Can); Courtney, 'Recognition of Canadian Political Parties in Parliament and in Law'.

65 More than three decades after its inception, the Supreme Court struck down the 50-candidate requirement in *Figueroa v Canada* (AG) [2003] 1 SCR 912. The consequences of the 50-candidate requirement had been greatly increased, with a federally registered political party that failed to nominate 50 candidates for a federal election subject to automatic deregistration and the stripping of its assets.

66 *Election Laws Amendment Bill* (Cth) s. 21.

67 Department of Prime Minister and Cabinet (September 1974) 'Confidential Notes on Cabinet Submission No. 1332: Proposed Additional Amendments to the Commonwealth Electoral Act 1918–1973', in *Cabinet Records*, NAA, CL21 Part 2, Document 24, p. 2.

In response to the worrying rumours about the ALP's electoral reform agenda, and the motives behind it, the federal organisation of the Liberal Party launched an extensive information-gathering exercise, led by its Research Department. The party examined a multitude of electoral reforms that it believed the ALP might propose, from lowering the one-vote, one-value tolerance in redistributions to adopting first-past-the-post voting, Senate representation for the Territories and the placement of party affiliations on ballot papers.[68]

Early in the Liberal Party's process, Federal Director Bede Hartcher sought the State party organisational leadership's opinions on these electoral reforms, as was common practice in the party.[69] The State organisations obliged with feedback, often detailed and contrasting, which was generally negative about legal recognition.[70] The Research Department of the Federal Secretariat produced a series of reports on electoral reform, including a report collating the positions of the State divisions on each reform issue.[71] Based on its research, and its conservative position against state regulation of the private sector, the organisation took a generally oppositional stance to the proposal for legal recognition and informed Senator Withers accordingly. For their part, Liberal Party Members of Parliament (MPs) developed and circulated numerous summaries of the likely impacts of the proposed reforms, including a 50-page document listing the pros and cons of each and every provision of the ALP's electoral reform agenda.[72]

In perfect asymmetry, the ALP organisation was not involved in Daly's policy development process. The result was that the ALP organisation was less informed about the proposals of its representatives in government, and the finer details of legal recognition and registration, than the Liberal Party. The absence of a decision-making role for the

---

68   Research Department of the Federal Secretariat, Liberal Party of Australia (26 February 1973) 'Notes on the Commonwealth Electoral Act: Possible Labor Amendments [Research Note 4/73]', in *Sir Billy Snedden Papers*, NLA, MS6216, Series 10, Box 195, Folder 510.

69   John, Experience and Expectation, Ch. 6.

70   Research Department of the Federal Secretariat, Liberal Party of Australia (6 December 1973) 'Liberal Party Views on Electoral Reform', in *Liberal Party of Australia Records*, NLA, MS5000, Box 321.

71   Documents from ibid.: (26 June 1974) 'Proposed Government Electoral Legislation'; (26 April 1974) 'Federal Election Speakers' Notes—Electoral Reform'; 'Notes on the Commonwealth Electoral Act: Possible Labor Amendments'; and 'Liberal Party Views on Electoral Reform'.

72   Liberal Party of Australia (c. 1975) 'Confidential Attachment A', in *Alan Missen Papers*, NLA, MS7528, Box 302, Folder 'Commonwealth Electoral Act'.

organisation is striking, given the parliamentary ALP was formally bound by the decisions of the organisation, whereas the parliamentary Liberal Party was not. But, then, the ALP was less ideologically concerned about private rights and the limits of public power than the Liberal Party. Additionally, on the general idea of providing party affiliations on the ballot paper, the party organisation had been favourable for decades. And so, Daly largely designed his own scheme, subject only to the limitations imposed occasionally by Cabinet and, when remembered, political realities.

Daly's autonomy from the organisational wing was clearer in a second electoral reform proposal from the time, the Electoral (Disclosure of Funds) Bill 1974. This initiative reveals the extent to which Daly: 1) influenced the content of the ALP's electoral reform Bills, and 2) was influenced by his research trips to North America, especially Canada. In the United States, where Daly had toured in 1973, donation disclosure was considered to be the keystone of any campaign finance regulatory scheme.[73] In Canada, disclosure was a new and controversial idea, but absolutely central to the *Election Expenses Act 1974* (Can). It is striking that on Daly's return, disclosure became the cornerstone of the Whitlam Government's campaign finance reform package, even though it was nowhere on the radar, within the party or within the bureaucracy, when Daly left for his first research trip in June 1973. Indeed, at the time there were some within the ALP engaging in campaign financing practices they very much wanted to keep secret.[74]

In a typical model of regulation and recompense, the Canadian *Election Expenses Act 1974* introduced rigorous donation disclosure provisions and spending limits, while compensating parties for this regulation through public financing and tax deductions. Daly's disclosure proposals in the Electoral (Disclosure of Funds) Bill 1974 were virtually identical to the Canadian provisions, up to the point of a disclosure threshold of the identical amount ($100 or more) and very similar spending limits.[75] However, the Australian Electoral

---

73   The belief that timely and accurate disclosure is the central pillar of any campaign finance regulatory regime—or that 'sunlight is the best disinfectant'—was widely and sincerely held in the United States. For the origin of the phrase, see Louis D. Brandeis (1914) *Other People's Money*, New York: Frederick A. Stokes, Ch. 5.

74   See Paul Kelly (1976) *The Unmaking of Gough*, Sydney: Angus & Robertson, pp. 394–420.

75   Australian Government (March 1974) 'Cabinet Submission No. 964', in *Cabinet Records*, NAA, CL21 Part 1, Document No. 217, pp. 3, 11.

(Disclosure of Funds) Bill 1974 diverged from the Canadian *Election Expenses Act 1974* in that it did not contain public financing or any favourable tax provisions. A public funding proposal styled on the Canadian model was initially in the Bill, but had been quickly rejected by Cabinet.[76] This meant that the Electoral (Disclosure of Funds) Bill 1974 would have imposed *regulation* on parties without any *recompense*: no special treatment came with the Bill; only requirements to reveal hitherto secret information on campaign contributions and the imposition of arbitrary limits on spending, together with a threat that noncompliance would leave party officials liable for prosecution. It is no surprise, then, that the Bill failed.

Two things are surprising: that the ALP caucus voted in favour of the passage of the Electoral (Disclosure of Funds) Bill 1974 and the persistence shown by Daly on all his electoral reform Bills. He appears to have become engrossed in the policy development process and his enthusiasm for the Canadian reforms appears to have overtaken all else, including party interests. This, combined with a dash of political naivety, ensured that Australia's first serious move towards party regulation was dead on arrival.

Party motivations: Interests, concern and caution

The ALP likely deferred to Daly's agenda because it appeared, for the most part, to be in their electoral interests. The ALP had a long-established and genuine belief that the electoral system was unfairly and intentionally stacked against it, resulting in elections that yielded a majority of the vote but not a majority of the seats.[77] Daly's motives were complicated; he was certainly aware of the ALP's interests in moving beyond the legal status quo, yet he appears to have been motivated by a genuine desire to modernise Australian law and by his enthusiasm for the Canadian system.[78]

---

76 Australian Government (13 October 1973) 'Draft of Cabinet Minute (Decision 1436) without Submission', in ibid., A5931, CL21 Part 1, Document No. 135. Reference to public financing was omitted in the final version of the minute: Australian Government (15 October 1973) 'Cabinet Minute (Decision 1436) without Submission', in ibid., A5931, CL21 Part 1, Document No. 138.
77 John, Experience and Expectation, Ch. 7.
78 ibid., Ch. 7.

Initially, parts of the Liberal Party were open to supporting Daly's Bill.[79] However, Daly's secretive process—possibly the consequence of inexperience in government—engendered suspicion and resentment in the Opposition. Better handled, the proposal for legal recognition in the Electoral Laws Amendment Bill 1974 might have been relatively uncontroversial since it seemingly served the interests of both major political parties. Suspicion of ALP motives, combined with a cautious approach to governmental regulation and a disinclination to move beyond the status quo, contributed to the Liberal Party's eventual decision to vote against the Bill.

Whenever it had been mooted, legal recognition raised visceral fears in the Liberal Party organisation about compromising the party's cherished private association status, and the control and autonomy that came with that status. The concept of recognition *without* registration brought up recurring concerns about losing control of the Liberal Party brand. In 1956—before the concept of registration had become central to schemes of legal recognition—Federal Director J. R. Willoughby wrote to Cabinet, then constituted by the Liberal–Country Coalition, rebuffing Cabinet's proposals that party labels be placed on the ballot paper.[80] Willoughby explained that the idea was 'full of problems' and:

> confusion [was] likely to arise … in the case of a candidate using the name of an existing major Party in an electorate deliberately not contested by that Party—or again of a candidate forming his own Party and using the name of a Party already in existence.[81]

The Liberal Party organisation was worried that, under a scheme of recognition without registration, it might lose control over its label and have its strategic decisions undermined by someone else using the Liberal name.[82]

---

79 ibid., Ch. 6.

80 The Minister for the Interior's office concluded that '[w]ith adequate safeguard to ensure that unauthorised or inappropriate names were not used', party labels on the ballot paper would 'materially assist electors in voting according to their desires'. Attachment to a letter: L. W. Hamilton to J. R. Willoughby (November 1956), in *Liberal Party of Australia Records*, NLA, MS5000, Box 134, Folder 'Electoral Act'.

81 J. R. Willoughby to Allen Fairhall (22 November 1956), in ibid., p. 2. Emphasis in original.

82 Willoughby was also concerned that non-party candidates may gain an advantage if they were allowed to use the term 'Independent', which he believed was a 'somewhat attractive' designation: Willoughby, J. R. (18 January 1954) 'Registration of Parties', in ibid.

In 1973, after rumours about the ALP's regulatory plans had proliferated, the NSW division responded to a request for opinions from the Liberal Party's Federal Secretariat, characterising party labels as 'superficially attractive'. The division explained that party labels would lead to a loss of control of the party brand unless a system of party registration was also introduced. Party affiliations on ballot papers:

> would require the registration of political parties and some form of protection against false pretences (eg. 'The N.S.W. Liberals', 'True Liberals' etc.) It would be difficult to handle the matter when a political party changes its management and perhaps its name. Others could perhaps continue the old name.[83]

The NSW division had clearly engaged in some serious thinking about the proposal for party affiliations on ballot papers and all the possible scenarios that might arise under the system. Importantly, control over the party's brand was central, in the opinion of the NSW division.

On the other hand, whenever recognition *with* registration was suggested, the Liberal Party organisation was less concerned about control of its brand and more concerned with a loss of autonomy that might result from registration, if it were to set the precedent for regulation. When Liberal Senators endorsed party labels with registration in 1954, the party organisation countered that '[a]lthough, on the surface, there appears to be much to commend this proposal',[84] it should be avoided. Instead, the party organisation recommended recognition without registration—a list of candidates, with their party affiliation beside them, posted in each polling station—to avoid the risks of a register.[85] While the Liberal Party had, by 1975, concluded that registration was the '[s]implest way to implement the

---

83   Research Department, *Liberal Party Views on Electoral Reform*, p. 9.

84   J. R. Willoughby to Allen Fairhall (18 January 1954) 'Confidential', in *Liberal Party of Australia Records*, NLA, MS5000, Box 134, Folder 'Electoral Act'.

85   Liberal Party Federal Secretariat (c. 1953) 'Report on Confidential Meeting Comprising Federal Director, NSW General Secretary and Assistant General Secretary and Victorian General Secretary held in Canberra 8 August 1952', in ibid. This proposal, or course, raised concerns about the party's control of its label, which Willoughby would canvass two years later (see footnote 82, this chapter).

proposal to show party affiliations on ballot papers', it cautioned that registration 'could be interpreted by some as government interference in the administration of political parties'.[86]

In short, the party organisation feared autonomy and control could not coexist if political parties were legally recognised. This conclusion was arrived at because, in all of its deliberations, the Liberal Party organisation aimed for rational decision-making. It was considered and cautious, evincing a determination to make the most sensible decision that would ensure that it did not lose its cherished private association status. The party was prescient in recognising that a register of parties could open the door to state control (regulation) of a party and a whittling away of party autonomy to conduct its own affairs as it pleased, though, after more than 30 years of legal recognition in Australia, we can see that risks of serious incursion into party affairs were overstated.

Having served under the Coalition Government for the previous two decades, the federal bureaucracy was aware that recognition with registration was controversial for the Liberal Party and made that clear to the new government. The bureaucracy advised the new ALP Cabinet that a register of parties was:

> [a] most contentious proposal—it could be interpreted as a form of control over political parties. As the object is to enable candidates' political affiliations to be identified on ballot papers, would it not be sufficient for the Chief Electoral Officer to maintain a list of parties?[87]

A handwritten note in Cabinet records attached to this advice notes that '[r]egistration could raise contentious issues not canvassed in the submission'.[88]

Taken together, concerns about recognition *with* and *without* registration predisposed the Liberal Party organisation against any form of legal recognition. The oppositional stance of the Liberal Party organisation was cemented as the research process progressed. As the

---

86   Liberal Party of Australia (c. 1975) 'Confidential Attachment A', in *Alan Missen Papers*, NLA, MS7528, Box 302, Folder 'Commonwealth Electoral Act', p. 31.
87   Parliamentary Branch (26 February 1974) 'Notes on Cabinet Submission No. 925—Amendments to the Commonwealth Electoral Act', in *Cabinet Records*, NAA, A5915, CL21 Part 1, Document 180, [8].
88   ibid., [8].

proposal for placing party affiliation on the ballot received more press in 1973 and 1974, more Liberal Party voices with oppositional perspectives were heard. When the State party organisations were asked for their views, some divisions speculated that the party's electoral interests lay in maintaining the status quo—the longstanding position of official ignorance—in which parties were not recognised at all in law.

Jim J. Carlton, General Secretary of the NSW division, explained that his division did not favour the idea of legal recognition. He suggested that the Liberal Party in fact benefited from the reliance on how-to-vote cards—expense and labour intensity notwithstanding—explaining that party affiliation on ballot papers would 'diminish the importance of organizational superiority'. It would, he continued, 'only assist minor parties and independents'.[89] The WA division agreed, explicitly citing the weaknesses of the other parties. 'Both the ALP and Country Party', the secretary explained, were 'finding it difficult to man booths' to hand out how-to-vote cards. 'We believe that is to our advantage.'[90] Intriguingly, the WA division understood its interests to be separate from the interests of its coalition partner, the Country Party.

These views could have set the stage for a showdown between the parliamentary party and the organisation. Instead, suspicious and speculative voices supported by limited evidence gave the parliamentary party reason enough to pause. These suggestions that the party's immediate interests in party affiliation on ballot papers ran in the opposite direction to what had previously been thought—combined with the organisation's increasingly oppositional stance and a desire to achieve consensus within the whole party—were sufficient for the parliamentary party to consider deferring the advancement of the parliamentary party's long-held inclination towards party labels on ballots.

The detail of the registration scheme proposed by Daly also mattered to the Liberal Party's position, though not as much as the Liberal Party organisation's desire to retain control and autonomy. When introduced into the House of Representatives, clause 21 of the Electoral

---

89 Research Department, *Liberal Party Views on Electoral Reform*, p. 9.
90 ibid., p. 10.

Laws Amendment Bill 1974 required that a party field candidates in 20 per cent of seats in a State to qualify for registration in that State. The Liberal Party believed this discriminated against small parties.[91] Reg Withers—who, in 1968, had favoured party labels—was Leader of the Opposition in the Senate in 1974. Speaking for the party (rather than expressing his personal opinion), Withers remarked that clause 21 would 'require substantial amendment to meet the requirements of the Liberal Country Party'.[92] Withers advised the party to seek an amendment, 'but if unable to do so, oppose [the] clause'—which they did.[93] Their eventual decision to vote against the measure in the Senate killed the Bill because the ALP did not command a majority in that chamber.

The parliamentary Liberal Party was convinced that there would be no electoral consequences in advancing what the party organisation now saw as the party's electoral interest in the defeat of the Electoral Laws Amendment Bill 1974. In a document circulated to Liberal Senators, Withers revealed how aware he was of the absence of consequences for the Liberal Party if it cynically chose to block the Bill:

> If it is decided to oppose the [Electoral Laws Amendment] Bill outright again I do not think that it will have any adverse public reaction— public interest in electoral matters is small and there are too many issues which more directly affect electors now such as inflation, unemployment, and general economic dislocation for people to be concerned about laws politicians want to make to help themselves be re-elected. However, there are some Senators and Members who are keen to see some changes in the *Electoral Act*; some of the Daly proposals could be accepted without altering our electoral chances.[94]

Even though parts of the parliamentary party supported the policy changes, the political risks of opposing legal recognition were few. Thus, the Liberal Party deferred to the organisation's wishes and voted down the Bill in the Senate.

91   Liberal Party of Australia (c. 1974) 'Electoral Laws Amendment Act 1974 (clause by clause)', in *Alan Missen Papers*, NLA, MS7528, Box 223, p. 3.
92   ibid.
93   ibid. By 1975, his views had hardened. Withers wrote that '[i]t is not really practical to show candidate affiliations on ballot papers unless there is a register of parties. Certainly the register suggested by Daly is not desirable. If it was wished to show party affiliations on ballots a much more simple requirement for registration of parties could be worked out.' R. G. Withers (4 April 1975) 'Electoral Laws Amendment Bill', in *Alan Missen Papers*, NLA, MS 7528, Box 223.
94   ibid.

In the case of the Liberal Party organisation, direct interests in monetary and labour savings were far less influential in determining their position on reform than their fears about possible future loss of control. This stance, we saw, was reinforced once the State divisions began to speculate that the party's competitive advantage lay in the status quo. Reflecting that these positions were speculative and not evidence-based, they would prove to be wrong. The expense of how-to-vote cards and the difficulties in mobilising a volunteer army to distribute them only increased. Correspondingly, calls for party labels on ballots continued, and intensified, even within the Liberal Party.

By 1982, one year before party labels and legal recognition were legislated nationally, the Young Liberal Movement expressed its annoyance with the persistence of old-fashioned how-to-vote cards and argued fiercely for party affiliations to be placed on ballots:

> Reforms must also be instituted in the basic machinery of the electoral system. The traditional 'how to vote' cards, for example, are a clumsy and wasteful method of indicating a political party's preferred voting pattern. The electoral act should be amended to provide for party names to be shown on ballot papers, and for 'how to vote' cards to be displayed in polling booths (in a form approved by the electoral office).

> Under this more equitable arrangement the need to physically distribute cards is removed and most importantly, every voter will know precisely which party he is voting for. The number of informal votes is therefore likely to fall.[95]

For all its caution and deliberateness in the early 1970s, the Liberal Party succumbed to speculation and did not accurately foresee the extent to which its interests lay in legal recognition with registration. Nor did it foresee the inevitability of legal recognition.

When, in 1983, the ALP again took government, it, in the words of the Australian Electoral Commission, 'eschewed the confrontational style which had limited the success of its predecessor, and established a parliamentary committee, the Joint Select Committee on Electoral Reform'[96] (JSCER) to explore recognising, registering and regulating

---

95   Young Liberal Movement of Australia (12 December 1982) 'Press Release: Reforming our Democracy', in *Alan Missen Papers*, NLA, MS7528, Box 293, Folder 'Electoral Reform', p. 2.
96   Australian Electoral Commission (AEC) (28 January 2011) *A Short History of Federal Election Reform in Australia*, Canberra: AEC, available at: aec.gov.au/Elections/australian_electoral_history/history.htm.

political parties. The legacy of the failed early 1970s foray into party recognition and regulation was that there was voluminous party research and knowledge, a greater level of bureaucratic expertise and multiple draft Bills that could be used as a starting point on which JSCER and the parties could build. Additionally, by 1983, a decade had passed, allowing time for the Liberal Party to get used to the concept of legal recognition and registration. Furthermore, the politics of reform was executed more deftly, with secrecy replaced with a more cartel-like process in which all major political parties could contribute and advance their views and interests. Perhaps reflecting that this was a cartel-like process, recognition with registration and reward (a much more beneficial arrangement for the parties than had been proposed in the early 1970s) emerged out of JSCER as the model of regulation in Australia.

The Liberal Party was facing a bigger, more offensive challenge than mere legal recognition. The 1983 reform package included *recognition with registration*, slight *regulation* of party campaign finance *and reward*, in the form of public funding of party expenses, following in the footsteps of NSW two years earlier. Throughout JSCER and after the committee's two reports, the Liberal Party remained cautious about legal recognition of political parties, still fearful of the loss of control and autonomy that might follow. But, in 1983, the Liberal Party directed most of its efforts to opposing the public financing of party expenses.[97] In terms entirely consistent with its internal, private reasoning a decade earlier about where legal recognition with registration might lead, the Liberal Party argued that political parties 'should remain essentially voluntary organisations'[98] and that public funding of party expenses could 'have the effect of undermining volunteerism and reducing levels of membership participation within political parties',[99] 'entrench existing parties' and 'create a stale and moribund atmosphere'.[100] The registration of political parties was still not looked on favourably, with Steele Hall noting that '[r]egistration is part of the paraphernalia that will inevitably swell the bureaucracy when public funding is introduced'.[101] However, in 1983, unlike 1973–75,

---

97 See the dissenting reports in Joint Select Committee on Electoral Reform (JSCER) (September 1983) *First Report*, Canberra: Commonwealth of Australia, pp. 223–80.
98 Sir John Carrick, 'Dissenting Report', in ibid., p. 238.
99 JSCER, *First Report*, p. 149.
100 Steele Hall (30 August 1973) 'Dissenting Report', in ibid., p. 244.
101 ibid., p. 247.

the Liberal Party could not veto the passage of laws by blocking them in the Senate. The reforms passed and came into operation in time for the 1984 federal election.

Conclusion: Fearing the slippery slope

In many democracies, political parties have transitioned from private organisations with public functions unrecognised in law to largely publicly supported, sometimes regulated, organisations with protected private rights. The different points on the scale between official ignorance (with fully private status) and legal recognition with reward or recompense possess differing characteristics that make them more or less appealing to political parties, stable in practice and sound in theory.

It is the beneficial nature of the two most common types of relationship between party and state—regulation with recompense and recognition with registration and reward—that engenders suspicion that political parties have used their monopoly in the legislature to actively and presciently advance their own interests. At first blush, rational choice theory appears to explain well the likely role of parties in legislating the increasing resources the state provides to them and the barriers imposed on new political entrants.

By utilising hitherto private party records, the Australian case study of putting party affiliations on ballots in the early 1970s shows that political parties have not necessarily conformed to the rational choice expectation of deliberate and active use of the law to their own ends. Indeed, the case study shows that political parties approached the transition from a position of official ignorance to legal recognition with a good deal of caution, especially in the case of the party naturally more averse to governmental regulation, the Liberal Party.

Parties aimed to be rational in their approach to their interests and reform. Parties were meticulous researchers, believing that cautious and detailed study would enable them to be fully apprised of the short-term advantages and, especially, the long-term risks of recognition, and to avoid costly, and perhaps irrevocable, errors. This ensured that party elites largely understood the potential implications of recognition and regulation. International experience was key on the government side, where plentiful resources permitted detailed study trips and meetings with senior bureaucrats. While Daly and the ALP Cabinet were not very politically savvy in their pursuit of electoral reform, they were genuine in their views and operated from well-researched, if not well-disseminated, policy positions.

It is important to observe that, at least in the 1970s, Australian parties were not active manipulators of their monopoly over the legislature; they did not overtly seek advantage through legal recognition. Instead, as had been the case for decades, there was tremendous trepidation and caution within the Liberal Party about using the law for self-serving legal recognition purposes in case such use backfired and led either to a loss of control of the party brand or to a loss of control by setting the precedent for legal regulation.

In contrast, both parties initially saw significant potential advantages in *recognition* by the law: more votes for their party (ALP) and reduced expenditure in election campaigns (Liberal Party). Yet, the primary goals of maintaining control and autonomy, and the fear of a slippery slope from registration to regulation, concerned the Liberal Party organisation so much that the parliamentary party, in the absence of apparent electoral consequences, was willing to forgo any perceived advantages. Opposition to legal recognition was ensured once suspicious and speculative voices started suggesting that the Liberal Party's immediate electoral interests lay in the status quo.

Despite intentions, both parties fell short of truly rational decision-making. In the Liberal Party, the policy development process changed course based on largely speculative accounts about the weaknesses of other parties (including their coalition partner), even though they flew in the face of years of collective understanding about where the party's electoral interests lay. Within the ALP, a romanticised view of the Canadian system ensured that an objective assessment of the full range of recognition and regulatory regimes became impossible, and an assessment of the ALP's interests in the reforms was jettisoned from the process—as the pursuit of the Electoral (Disclosure of Funds) Bill 1974 demonstrated. And so, while the parties initially intended to rationally pursue their interests, they ended up muddling through the process. As it turned out, the failure of the Electoral Laws Amendment Bill 1974 was probably to the detriment of both major political parties.

In the end, Australian political parties, thus stymied, did not take the plunge into legal recognition until 1983. The 1983 reforms were of a different character—not recognition with registration but recognition with registration and reward—and were developed in a remarkably different context: a joint committee process, much more like Canada's process in the 1970s, rather than the inexperienced, secretive and Cabinet-driven process of the Whitlam Government. While, in 1983, the Liberal Party remained opposed, in principle, to regulation and public financing, they were in no position to prevent it. Australian parties jumped—in one fell swoop—all the way from being virtually unknown to the law to having legal recognition with registration and reward, without any serious regulation of party affairs.

3

Party registration and political participation: Regulating small and 'micro' parties

Norm Kelly

In the year before the 2013 federal election, 22 new political parties were registered. Many of these parties did not require their members to be active within the party or to pay fees; members were primarily used to meet registration requirements. The proliferation of these new parties would have been a trivial aside to the 2013 election, except that four went on to win six influential seats in parliament, including two parties that achieved less than 1 per cent in primary vote support. Because of the fine balance in the Senate after the election, where neither the Liberal–National Coalition Government nor the Labor Opposition held a majority of seats, these microparties wielded considerable power in determining contested legislative outcomes. These parties' electoral successes, which were based on a very tight exchange of preferences between many of these new microparties, have resulted in the new parties being accused of 'gaming' the system.[1]

---

1   For example, see Antony Green (2014) *Is It Time for a Fundamental Review of the Senate's Electoral System?*, Papers on Parliament No. 62, Canberra: Parliament of Australia, available at: www.aph.gov.au/~/~/link.aspx?_id=6EAB2F2521E8462CBBBF9EAE79C5229C&_z=z; Joint Standing Committee on Electoral Matters (JSCEM) (2014) *Interim Report on the Inquiry into the Conduct of the 2013 Federal Election: Senate Voting Practices*, Canberra: Parliament of Australia, available at: www.aph.gov.au/Parliamentary_Business/Committees/Joint/Electoral_Matters/2013_General_Election/Interim_Report.

The term 'gaming the system' in this context refers to the ability to produce successful election outcomes that do not necessarily correspond to voters' wishes, or to the relative support for the different parties. In fact, what these newer parties have done is utilise the established Senate ticket voting system to their own advantage, thereby outmanoeuvring the major parties that established the system 30 years ago. The major parties had been reluctant to reform the system, despite a growing understanding that Senate results could be 'gamed' in this way. As a result, the major parties suffered at the 2013 election.

This chapter explores the rise of the 'microparty' in Australia and its relationship to federal electoral regulation. It also asks whether Australia's party registration regime has a positive effect on the political participation function of parties discussed in Chapter 1. The following sections examine the legislative foundation for the regulation of political parties and the environment this has created for participation, both for internal member participation and for external electoral competition. A typology of microparties in the federal context is provided, and party registration trends since the commencement of the regulatory era in 1983 are analysed. This is followed by a discussion of the two-tiered membership threshold, which requires either 500 members or a sole parliamentarian to register a party. The role of regulation to encourage internal party democracy is assessed, as is whether legislators ought to provide controls or incentives—for example, by being more prescriptive on matters to be included in a party's constitution. Finally, an appraisal is provided of relevant aspects of the reform process, from the introduction of the party registration scheme in 1983 to the 2014 recommendations of the Joint Standing Committee on Electoral Matters (JSCEM) and, briefly, the 2016 Senate voting reforms.

The regulation of political parties

Political parties have a number of potential roles, including the recruitment of citizens into democratic processes and political activism.[2] The experience of party regulation in Australia, however, suggests that genuine citizen engagement has been of little consideration. The main reasons given in 1983 for introducing a political party registration scheme at the federal level were to enable parties to access public funding, provide recognition on ballot papers, introduce financial disclosure and reporting requirements, and reduce the level of informal Senate voting by allowing for the distribution of Senate preference votes through registered party tickets.[3]

While it can be argued that a membership threshold creates an uneven playing field for electoral competition, the new legislation at least provided a set of rules that clearly established the requirements for playing the political game. The introduction of this scheme strengthened the role of the existing parties, but also provided a framework with which emergent parties could work. But while providing a framework for party competition, the legislation was largely silent on the question of promoting political participation, allowing parties to carry out this purpose as they saw fit.

The growth and influence of the new microparties, without an obvious corresponding increase in party activism, appear to be an example of political opportunism, but can also be considered a reaction against a party cartel's control of the electoral system.[4] On one hand, this trend can be seen as indicative of efforts to 'game' the voting system. But gaming the system might also be seen as learning to better

---

2   Benjamin Reilly, Per Nordlund and Edward Newman (2008) *Political Parties in Conflict-Prone Societies: Encouraging Inclusive Politics and Democratic Development*, Tokyo: United Nations University.

3   The single transferable voting system is used to elect Senators. In a normal half-Senate election, six Senators are elected from each of the six States, with a quota being 14.3 per cent of the vote. Two Senators are also elected from each of the two mainland Territories. Parties are able to lodge group voting tickets (GVTs), which direct the preferences for voters who vote for the party 'above the line'. Although voters can choose to direct where their preferences go by voting 'below the line', less than 5 per cent do so, largely because of the complexity and time required to fill out the ballot paper.

4   For example, see Senator John Madigan, in Lenore Taylor (2016) 'Senate Voting Changes: Coalition Wins over Nick Xenophon and Greens', *The Guardian*, 12 February, available at: theguardian.com/australia-news/2016/feb/12/senate-voting-changes-coalition-wins-over-nick-xenophon-and-greens.

compete within the rules of the system, as laid down by the governing powers. Thus the creation and manoeuvring of newer microparties might be more broadly regarded as a legitimate strategy to break into a political system that has been controlled largely by the two major parties (Labor and the Liberal–National Coalition) for decades. The overriding questions then become: Does the proliferation of parties promote genuine participation of citizens in political debate? Should legislation explicitly encourage such participation? Is this healthy for Australia's democracy?

At a time when political parties in Western democracies, including Australia, are experiencing a decline in membership,[5] Australia has witnessed this significant increase in the number of parties contesting elections (see Figure 3.1). Could the new parties be filling an identified gap in the spectrum of possibilities for political expression and political participation? Is Australia's party registration regime, combined with the Senate single transferable vote (STV) voting system, doing anything to promote genuine political participation? Or is the growth in the number of parties simply a reflection of political expediency brought about by the inaction of legislators since party registration was introduced in 1983?

Interest in the number of political parties contesting federal elections reached a peak at the 2013 election—primarily because of Senate counts that resulted in two parties that initially received less than 0.04 of a quota in primary votes eventually winning seats. This was achieved primarily by staying ahead of other parties with fewer votes and then receiving their preference allocations.[6] These results were possible through tightly controlled preference exchanges between several parties, each with a small share of the primary vote, but collectively able to combine to achieve a significant share of the vote. Also of concern was the impact on voters, with electors

5   For example, see Marian Sawer, Norman Abjorensen and Phil Larkin (2009) *Australia: The State of Democracy*, Sydney: The Federation Press; Anika Gauja (2012) 'The "Push" for Primaries: What Drives Party Organisational Reform in Australia and the United Kingdom?', *Australian Journal of Political Science* 47(4): 641–58; Ingrid van Biezen and Thomas Poguntke (2014) 'The Decline of Membership-Based Politics', *Party Politics* 20(2): 205–16; Zsolt Enyedi (2014) 'The Discreet Charm of Political Parties', *Party Politics* 20(2): 194–204.
6   In Western Australia, the Australian Sports Party's primary vote share was 0.23 per cent or 0.016 of a quota. In Victoria, the Australian Motoring Enthusiast Party received 0.51 per cent of primary votes (0.0354 of a quota). The result in Western Australia was later declared void due to missing ballot papers.

needing magnifiers to read large ballot papers, and the difficulty of making an informed choice between a larger number of candidates and parties.[7]

Much of the subsequent commentary on the 2013 election results has centred on the Senate voting system and the ability to 'game' the system through compulsory preferential voting and the use of group voting tickets (GVTs).[8] As Antony Green has shown, the preferences expressed by minor party voters when voting below the line were very different from the way their preferences were distributed through the GVTs registered by parties.[9] Less attention has been given to the growth in the number of registered political parties and the impact that the regulatory regime for political parties may be having on democratic participation in Australia. In its inquiry into the 2013 federal election, the JSCEM's interim report focused on Senate voting practices. In regard to the party registration regime, JSCEM recommended changes to minimum membership requirements— to raise the bar against new party entrants contesting elections— but the role of political parties as forums for promoting political participation remained relatively unaddressed.

Australian microparties

In the Australian context, 'microparties' can be defined in several ways. The term is usually used in a pejorative sense, often by larger parties that see these minor parties as having a disproportionate influence in relation to their membership, parliamentary size and level of electoral support. Microparties themselves will understandably not use the term for self-identification, and a specific definition can be difficult, but microparties will typically be identified as having small or minimal party membership, low electoral support, low or non-existent parliamentary representation and a narrow issue-based or ideological policy focus.

---

7   In New South Wales, 44 groups and 110 candidates contested the Senate election.
8   See JSCEM, *Interim Report on the Inquiry into the Conduct of the 2013 Federal Election*.
9   See Antony Green (2014) 'Below the Line Preference Flows at the 2013 WA Senate Election', *ABC Elections*, [blog], 4 April, available at: blogs.abc.net.au/antonygreen/2014/04/below-the-line-preference-flows-at-the-2013-wa-senate-election.html.

The term microparty is essentially a subjective description of a party that is smaller than a 'minor party'. Typically, a *minor party* would record a low rating for at least one of the four identifiers—membership base, electoral support, parliamentary representation, policy base— but a *microparty* could be expected to exhibit low ratings for at least three, if not all four, of the identifiers.

Typically, the microparty may be one or a combination of the following three types. First, the party may be a vehicle for an individual's political aspirations. The formation of these parties is often based on a leader such as an existing Senator or Member of Parliament (MP), and often a parliamentarian who was first elected as a member of another party. This is facilitated by the section 123(1)(a)(i) provision of the *Commonwealth Electoral Act 1918* that allows a sole MP or Senator to register a party, with no requirement for a minimum number of party members. Characteristically, these parties rely on the success of the founder, and will often use the founder's name in the registered party name.

The Tasmanian Independent Senator Brian Harradine Group, for instance, existed for 21 years as a support mechanism for Senator Harradine, and was voluntarily deregistered when Harradine retired from parliament. Similarly, the Australian Progressive Alliance (APA) was deregistered after the parliamentary term of its founder, Senator Meg Lees, ended in 2005. Lees had registered the APA in 2003, following her resignation from the Australian Democrats. The 2015 registrations of the Jacqui Lambie Network, Glenn Lazarus Team and John Madigan's Manufacturing and Farming Party are recent examples of this type of microparty. Lambie's and Lazarus' parties were registered following their resignations from the ironically named Palmer United Party, another 'personal' party dependent on its founder-leader for survival.[10]

A second type of microparty is formed to pursue a specific narrow policy agenda. These 'single-issue' parties may be successful in achieving their desired policy outcome simply by competing electorally and not necessarily winning seats. For example, the mere threat of a single-issue

---

10   Glenn Kefford and Duncan McDonnell (2016) 'Ballots and Billions: Clive Palmer's Personal Party', *Australian Journal of Political Science*, 5 February, available at: tandfonline.com/doi/full/ 10.1080/10361146.2015.1133800.

microparty competing at an election may be sufficient for government and opposition parties to adopt a policy position on that particular issue. For instance, in the 2000s, the Fishing Party had some success in influencing changes in major party policies on access for recreational fishing. The ability to use GVTs to direct preferences, either towards or away from these major parties, has given the microparty significant influence. At the very least, the registration of single-issue parties promotes their issues in public political debate.

When single-issue parties are successful in winning seats—for example, the Australian Motoring Enthusiast Party (AMEP) winning a Senate seat in 2013—the question arises of how these parties' representatives will then act on legislation unrelated to their raison d'être. Although unsuccessful in winning seats, the Save the ADI Site Party (SASP) is an example of the transient nature of some of these single-issue parties. The SASP was registered in 2001 with the primary objective of preventing the development of government-owned bushland near Penrith, in Sydney's western suburbs. The party contested two federal elections, in 2001 and 2004. However, after the Australian Defence Industries (ADI) site was sold to private interests in 2004, the party had no further purpose and was voluntarily deregistered in 2005.[11] The current register of parties (April 2016) includes many single-issue microparties, such as the Australian Cyclists Party, Australian Antipaedophile Party, Voluntary Euthanasia Party, Smokers Rights Party and Bullet Train for Australia.

The Nick Xenophon Team (NXT) provides a good example of a microparty that exhibits elements of the above types. The NXT has evolved from the Xenophon-led Independent No Pokies ticket, a party grouping that was never registered at the federal level, but played a significant role in South Australian (SA) politics. Xenophon was elected to the SA Parliament in 1997, with less than 3 per cent of the vote, on the single issue of abolishing poker machines. Following his election to the Federal Parliament as an Independent Senator, Xenophon subsequently established the NXT in 2013. From its origins as a single-issue State-based party, the NXT has developed a far broader policy agenda and support base, but primarily remains a vehicle for a single politician.

---

11 See Norm Kelly (2012) *Directions in Australian Electoral Reform: Professionalism and Partisanship in Electoral Management*, Canberra: ANU E Press, pp. 85–6.

A third type of microparty may be formed primarily as a harvester of preferences, often with a 'feel-good' name that can in itself attract votes (for example, Coke in the Bubblers was registered from 2013 to 2015). If several parties established on this basis form a syndicate, their GVTs can distribute their vote preferences within the syndicate. In the Senate context, if there are sufficient syndicate party votes to reach a quota (or at least remain ahead of non-syndicate parties), the lead candidate of one of the syndicate members will be elected.

It appears that the rise in the number of political parties at the federal level has more to do with political expediency, in furthering the interests of a few individuals, than with an increase in broader political participation. This may be for legitimate policy-driven reasons or for personal gain and influence. From a regulatory viewpoint, though, the challenge lies in providing a reasonable balance between allowing the formation of multiple parties to represent diverse policy-based interests and restricting the entry of frivolous or narrowly focused single-issue parties. And there is the prior question of whether this is actually the role of the regulator.

A disconcerting aspect of the increase in prominence of microparties is the deleterious impact it may have on the level of women's representation. Where microparties can win seats (through the lack of a threshold party vote), as in the Australian Senate, this can result in fewer women being elected. This is due to microparties tending to have male leaders who win their only seat.[12] In the 2013 Victorian Senate election, for instance, only four of 34 minor and microparty leading candidates were women.[13] This gender disparity was similar in other States.

---

12   See Richard E. Matland (2005) 'Enhancing Women's Political Participation: Legislative Recruitment and Electoral Systems', in Julie Ballington and Azza Karam (eds) *Women in Parliament: Beyond Numbers*, Stockholm: International Institute for Democracy and Electoral Assistance, pp. 93–111.

13   Two major party groups, the Coalition and Labor, had male lead candidates. The Greens had a woman lead.

Promoting and restricting participation

In the electoral context, participation takes two forms: the *internal* democratic participation of individuals and organisations within political parties, which can take a variety of different forms,[14] and the *external* participation between competing political parties at elections. To date, legislators in Australia have been reluctant to interfere in the internal machinations of parties. As Gauja argues in this volume, this reluctance stems from both a concern to maintain the associated freedoms of parties and a normative disagreement over what might constitute the most appropriate form of intraparty democracy. At the federal level, registered parties are required to have a written constitution that sets out the aims of the party,[15] but the legislation is otherwise silent on matters to be included in the constitution (for example, administrative structures or governance).

Legislators have usually taken action only after some form of political scandal, with the most obvious example being Queensland's legislation directing the manner in which party preselections are conducted. This general reticence is understandable, as legislators could either be working against the interests of their own parties or, conversely, be overly partisan in their approach. The question of what it means to be a member of a party has not been comprehensively dealt with in legislation. There may be good reason for this and, as Orr points out, under contract law it can be up to the party itself to determine what constitutes a 'member'.[16] Queensland's *Electoral Act* provides limited help, saying that *a member of a political party means a person who is a member of the political party.*[17] Other jurisdictions do not even include such a concise interpretation.

---

14   See William P. Cross and Richard S. Katz (eds) (2013) *The Challenges of Intra-party Democracy*, Oxford: Oxford University Press; Ian Marsh and Raymond Miller (2012) *Democratic Decline and Democratic Renewal: Political Change in Britain, Australia and New Zealand*, Cambridge: Cambridge University Press.

15   Section 123(1)(b) of the *Commonwealth Electoral Act 1918*.

16   Graeme Orr (2010) *The Law of Politics: Elections, Parties and Money in Australia*, Sydney: The Federation Press, pp. 133–4. See also Anika Gauja (2015) 'The Construction of Party Membership', *European Journal of Political Research* 54(2): 232–48.

17   Section 2 of the *Electoral Act 1992*.

Parliaments have been more proactive in regulating the eligibility for parties to fully participate at elections, including party name recognition on ballot papers and public funding.[18] This may seem to support the cartelisation thesis regarding restriction of competition,[19] but can also be argued as necessary to ensure voters can make a considered and informed choice between serious candidates and policy options. This rationale is particularly prominent in relation to federal reforms designed to limit the participation of parties such as the Democratic Labor Party (DLP) and Liberals for Forests (LFF). After parliament increased the powers of the Australian Electoral Commission (AEC) to deregister parties in 2000, the DLP refused to provide a membership list to the commission, resulting in parliament further amending legislation in 2001 to strengthen the AEC's powers.[20] In the LFF case, the Liberal–National Coalition Government was successful in 2004 in legislating to limit the ability for new parties to use names that might misleadingly suggest a connection or relationship with previously registered parties.[21] However, this could not apply to existing parties, so the government passed further legislation in 2006 to deregister all parties and require them to reapply for registration, thus eliminating the LFF, which had been registered since 2001.[22]

The contestation of ideologically based party names can be seen in the registration process for the Liberal Democratic Party (LDP). The LDP was advised by the AEC in 2007 that the commission would likely reject an application to register the party as the Liberal Democratic Party, due to possible confusion with the existing Liberal Party name.[23] The party then applied, and was registered, as the Liberty and Democracy Party. The following year, the LDP applied to change its registered name to the Liberal Democratic Party. Despite objections from the Liberal Party, Australian Democrats and the Liberal National Party of Queensland, as well as the AEC's own doubts, the AEC approved the

---

18   While unregistered parties are able to stand candidates at elections, these candidates have a similar standing as Independent candidates.

19   See Kelly, *Directions in Australian Electoral Reform*, pp. 24–5.

20   Laurie McGrath (2011) *Law Reform and Political Party Registration Case Study: Democratic Labor Party (DLP)*, Research Paper, Brisbane: Australian Electoral Commission (Queensland), 2 July, available at: aceproject.org/ero-en/regions/pacific/AU/law-reform-and-political-party-registration-case.

21   *Electoral and Referendum Amendment (Enrolment Integrity and Other Measures) Act 2004*, amending section 129 of the *Commonwealth Electoral Act 1918*.

22   Kelly, *Directions in Australian Electoral Reform*, pp. 97–8.

23   See AEC decision at: aec.gov.au/Parties_and_Representatives/party_registration/Registration_Decisions/2007/ldp.htm.

name change.[24] The result of the 2013 NSW Senate election renewed debate about the consequences of the similarity in the LDP's and Liberal Party's registered names. At that election, the LDP, using their registered short name of 'Liberal Democrats', and fortunate in drawing the first allocated group position on the Senate ballot paper, achieved 9.5 per cent of the vote,[25] an increase of 7.19 per cent from the 2010 election (when they drew the final group position). The LDP's success in winning a NSW Senate seat can be attributed to the mix of a favourable ballot position, favourable preference flows, possible confusion with the Liberal Party (which used the short name of 'Liberals and Nationals' in a joint ticket in the 25th allocated group) as well as genuine support for the party. The degree of importance attributable to each of these factors, though, is difficult to determine.

Party registration trends

Prior to 1983, there had been little specific reference to political parties in Australian statutes. Political parties had historically been considered voluntary associations[26] and the courts were reluctant to interfere in internal party issues. The only pieces of federal legislation that dealt specifically with political parties in the first 80 years of Federation were the *Commonwealth Electoral (War-Time) Act 1917*, which simply referred to the 'Ministerial' and 'Opposition' parties; the *Communist Party Dissolution Act 1950*, later ruled by the High Court to be unconstitutional; and the *Constitution Alteration (Senate Casual Vacancies) 1977*, which facilitated the first reference to political parties in the Australian Constitution.

In more recent times, parties have been more accurately considered as professional organisations that exert considerable influence and power over state affairs, through the election of party candidates, influencing who is elected from other parties or the promotion of policies in an election environment. In addition, since the introduction of public funding regimes in the 1980s, parties have become the recipients

---

24   See   AEC   decision   at: aec.gov.au/Parties_and_Representatives/party_registration/
Registration_Decisions/2008/liberal_democratic.htm.
25   Australian Electoral Commission (AEC) (2010) *First Preferences by Candidate: NSW*, Virtual Tally Room, Canberra: AEC, available at: results.aec.gov.au/15508/Website/SenateStateFirstPrefs-15508-NSW.htm.
26   Anika Gauja (2010) *Political Parties and Elections: Legislating for Representative Democracy*, Farnham: Ashgate, p. 45.

of substantial taxpayer financial support. As a result, parties have increasingly been considered as legal entities and are increasingly subject to judicial interventions in their affairs.[27]

Since the introduction of the federal registration regime in 1983, 251 parties have been registered at the federal level (for the full list, see the Appendix to this volume). After State divisions and branches of several party groups (such as the Liberal, Labor, Greens and Christian Democratic parties) are consolidated, there remain about 170 specific parties during this 33-year period. While several parties have re-formed or been renamed over this period, the number of parties registered for each of the 11 elections held since the party registration regime was introduced has ranged from 32 to 77, with at least 50 parties registered at each election since 1990. The focus on the large numbers of Senate groups at the 2013 election has led to a media perception that the 77 parties registered for that election represented a high watermark. However, the same numbers of parties were registered for the 1998 election (see Figure 3.1).

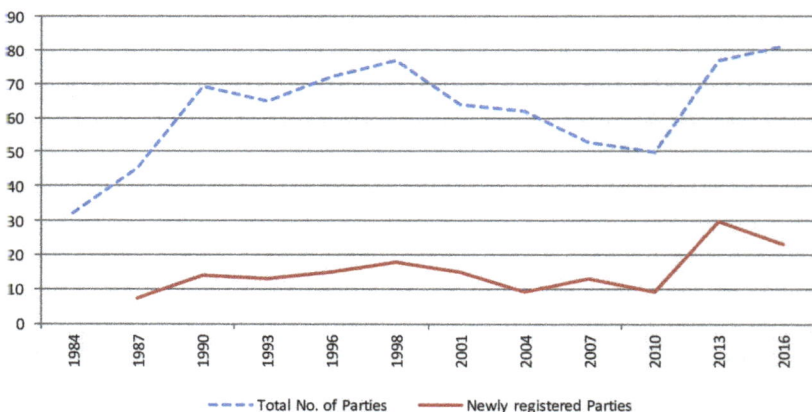

Figure 3.1 Number of registered parties at federal elections, 1984–2013

Notes: Total number of parties includes party divisions as separate parties. Newly registered parties: 1987 does not include seven State and Territory branches of the Australian Labor Party; 1990 does not include 14 State and local Greens parties; 1996 does not include six State and Territory divisions of the Call to Australia (Fred Nile) Group; 1998 does not include nine Christian Democratic parties—essentially a renaming of the Call to Australia Group.

Source: Australian Electoral Commission figures (aec.gov.au).

27   See Orr, *The Law of Politics*, pp. 117–41.

When the figures are broken down to identify the number of newly registered parties for each election, it can be seen that there was a significant increase between 2010 and 2013—almost double the number of newly registered parties in any previous inter-election period. Of the 30 newly registered parties, 22 were registered in the eight months prior to the election.[28] This may suggest an increase in political activism or the setting up of parties for the purpose of 'gaming' the Senate elections (or a combination of both). Since the 2013 election, a further 23 new parties have registered, with many of these likely to be inspired by the 2013 election results.

Table 3.1 Party groups contesting Senate elections, 1998, 2013 and 2016*

	NSW	Vic.	Qld	WA	SA	Tas.	ACT	NT	Total
1998	16	19	18	15	10	12	8	5	103
2013	42	37	34	27	31	23	13	12	219
2016	41	37	37	27	23	21	10	7	203

* Does not include unendorsed groups.

Source: Australian Electoral Commission election results (aec.gov.au).

Further analysis of the 2013 federal election shows that while the total number of parties in 2013 was the same as for the 1998 election, there was a doubling in the number of party nominations for Senate elections (see Table 3.1). This further supports the argument that the Senate voting system was being 'gamed', and is not necessarily an indication of increased political activism. For 2016, there has been only a small drop in the number of party groups contesting the Senate elections. This may indicate that the full effect of changes to the Senate voting system in 2016 is yet to be reflected in party competition. The influence that small parties can have on election outcomes, combined with the ease in harvesting membership names through internet-based and social media sources, suggests that gaming has been a driving factor. However, further analysis is required to determine whether these new parties are a sign of increasing political participation, gaming or possible disenchantment with established, older parties.

Often, these newer small parties have an online presence encouraging people to join, but typically do not provide a link to a party constitution so that this can be considered by intending

---

28   A list of parties registered between the 2010 and 2013 elections is in the Appendix to this volume.

members. This includes the Vote Flux Party, Australian Sex Party, AMEP, Australian Christians, Smokers Rights Party and, ironically, the Wikileaks Party—a party with a policy platform based on transparency. The Pirate Party Australia, another freedom of information party, does have its constitution available online.[29]

Analysis of the new parties' websites shows that many of the parties do not require intending members to pay a membership fee (see Appendix 3.1), which can be indicative of a lack of internal party activity and was the case for more than 70 per cent of the parties registered in 2013. On their membership application forms, several parties stress the need to ensure the application details are identical to those on the AEC's roll.[30] This is clearly designed to ensure that new members can be used to meet the 500-member registration requirement of section 123 of the Act. It appears that many parties are developing their membership simply as a database of enrolled voters, with no requirement to contribute financially to the party and with little opportunity for members to be involved in party activities.

A good example of the motives to establish new parties can be seen from the comments of one promoter of a party seeking registration:

> This is intended to be a single issue party, created to hopefully become a balance of power party in the Senate ... I need 500 signatures from people who think as we do, so that I can register the party.[31]

This comment is refreshingly honest and forthright, and highlights the three focuses of many new parties: signatures, a particular single issue and Senate influence. It also emphasises the importance of names and signatures, without mention of participation in internal party activity, such as policy development and campaigning.

This may be a consequence of the federal legislation not specifying requirements to be included in a party's constitution, but may also be in the interests of both a party and its membership. From a party's perspective, managing and organising a membership base can be time-consuming and costly. And if members have democratic rights—for

---

29   Available at: pirateparty.org.au/constitution/.
30   For example: 'I declare that I am enrolled on the Commonwealth electoral roll at my address as shown above.'
31   Russell Pridgeon, Australians Against Paedophiles Party, 31 March 2014, available at: hotcopper.com.au/threads/anti-pedophile-party.2250494/?vtrct=5&utm_expid=509771-17. U3wUhNlPTku4I_iccyMzSg.5&utm_referrer=https%3A%2F%2Fwww.google.co.nz%2F#. Vbv6R_OqpBc.

example, determining policies and/or executive members—this can be seen as threatening to a party's policy direction and leadership. From a member's perspective, assisting a party to become registered may be considered sufficient political engagement, with no expectation of or desire for further political activism. These can be mutually beneficial outcomes: the party is enabled to pursue its objectives in the electoral and political arenas and can concentrate on these objectives without diverting resources to service the membership, while members have expressed their support for a particular cause, with their activism at a level with which they are comfortable.

An example of this newer form of political activism can be seen in the recently registered Jacqui Lambie Network (JLN). Having been registered on the basis of the provision of the Act that allows a sole MP or Senator to register a party (section 123(1)(a)(i)), the JLN is not required to have 500 members. However, as with other parties, it is seeking electoral success. At the time of writing, the JLN does not have a website and its main interface with the public is a Facebook page.[32] In principle, a social media site can provide an active interface between a party and its supporters, though one controlled largely by the party itself.

Such forms of party engagement can be more attractive to citizens who may not be interested in the often more formalised structures and processes that exist in many of the older established parties.[33] While most established parties actively engage in social media to spread their messages and to generate financial support, this tends to support traditional party structures. Newer, smaller parties—for example, those using the section 123 provision—appear to concentrate on forms of 'clicktivism', where supporters are encouraged to click on electronic petitions to demonstrate their political participation. The Glenn Lazarus Team, registered in mid-2015, did not appear to have a party website three months after registration, but, through Senator Lazarus' parliamentary website, supporters could sign petitions, be linked to parliamentary inquiry websites and register for policy forums. The homepage is complete with links to Facebook, Twitter, Instagram

---

32   Available at: facebook.com/pages/Jacqui-Lambie-Network/881832031874477. Rather than seeking party members, Senator Lambie stated: 'Jacqui Lambie has called for people who would like to be part of her political Network to make contact through her Facebook.' 31 March 2015, available at: senatorlambie.com.au/2015/03/lambie-seeks-to-form-independent-network/.
33   Gauja, 'The Construction of Party Membership'.

and YouTube, and appears to be designed to provide supporters with easy access to opportunities for political expression,[34] and this can be particularly appealing to those who distrust established political parties.

The membership threshold

The difficulty of meeting the 500-member threshold is reflected in several rejections of party registration applications. In 2013, six applications to register new parties were refused—all due to failure to satisfy the membership threshold test (see Table 3.2). Once the AEC has identified at least 500 names on the electoral roll, it contacts a random sample of 18 to 50 names to ascertain whether they are genuine members of the party.[35] The majority of parties refused registration (and many that were registered in 2013; see Appendix 3.1) appear to represent extremely narrow policy interests. Typical of these refusals is the rejection of the Cheaper Petrol Party, where the AEC stated that in conducting a random sample of 50 members:

> [E]ight of these people denied being members of the Party. Five of the eight people remembered signing a petition for lower petrol prices, but were quite clear that they had not joined a political party and did not want to do so. The other three people had no idea where the Party had sourced their details from and did not remember having any contact with the Party.[36]

Partly as a result of the use of petitions to build membership lists, the JSCEM has recommended that legislation be amended to require the AEC to validate all memberships submitted to meet the minimum membership threshold.[37] If legislators endorse the recommended trebling of the minimum threshold, the higher level will have little, if any, impact on the major established parties. The increase is designed to eliminate microparties or at least make it difficult for them to survive. A comparison of member threshold requirements in Australian jurisdictions is provided in Table 3.3. When the membership threshold is considered as a ratio against total numbers on the electoral roll,

34 See: senatorlazarus.com/.
35 Details of how the numbers are determined are in Appendix 3 of the AEC's *Party Registration Guide: Federal Registration of Political Parties* booklet, available at: aec.gov.au/Parties_and_Representatives/Party_Registration/files/party-registration-guide.pdf.
36 Available at: aec.gov.au/Parties_and_Representatives/party_registration/Registration_Decisions/2013/5204.htm.
37 JSCEM, *Interim Report on the Inquiry into the Conduct of the 2013 Federal Election*, p. 57.

it can be seen that the federal threshold is the lowest of all Australian jurisdictions, and will remain so even if the threshold was to increase to 1,500 members.

Table 3.2 Parties refused registration in 2013: 500-member test

Party	Verified on roll	Contacted	Denied being a member
Liberal Movement	533	38	12
Cheaper Petrol Party	549	50	8
No Parking Meters Party	502	18	2
Australian Rock N Roll Party	419	0	0
The Burger Urge Party	500	18	5
Natural Medicine Party*	Not specified	34	4

* The AEC could identify only 489 members of the Natural Medicine Party on the electoral roll from its initial application. A second application was received on 13 June 2013, which was refused due to four people denying being members. A third application was approved in November 2013.

Source: Australian Electoral Commission (www.aec.gov.au/Parties_and_Representatives/party_registration/index.htm).

Table 3.3 Party membership requirements for registration

Jurisdiction	Minimum required members	Enrolled at most recent election (year)	Enrolled: minimum required members ratio	Parties contesting most recent election[1]
Commonwealth	500	15,671,551 (2016)	31,343	64
Commonwealth (JSCEM recommendation)	1,500	15,671,551 (2016)	10,448	N/A
New South Wales	750	5,040,662 (2015)	6,721	17
Victoria	500	3,806,301 (2014)	7,613	20
Queensland	500	2,981,145 (2015)	5,962	7
Western Australia	500	1,412,533 (2013)	2,825	10
South Australia	150	1,142,419 (2014)	7,616	22[2]
Tasmania	100	366,442 (2014)	3,664	7
Australian Capital Territory	100	256,702 (2012)	2,435	7
Northern Territory	200	123,805 (2012)	619	5

[1] Separate divisions of a party (for example, Liberal NSW, Victoria; Labor, Country Labor, and so on) or cooperative alliances (for example, Australian Greens, Greens NSW) are counted as one party.

[2] Includes eight 'Independent' groups, such as the Nick Xenophon Team and Palmer United Party.

Sources: Electoral commissions' election data, updated from Norm Kelly (2012) *Directions in Australian Electoral Reform: Professionalism and Partisanship in Electoral Management*, Canberra: ANU E Press, p. 85.

Regulating for internal party democracy

A way to encourage greater political participation in political parties is to provide members with genuine opportunities to be involved in decision-making, including for preselections, policy platforms and electing party officials. The existence of a registration regime provides the state with an opportunity to require certain standards or principles of internal party democracy and behaviour. There are competing arguments on whether increased internal party democracy is more empowering for the general party membership or for the party leadership.

For example, Susan Scarrow puts forward the proposition that increased internal democracy can create a 'virtuous circle' whereby the general membership is more closely linked to ordinary citizens and democratic decisions will result in parties better reflecting citizens' views and, as a result, governments become more stable and legitimate.[38] It is also argued that by including the general membership in decision-making, a party will offer voters more informed choices, as a result of more broad-based input. Conversely, though, the economic theory of democracy argues, as Sawer and Gauja note in Chapter 1, that internal party democracy can detract from a party's ability to be electorally competitive. In such cases, what a party may be seeking are 'fans', as Scarrow describes them: members who are willing to express loyalty and contribute financially, without seeking active involvement in a party's decision-making processes.[39] Otherwise, ideologically adherent members (again using Scarrow's typology) may stymie electoral effectiveness due to these members being more extremist than the general population.

In Australia, issues of internal party democracy have generally related to candidate preselections, and often in a negative sense following claims of 'branch-stacking' for the purpose of controlling preselection

---

38   Susan Scarrow (2005) *Political Parties and Democracy in Theoretical and Practical Perspectives: Implementing Intra-party Democracy*, Washington, DC: National Democratic Institute for International Affairs, p. 3.
39   Susan Scarrow (2014) Multi-Speed Membership Parties: Evidence and Implications, Paper prepared for Contemporary Meanings of Party Membership, ECPR Joint Sessions of Workshops, Salamanca, Spain, available at: ecpr.eu/Filestore/PaperProposal/e6c836a5-f1b2-4717-814c-786275ce2da2.pdf. Also see Richard Gunther and Larry Diamond (2003) 'Species of Political Parties: A New Typology', *Party Politics* 9(2): 167–99.

outcomes. For the Australian Labor Party (ALP), internal democracy issues have also related to the election of parliamentary leaders and the degree of voting influence that affiliated trade unions have in preselections. To re-energise the party at the grassroots level, an ALP review committee recommended in 2010 that party executives and trade unions should have less influence in preselections, and that a system of primaries be introduced that would include non-members.[40]

In 2013, ALP members were able to vote in the parliamentary leadership ballot, with the total of members' votes given equal weight with parliamentary party votes. Although Bill Shorten lost the general membership vote (40 per cent), he was elected leader due to his high level of support in the caucus room (64 per cent).[41] The ALP also trialled community preselections ahead of the 2015 NSW State election.[42] While the concept of a party reaching beyond its membership to make preselection decisions appears to be a healthy democratic development in Australia, it does raise many new regulatory questions. For example, the question of regulating preselection campaign expenditure is an emerging issue.

The most directly democratic of the Australian parties has been the Australian Democrats, which provided all members with a vote on parliamentary leadership positions, preselections, executive positions and policies. This approach, while inherently altruistic, resulted in several problems and issues within the party. For example, through the 1990s, policy positions were often decided by only 1 to 3 per cent of the membership, allowing small numbers of members to exert a large influence on the party's policy positions.[43] Because of a reliance on mail-based ballots, there can be long periods when the party leadership remains undecided, and leadership votes by the general

40   Steve Bracks, John Faulkner and Bob Carr (2010) *2010 National Review: Report to the ALP National Executive*, Canberra: Australian Labor Party.
41   Emma Griffiths (2013) 'Bill Shorten Elected Labor Leader over Anthony Albanese after Month-long Campaign', *ABC News*, 13 October, available at: www.abc.net.au/news/2013-10-13/bill-shorten-elected-labor-leader/5019116.
42   In the seats of Balmain, Campbelltown, Londonderry, Newtown and Strathfield. Party members and the general community each receive a 50 per cent vote weighting. Female candidates receive a vote weighting according to Labor's affirmative action policy. See Alexis Carey (2014) 'Former Balmain State Labor MP Verity Firth Wins Community Pre-selection for the Seat of Balmain', *Inner West Courier*, 5 May, available at: dailytelegraph.com.au/newslocal/inner-west/former-balmain-state-labor-mp-verity-firth-wins-community-pre-selection-for-the-seat-of-balmain/story-fngr8h4f-1226905718944.
43   Author's personal communications.

membership can be in conflict with the view of the party's caucus room. For example, in 2001, Senator Natasha Stott Despoja defeated Senator Meg Lees for the party leadership position with about two-thirds of the membership vote. However, Stott Despoja did not have majority support in the caucus room and was forced to resign the leadership the following year, while Lees had already left the party.

Currently, when a political party applies for federal registration, it is required to provide a copy of its constitution, but the legislation has limited requirements for what needs to be included in this constitution (see Chapter 7, this volume).[44] In 2009, the Rudd Labor Government's *Electoral Reform Green Paper* put forward a range of measures to regulate party constitutions. The paper suggested that constitutions be available on the AEC website, that they contain minimum requirements in regard to membership, structure and amending the constitution and that they could include internal democracy provisions.[45] Such reforms had earlier been suggested in the JSCEM's report into the 2004 election. However, internal party democracy was not addressed in the JSCEM report, except in the Australian Democrats' minority report. The Democrats subsequently introduced legislation to require internal democracy measures, but the Bill lapsed without debate in 2010.[46]

At the State level, Queensland has been the only State to legislate for internal party democracy and, as noted earlier, this was a result of concerns of corrupt and fraudulent practices within parties.[47] Following amendments in 2002, the *Electoral Act 1992* is now quite prescriptive of what is required in a registered party's constitution, including that a preselection ballot must satisfy the general principles of free and democratic elections.[48] The following subsection details what these principles are, including that only party members may vote, each member has only one vote and voting is to be conducted by secret ballot. Further, Electoral Commission Queensland (ECQ) can intervene in a party's preselection processes, either on its own initiative

---

44   Section 126(2)(f) of the *Commonwealth Electoral Act 1918*.
45   Australian Government (2009) *Electoral Reform Green Paper: Strengthening Australia's Democracy*, Canberra: Commonwealth of Australia, p. 117.
46   Electoral (Greater Fairness of Electoral Processes) Amendment Bill 2007.
47   Scott Bennett (2002) *Australia's Political Parties: More Regulation?*, Department of the Parliamentary Library Research Paper No. 21, Canberra: Parliament of Australia, p. 20.
48   Section 76(1) of the *Electoral Act 1992*.

or after receiving a complaint.[49] Section 71 of New Zealand's *Electoral Act 1993* contains similar provisions for member participation in preselections, including an allowance for preselections to be decided by delegated authority.

JSCEM recommendations

The reforms of 1983 were designed to provide the major parties with control over the Senate voting system. Although the rising level of informal voting for the Senate had been a catalyst for change, the possibility existed to reform the system without removing voters' control over the flow of their preferences. In 1983, the ALP recommended the introduction of optional preferential voting (OPV) for both the Senate and the House of Representatives. The (Labor-majority) Joint Select Committee on Electoral Reform (JSCER) noted that:

> [T]he full preferential system leads to an increased informal vote, and may force voters to cast a preference in favour of candidates to whom they feel antipathy, or feel no sympathy, or about whom they do not care.[50]

However, the Liberal–National Coalition opposed Labor's OPV proposal. This was understandable given that the Coalition was the major beneficiary of preference flows at the time. The proposal was therefore abandoned in the desire to achieve broader bipartisan reform.

In May 2014, the (Coalition-majority) JSCEM released an interim report into the 2013 election and reprised the comment from the 1983 committee that 'electors felt their votes had been devalued by preference deals and that they had been disenfranchised by being forced to prefer unpreferred candidates'.[51] The 2014 report recommended that OPV be introduced for above-the-line voting and that GVTs be abolished. While the JSCEM report supported this recommendation by making reference to the altruistic ideals of 'enfranchising voters by returning to them full control of preferences' and 'ending voter frustration',

---

49   ibid., s. 168.
50   Joint Select Committee on Electoral Reform (JSCER) (1983) *First Report*, Canberra: Parliament of the Commonwealth of Australia, p. 63.
51   JSCEM, *Interim Report on the Inquiry into the Conduct of the 2013 Federal Election*, p. 2.

it also referred to the political objectives of providing a disincentive to the proliferation of 'minor "front" parties' and 'removing the incentive to "game" the system'.[52]

Once again, the approach to possible reform was influenced by perceptions of electoral advantage from the existing system—with the Coalition Government in the midst of negotiating legislation through a noncompliant Senate at the time, due to the balance of power held by the microparties. It was therefore seen as electorally and politically advantageous to remove these microparties. The difficulty with this strategy is that the Coalition requires support from one of the larger parties—the ALP or The Greens—to bring about change, as the microparties will be steadfast in opposing any reform that is likely to result in their demise.[53]

Between the 1983 and 2014 reports, the (Coalition-majority) JSCEM report on the 1996 election stated it would prefer reducing the number of candidates standing for the Senate, to moving to an OPV system. However, since that report, Senate candidate numbers have more than doubled (see Table 3.4) and the JSCEM was largely silent on this issue until its 2014 report.

Table 3.4 Candidates contesting Senate elections, 1983–2016

1983	1984	1987	1990	1993	1996	1998	2001	2004	2007	2010	2013	2016
244*	202	255*	223	266	255	329	285	330	367	349	529	631*

* 1983, 1987 and 2016 were double-dissolution elections, meaning that all Senate seats were up for election, resulting in higher than normal numbers of candidates.

Source: Australian Electoral Commission election results (aec.gov.au).

The 2014 report contained only three core recommendations in relation to party registration: increase the membership threshold to 1,500 members, with lower thresholds for parties that wish to nominate candidates only in specific States or Territories; require new and existing parties to meet the new thresholds; and require more

---

52   ibid., p. 52.

53   See Lenore Taylor (2015) 'Turnbull Government Faces Battle to Change Voting Rules for Senate', *The Guardian*, 22 September, available at: theguardian.com/australia-news/2015/sep/22/turnbull-government-faces-battle-to-change-voting-rules-for-senate; and Heath Aston (2015) 'Micro-parties Threaten Election War against Coalition, Greens over Senate Change', *The Canberra Times*, 23 September, available at: canberratimes.com.au/federal-politics/political-news/microparties-threaten-election-war-against-coalition-greens-over-senate-change-20150923-gjt29b.html.

detail in party constitutions. While this is a minimalist approach to an opportunity to overhaul the registration regime, it is understandable given that the inquiry was primarily focused on the Senate election outcomes and possible 'gaming' of the system.

As part of its recommendations, JSCEM proposed that the AEC check the membership validity of each person submitted to meet the threshold and that these verification checks be conducted for each party every three years. If this provision were to be adopted, along with the accompanying recommendation to increase the minimum membership threshold to 1,500, this would create a significantly higher administrative burden on the AEC. This would be met from central funds, but the JSCEM has also recommended that there should not be any increase in the cost to apply for registration (currently $500). Hence, there is little monetary penalty for party applicants to ensure their membership lists are accurate; it is the AEC that has the financial burden of verifying applications. A better system may be to increase the application fee substantially, with the major proportion of the fee refunded once a party is registered. This would provide all parties with a severe penalty if their membership lists were noncompliant.

The JSCEM recommendation to require parties to provide more detail in their constitutions is based on the Queensland legislation, with details required including party objectives, rules of membership, selection of officials and preselection rules.[54] This appears to be a common sense approach, not dictating to parties how to run their affairs, but requiring information that is beneficial to intending members. Ideally, this would create greater transparency in relation to internal processes, while leaving it to the parties to decide the manner in which these issues are dealt with—a natural progression in the way that party administration has evolved from the private to the public realm.

---

54   JSCEM, *Interim Report on the Inquiry into the Conduct of the 2013 Federal Election*, pp. 58–9.

2016: Reform at last

In March 2016, reform of the Senate voting system was passed by the Parliament.[55] These changes did little in the area of party registration, with the primary change being to allow the use of party logos on ballot papers—partially a response to questions of confusion for voters, as discussed earlier in relation to the LDP. Two major reforms of the voting system occurred. First was the removal of voting tickets, therefore removing the ability for parties to direct the preferences of voters. Second, partial optional preferential (POP) voting for the Senate was introduced, so that voters now only need to express six preferences above the line or 12 below the line to make a formal vote.[56] Now that voters no longer have the convenience of stating a single preference, POP voting eases the burden for the voter that a full preferential system would create. This also avoids the complexity and high informal rate that would most likely occur under a full preferential system.

The Coalition Government was able to pass the legislation with the support of the Australian Greens, a party that would also benefit from the reduced influence, and seat-winning ability, of the microparties. Although there may be strategic advantages to The Greens, the party also has a significant history of Senate electoral reform attempts, so their actions in 2016 can be viewed as a convergence of party policy and pragmatic positioning. The reaction from the microparties was understandable, with arguments that, for example, the reform 'strips democracy from the people'[57] and 'will crucify democracy in this country'.[58] However, the microparties are essentially victims of their own success and their arguments are not consistent with the democratic principle of fairness. Despite any strategic reasons the Coalition and

---

55   Commonwealth Electoral Amendment Bill 2016.
56   There are additional saving provisions to ensure that voters who continue to use the previous system—that is, just voting '1' above the line—will have this recorded as a formal vote. See the explanatory memoranda, available at: aph.gov.au/Parliamentary_Business/ Bills_ Legislation/Bills_Search_Results/Result?bId=r5626.
57   Senator Ricky Muir (2016) *Hansard*, 17 March, p. 2328.
58   Senator Glenn Lazarus (2016) *Hansard*, 16 March, p. 2232.

Greens may have for the reforms, the reality is that, as Antony Green states, 'it is fairer as [the reform places] the power over preferences into the hands of voters'.[59]

Conclusions

The founders of the microparties that have been registered in recent years cannot be blamed for engaging in their strategic manoeuvres to win Senate seats at the 2013 election. They achieved success by forming syndicates that worked together to exploit the weaknesses in the system designed by their political opponents. In this setting, the microparties have exhibited more astute strategic positioning and agility than the older governing parties that established and maintained this electoral environment over the past 30 years. The Labor/Coalition governing parties' cartel has failed to reform a flawed voting system, despite its weaknesses being obvious for many years. The major governing parties are the ones who have controlled the outputs of the JSCEM over the past 30 years, and who are responsible for creating this situation. Because these microparties gained seats in the Senate, it became difficult for the government to amend the Senate voting system in a way that would disadvantage these microparties, at least until a willing ally in the Senate was found.

A benefit of the increased number and influence of microparties has been the prominent attention given to several narrow policy areas— for instance, the interests of motoring enthusiasts appear to be well served by the election of the AMEP's Ricky Muir to the Senate. However, the increase in the number of registered parties since 2010 has not been in response to public demand for new outlets for political activism and political expression. And while the 1983 reforms were designed to encourage stronger parties, it was never a specific intent of the legislation to promote participation.

Party defections have occurred since the 2013 election, with newly Independent Senators Lambie, Lazarus and Madigan now forming their own microparties through the section 123(1)(a)(i) provision of the

---

59   Antony Green (2016) 'Q&A: Open Post for Questions on the New Senate Electoral System', *ABC Elections*, [blog], 9 March, available at: blogs.abc.net.au/antonygreen/2016/03/qa-open-post-for-questions-on-the-new-senate-electoral-system.html.

Act. This provision negates any sense that the 1983 legislative reforms may have been designed to promote political participation, though founders of these parties may argue that they are filling an unmet need in political debate. The 'single-member' party is one that needs neither party membership support nor substantial levels of voter support to survive. The control of GVT preference flows—in both receiving and dispersing these preferences—has allowed these parties to wield significant influence, far in excess of their levels of member or voter support.

The 2016 Senate voting system reform package is a positive outcome for democratic choice. The removal of voting tickets and, to a lesser extent, the introduction of POP voting above the line, shift power away from party brokers. These preference dealers, from both major and smaller parties, have controlled voters' preferences as a result of the difficulty voters had in expressing their own choices. Now voters are able to exercise the power—and the responsibility—to indicate their own preferences.

The 2016 general election provides an interesting case study of the response to electoral reform in terms of how parties reacted to these changes through their campaigning techniques and how-to-vote card designs. Voters appear to have embraced this newfound level of direct influence over election outcomes by shifting away from the major parties, with record numbers of voters supporting minor parties and Independents in both the House of Representatives and Senate.

Appendix 3.1: New party registrations, 2010–16

Table A3.1 Parties registered between the 2010 and 2013 federal elections

Registration	Party	Membership fee ($)
23 September 2010	Stable Population Party of Australia	20
23 September 2010	Help End Marijuana Prohibition (HEMP) Party	0
6 January 2011	The First Nations Political Party	?
18 January 2011	Australian Protectionist Party	20
3 May 2011	Animal Justice Party	20
26 July 2011	Country Alliance	30

Registration	Party	Membership fee ($)
27 September 2011	Katter's Australian Party	33
15 December 2011	Australian Christians	20
3 February 2012	Rise Up Australia	20
15 January 2013	Pirate Party Australia	20
21 February 2013	Bank Reform Party	0
20 March 2013	Carers Alliance (re-registration) (originally registered in 2007, deregistered in 2012)	0
22 May 2013	Bullet Train for Australia	0
5 June 2013	Uniting Australia Party	?
1 July 2013	Nick Xenophon Team	?
1 July 2013	Voluntary Euthanasia Party	0
1 July 2013	The Wikileaks Party	20
2 July 2013	Australian Sovereignty Party	0
2 July 2013	Australian Voice Party	30
2 July 2013	Drug Law Reform Australia	0
2 July 2013	Future Party	0
2 July 2013	The 23 Million	0
5 July 2013	Palmer United Party	20
5 July 2013	Outdoor Recreation Party (Stop The Greens)	0
9 July 2013	Australian Motoring Enthusiast Party	20
9 July 2013	Australian Sports Party	0
9 July 2013	Republican Party of Australia	0
16 July 2013	Coke in the Bubblers Party	0
16 July 2013	Smokers Rights Party	0
16 July 2013	Australian Independents	0
23 July 2013	Stop CSG Party	0

Source: Australian Electoral Commission (www.aec.gov.au/Parties_and_Representatives/ party_registration). Membership fees as provided on party websites.

Table A3.2 Parties that applied prior to the 2013 election and registered after the 2013 election

Registration	Party	Membership fee ($)
7 November 2013	21st Century Party	0
7 November 2013	Single Parents' Party	0
7 November 2013	Natural Medicine Party	20

Source: Australian Electoral Commission (www.aec.gov.au/Parties_and_Representatives/ party_registration). Membership fees as provided on party websites.

Table A3.3 Newly registered parties, 2014–16

Registration	Party	Membership fee ($)
6 August 2014	The Arts Party	20
20 August 2014	Australian Cyclists Party	0
9 October 2014	Australian Equality Party	30
17 February 2015	Australian Progressives	0
4 March 2015	Seniors United NSW	20
14 May 2015	Jacqui Lambie Network	?
18 May 2015	John Madigan's Manufacturing and Farming Party	0
15 June 2015	Australian Defence Veterans Party	50
9 July 2015	Glenn Lazarus Team	0
28 July 2015	Australians Against Paedophiles Party	0
28 July 2015	Australian Liberty Alliance	10
25 February 2016	The Australian Greens—Victoria	30 / 135*
7 March 2016	Consumer Rights & No-Tolls	0
11 March 2016	The Australian Mental Health Party	0
22 March 2016	Renewable Energy Party	0
29 March 2016	VOTEFLUX.ORG | Upgrade Democracy!	0
14 April 2016	Mature Australia Party	30
14 April 2016	Derryn Hinch's Justice Party	20
14 April 2016	CountryMinded	0
9 May 2016	Australian Recreational Fishers Party	10

Source: Australian Electoral Commission (www.aec.gov.au/Parties_and_Representatives/party_registration). Membership fees as provided on party websites.

* Scaled, depending on income.

4

Who gets what, when and how: The politics of resource allocation to parliamentary parties

Yvonne Murphy

> People don't like their politicians to be comfortable. They don't like you having expenses. They don't like you being paid. They'd rather you lived in a ... cave.[1]

While the source of this declaration is the bad-tempered fictional government press secretary Malcolm Tucker, as portrayed in the BBC's *The Thick of It*, it would be difficult to find a more apt way to describe the general public sentiment that surrounds the topic of politicians' salaries and allowances. Any mention of the subject is generally met with cynicism, suspicion and, often, a sense of outrage—a state of affairs that is not aided by periodic scandals concerning misconduct over claims for expenses. Understandably, recent decades have seen an increasing public appetite for closer scrutiny, increased transparency and more effective oversight of how public monies are spent on politicians and political parties—including calls from politicians themselves. And, since the 1970s, there has been a shift in Australia towards addressing such calls through the establishment of bodies

1   British Broadcasting Corporation (BBC) (2009) *The Thick of It*, [video recording], Series 3, Episode 1.

such as the Commonwealth Remuneration Tribunal and periodic audits to review, report on and offer recommendations on the regularisation of such spending.[2]

Yet one set of taxpayer-funded allowances has consistently escaped the gaze of such reviews and has received little attention from scholars: the staffing, office space and information and communication technology (ICT) equipment provided to qualifying parliamentary parties to facilitate them in organising and supporting their members and working with government and other parties to coordinate parliamentary business. Existing scholarship has examined the provision of resources to individual parliamentarians and parties in terms of its effect on both intraparty and interparty dynamics and in facilitating the professionalisation of politics.[3] For example, studies of the public financing of political parties have explored the impact of this funding on public attitudes to politics, party behaviour and the relationship between parties and the state (see chapters 1 and 6, this volume).[4] Nevertheless, scholars have not systematically examined the direct provision of resources to legislative parties with regard to either Australia or other jurisdictions. This is also true of the impact that such resource provision has on intra-parliamentary dynamics.

This is not really surprising, given that resources of this sort tend to be distributed on a discretionary basis and such in-house decision-making limits visibility. They are little discussed, even among parliamentarians, with many taking for granted the presence or absence of party-based support services. Moreover, apart from the work of Norm Kelly, these facilities and resources are little talked about in terms of their impact on democratic representation—that is,

2   See, for example, Cathy Madden (2015) 'Parliamentary Entitlements: Inquiries and Reports', *Flagpost*, 10 August, Canberra: Parliamentary Library, available at: aph.gov.au/About_Parliament/ Parliamentary_Departments/Parliamentary_Library/FlagPost/2015/August/Entitlements.

3   Nicole Bolleyer and Anika Gauja (2011) 'Parliamentary Salaries as a Party Resource: Party Organizational Power in Westminster Democracies', *Party Politics* 19(5): 778–97; Richard S. Katz and Peter Mair (1995) 'Changing Models of Party Organization and Party Democracy: The Emergence of the Cartel Party', *Party Politics* 1(1): 5–28; Kate Jones (2006) 'One Step at a Time: Australian Parliamentarians, Professionalism and the Need for Staff', *Parliamentary Affairs* 59(4): 638–53.

4   Fernando Casal Bertoa, Fransje Molenaar, Daniela R. Piccio and Ekaterina R. Rashkova (2014) 'The World Upside Down: Delegitimising Political Finance Regulation', *International Political Science Review* 35(3): 355–75; Ingrid van Biezen (2004) 'Political Parties as Public Utilities', *Party Politics* 10(6): 701–22; Katz and Mair, 'Changing Models of Party Organization and Party Democracy'.

how they impact on the capacity of members and legislative parties to participate effectively in the functions of parliament.[5] This is perhaps a symptom of the fact that they fall into the cracks between electoral funding, wider party financing and parliamentary resource provision for individual members. Qualification criteria for the allocation of resources tend to vary from legislature to legislature—as highlighted in Kelly's Democratic Audit of Australia Discussion Paper[6]— ranging from provision being made for individual Independents at the federal level to a parliamentary party qualification threshold of 11 parliamentarians in the Victorian State legislature. To the extent that we cannot depend on uniform standards or statutory provisions to inform us of who gets what, when and how, parliamentary allowances for staff, office space and ICT constitute a somewhat 'invisible' form of state support for the parliamentary wing of political parties.

A systemic examination of resources allocated to parliamentary parties is therefore overdue. We need to better understand how legislative parties operate, how this is supported within the parliamentary system by the provision of these resources and what consequences this might have for representative democracy. This chapter addresses these issues in several sections. The first examines the history of the provision of parliamentary resources in Australia and places them in an international context. The second sets out the distinctions between 'tools of the trade' parliamentary party allowances (covering staffing, office space and so on) and others found within the Australian political system. This is then followed by analysis of how allowances are allocated and overseen in the Australian context and the role of discretion and bargaining in the process. The chapter concludes with a brief consideration of some of the democratic implications of the present system of parliamentary party resource allocation.

Analysis is based on qualitative data gathered on the practices surrounding parliamentary party resource provision in Australian parliaments, with particular emphasis on the Federal Parliament. Data consist of first-hand accounts by serving and former parliamentarians gathered through parliamentary debates, official

---

5   See Norm Kelly (2004) *Determining Parliamentary Parties: A Real Status Symbol*, Democratic Audit of Australia Discussion Paper, Melbourne: Australian Policy Online, available at: apo.org. au/node/585.
6   ibid.

statements and media interviews. Similarly, documentary evidence of resource allocation practices has been gathered from online parliamentary repositories, formal reviews of allowance frameworks conducted by bodies such as review committees and remuneration tribunals and statements by parliamentarians, government ministers and spokespeople. This approach was required because of the lack of formal guidelines governing the allocation of parliamentary party resources and the lack of formal review mechanisms. As will be shown, this is an area of parliamentary life ruled by convention rather than formal regulation, discretion rather than certainty and backroom negotiations rather than transparency.

The historical origins and expansion of parliamentary allowances

As noted by Gauja and Sawer in Chapter 1, there have been increasing moves towards the regulation of political parties in Australia since the 1980s, not least due to the introduction of new and increasing levels of state subventions. Financial support for politics—in the form of payments to politicians—is not, however, a new phenomenon. In the United Kingdom, it dates back as far as the thirteenth century when shires and boroughs made payments to Members of Parliament (MPs)—a practice that continued until the late seventeenth century.[7] The US Congress employed a similar system until standardised per diem and eventually per annum salaries were introduced in 1789 and 1815, respectively.[8] The introduction of payments such as those in the United States was intended to limit financial dependence on vested interests and to bolster the capacity of members to engage in independent and nationally focused decision-making. This is an important point to note in relation to modern-day moves towards the standardisation and regulation of public subventions for political activity, the aim of which has been, inter alia, to insulate parliamentary actors from reliance on vested interests. France, Holland, Belgium, Sweden and Brazil followed suit by introducing annual salaries for politicians,

---

7   House of Commons Information Office (2009) *Members' Pay, Pensions and Allowances*, No. M5, London: House of Commons Information Office.
8   Ida A. Brudnick (2014) *Salaries of Members of Congress: Recent Actions and Historical Tables*, Washington, DC: US Congress.

and Canada, New Zealand, Portugal and Norway adopted sitting day allowances, all of which occurred in the first half of the nineteenth century. It is within this broader international context that salary payments were first introduced for parliamentarians in Australia.

Payment for MPs and removal of existing property qualifications were two of the demands of the Chartist movement, and were seen as a prerequisite for working-class representation in parliament. The Parliament of Victoria led the way in introducing MPs' pay in 1870[9] and, despite delays caused by opposition in conservative upper houses, the other Australian colonies followed suit during the 1880s and 1890s. A salary allowance was also introduced in the Commonwealth Parliament on its establishment in 1901. Yet, not everyone endorsed the measure. John Stuart Mill, for example, objected on the basis that it would encourage the emergence of a class of professional politician, interested only in money.[10] The reality on the ground, in Westminster at least, was that the reward of public service was not the only motivating factor for many who aspired to win a seat in parliament in the nineteenth century. Salary allowances may not have existed, but substantial material rewards came in the form of lucrative pensions and appointments. Becoming a parliamentarian was, in fact, so desirable that many were willing to pay for the privilege.[11] Therefore, while Mill's argument in favour of preserving the purity of public service was not without merit, it was undermined by the presence of indirectly administered material rewards that were controlled by private interests.

As noted in the Victorian debates, the alternative proposed by Mill was that representatives ought to be supported by contributions from their constituents. However, this approach had been tried, tested and rejected in the seventeenth and eighteenth centuries by Westminster and the US Congress, respectively, owing to the conflict of interest it created for members forced to decide between local and national interests. In 1909, the Osborne judgement in the United Kingdom

---

9   Kate Jones (2007) 'Daring and Discretion: Paying Australian Legislators', *The Journal of Legislative Studies* 13(2): 235–53; House of Commons Information Office (2004) *Members' Pay, Pensions and Allowances*, London: British House of Commons; *Constitution of the Irish Free State* (1922), Dublin: Stationery Office.

10   Marian Sawer (2001) 'Pacemakers for the World?', in Marian Sawer (ed.) *Elections: Full, Free and Fair*, Sydney: The Federation Press, p. 14.

11   House of Commons Information Office (2009), *Members' Pay, Pensions and Allowances*.

rendered it illegal for trade unions to make payments to working-class MPs—a practice that could be seen as analogous to constituency contributions.[12]

A positive effect of introducing salaries for parliamentarians was that it opened up the prospect of parliamentary participation from across the socioeconomic divide. Prior to the introduction of parliamentary salaries, those hailing from working-class backgrounds faced tremendous barriers to political involvement. For example, stonemason Charles Jardine Don, who was elected in 1859 in Victoria, had great difficulty combining parliamentary duties with earning a living.[13]

Owing to their origin as a modest form of support for individual MPs, and perhaps reflecting the elite/cadre model of party politics that prevailed in Australia until the 1890s,[14] parliamentary allowances were initially provided exclusively to members without reference to their parliamentary parties. Despite the consolidation of the Australian party system over the course of the twentieth century, this form of individual allowance has persisted, increased and indeed expanded over the years. Initially introduced at £400 per annum in 1901,[15] salaries in the Commonwealth Parliament increased on an ad hoc basis according to 'no fixed pattern of approach' until the Remuneration Tribunal was established in 1973.[16] Further changes included the introduction of an income tax–exempt electorate expense allowance in 1952;[17] the provision of subsidised printing, postage and home telephone calls and increased travel assistance in the 1960s;[18] and expanded staffing and accommodation provisions in 1975.

---

12   Paul Seaward (2010) 'Sleaze, Old Corruption and Parliamentary Reform: An Historical Perspective on the Current Crisis', *Political Quarterly* 81(1): 39–48.
13   See the entry for Don, Charles Jardine (1820–1866) in S. Merrifield (1972) *Australian Dictionary of Biography. Volume 4*, Melbourne: Melbourne University Press, available at: adb.anu.edu.au/biography/don-charles-jardine-3423.
14   Katz and Mair, 'Changing Models of Party Organization and Party Democracy'; Peter Loveday, Allan W. Martin and Robert S. Parker (1977) *The Emergence of the Australian Party System*, Sydney: Hale & Iremonger.
15   Jones, 'Daring and Discretion'.
16   Justice Kerr ['Kerr Report'] (1971) *Salaries and Allowances of Members of the Parliament of the Commonwealth: A Report of Inquiry by Mr Justice Kerr*, Canberra: Commonwealth Parliament of Australia.
17   ibid.
18   John Wilkinson (2002), *MPs' Entitlements*, Occasional Paper No. 8, Sydney: NSW Parliamentary Library Research Service.

4. WHO GETS WHAT, WHEN AND HOW

Since 2007, all Senators and MPs have also been allowed to hire four electorate staff, with the possibility of additional 'personal positions' being allocated on a discretionary basis.

A similar evolution of allowance structures can be found across Australia's State parliaments and, indeed, the parliaments of other jurisdictions. For example, the 1923 Irish parliamentarian received a salary 'allowance' of £30 per month and 'first class railway travelling facilities' to facilitate travel to and from parliamentary sittings.[19] Over the years, this evolved into salary provisions comparable with those received by senior civil servants. The first-class railway travel facility has also been replaced with the Travel and Accommodation Allowance (TAA), calculated according to the distance of the MP's principal private residence from the National Parliament in Dublin.[20] A suite of other allowances is also provided, such as mobile phone and postage allowances, staffing provisions and the Parliamentary Standard Allowance, which has a range of constituency-related uses, including the maintenance of a constituency office.[21]

In addition to these allowances supporting individual parliamentarians, support for parliamentary parties has also expanded in recent decades to include increased travel and staff allowances for office-holders. However, the significant leeway given to individual legislators in the deployment and use of their individual allowances allowed parliamentary parties to benefit from the general expansions seen in earlier decades. As highlighted by Bolleyer and Gauja,[22] there is little in the way of regulatory deterrents to prevent practices such as the use of allowances for party political purposes. This issue came to prominence most recently in 2015 when Liberal Speaker of the House of Representatives Bronwyn Bishop used her parliamentary travel entitlements to attend a Liberal Party fundraiser. There is therefore substantial potential for intermingling between allowances paid to individual members and those paid to parliamentary parties, and this exacerbates the lack of transparency surrounding the extent and sources of allowances made available to parliamentary parties in

19   *The Oireachtas (Payment of Members) Act* (1923), Dublin: Stationery Office.
20   *Parliamentary Standard Allowance (PSA)* (2014), Dublin: Houses of the Oireachtas Commission, available at: oireachtas.ie/parliament/tdssenators/salariesallowances/.
21   ibid.
22   Nicole Bolleyer and Anika Gauja (2015) 'The Limits of Regulation: Indirect Party Access to State Resources in Australia and the United Kingdom', *Governance* 28(3): 321–40.

particular. One such source that has received little scholarly attention up to this point is the 'tools of trade' category of allowances provided to parliamentary parties in their own right.

Equipping parliamentary parties with the 'tools of trade'

'Tools of trade' allowances are allocated to legislative parties in all of Australia's parliaments except the Northern Territory (NT) and the Australian Capital Territory (ACT). Where they are provided, they include staffing, office space, meeting space and additional travel allowances for office-holders; their purpose being to provide parties with the 'tools of trade'[23] required to function effectively in the parliamentary setting. Australian legislative parties do not receive monetary support comparable with the provision of 'Short Money' in Westminster or the Parliamentary Activities Allowance (PAA) paid to party leaders in respect of their party's MPs and to Independents in the Irish Parliament. Therefore, it is not necessary to examine financial resources in the context of tools-of-trade resource provision in Australia, as the government does not provide direct funding to parliamentary parties. This simplifies matters somewhat.

Tools-of-trade allowances allocated to legislative parties can be distinguished from a similar suite of salary and tools-of-trade allowances provided directly to individual parliamentarians for their own direct use—that is, base salaries, salary top-ups for office-holders, individual electorate allowances and other benefits. It is important to note that the last category can and indeed has been used by or for the benefit of legislative parties. For example, Bolleyer and Gauja document the practice of salary tithing by parliamentary parties in their 2011 and 2015 studies.[24] However, irrespective of the level of institutionalisation the practice attains, it constitutes a transaction between the parliamentarian and their party. The state provides a resource to the MP—their private salary in this case—and the MP then passes a portion on to the party. The transaction is therefore

---

23   Committee for the Review of Parliamentary Entitlements ['Belcher Review'] (2010) *Review of Parliamentary Entitlements*, Canberra: Parliament of Australia, p. 9.
24   Bolleyer and Gauja, 'Parliamentary Salaries as a Party Resource'; Bolleyer and Gauja, 'The Limits of Regulation'.

between the parliamentarian and the party, not between the state and the party. This is also the case where an MP informally gifts a non-monetary allowance to their party—for example, where they surrender a member of their personal staff to the central party for an individual task, project or set period. While this is a rare occurrence within large, well-staffed parties, newly formed and minor parties with little in the way of staffing and resources often call on members to help them in such ways.

Resources allocated to parliamentary parties, as opposed to resources allocated to parliamentarians, introduce a new variable into the parliamentary dynamic as they create a separate space for the legislative party to function in parliament in its own right. As a result, instead of a legislative party's ability to operate depending solely on its ability to appropriate or pool resources allocated to members on an individual basis—such as the tithing of members', office-holders' or ministers' salaries and the pooling of print, communications and graphic design allowances[25]—this separate layer of parliamentary support entitles parties to resources in their own right. One interesting feature of this support is that it is provided in addition to the sum of available pooled resources, which means that qualifying parties gain additional resources simply by virtue of attaining the status of a parliamentary party. This perhaps supports Bowler's description of such resources as constituting 'material rewards', as, in effect, they constitute an institutional reward for parties.[26]

It must be acknowledged that legislative parties and their members are not the only ones who profit from the provision of this support for tools of the trade. Parliament itself benefits substantially from parliamentary parties having the capacity to operate cohesively and effectively. Nevertheless, this important function is somewhat undermined by the differential level at which support is provided to different party groups, how it is allocated and how it is overseen.

---

25   Bolleyer and Gauja, 'Parliamentary Salaries as a Party Resource'; Bolleyer and Gauja, 'The Limits of Regulation'.
26   Shaun Bowler (2000) 'Parties in Legislatures: Two Competing Explanations', in Russell J. Dalton and Martin P. Wattenberg (eds) *Parties without Partisans: Political Change in Advanced Industrial Democracies*, Oxford: Oxford University Press, pp. 157–79.

Allocating and overseeing the provision of tools-of-trade resources

The authority to set the level of parliamentary allowances and to determine the ways in which these allowances are distributed originates and rests with parliamentarians themselves.[27] This has its roots in the doctrine of the separation of powers and the principle of maintaining the independence of parliament as a distinct and inviolable organ of the state.[28] Members of Parliament should not be beholden to external forces for subsistence: to support the basic functioning of the institution, parliament must either directly sign off on the provision of finance and resources for its operation or delegate that responsibility to another authority such as a remuneration tribunal or a ministerial department.[29] It is important to note, however, that where a body is entrusted with such responsibility, it is on the basis of delegated authority, which leaves it open for parliament to revisit the arrangement at a later time. The rationale for this is to ensure that members are free to discharge their duties without fear of monetary reprisal from vested interests.[30] For example, members of the US Senate were paid directly by their sending States between 1787 and 1789 until the Constitutional Convention vested Congress itself with authority to pay members. This action was taken in a bid to strengthen central government by providing members with a level of independence from State administrations so they could exercise autonomy in decision-making.

Placing the power to determine salaries and allowances in the hands of parliament itself is therefore sensible in many respects. This is despite the inherent 'paradox'[31] presented by the fact that those who stand to benefit from parliamentary allowances are the ones who determine who gets what, when and how.[32] As a means of addressing this shortcoming, the general trend since the 1970s has been to delegate varying levels of authority to independent statutory bodies so that they may make recommendations and determinations, inquire into

---

27 Wilkinson, *MPs' Entitlements*.
28 See Seaward, 'Sleaze, Old Corruption and Parliamentary Reform'.
29 Wilkinson, *MPs' Entitlements*.
30 ibid.
31 Ekaterina Rashkova and Ingrid van Biezen (2014) 'The Legal Regulation of Political Parties: Contesting or Promoting Legitimacy?', *International Political Science Review* 35(3): 265–74.
32 Belcher Review, p. 47; Wilkinson, *MPs' Entitlements*, p. 27.

and oversee salary and allowance allocations. In Australia, this has come in the form of a number of remuneration tribunals. The first of these was the Commonwealth Remuneration Tribunal, which was founded in 1973 following a report by Justice Kerr concerning salary and allowance determination practices.[33] Up to this point, decision-making had been the sole preserve of parliament and the executive government; indeed, even after its establishment, the Remuneration Tribunal did not fully assume authority over salaries and allowances until 2012.[34] Between 1990 and 2012, its remit was to provide inquiry and advisory services, which facilitated a more transparent decision-making process concerning allowance allocations while leaving ultimate decision-making authority in the hands of parliament and the executive government. In addition to increased transparency, the Remuneration Tribunal provided a forum for parliamentarians to volunteer information on their own experiences of parliamentary life and the resources they wished to see introduced. This resulted in an increase and expansion of resources such as staff allowances in the years following establishment of the tribunal, the result of which were increased costs for parliament, which is ultimately why the responsibilities of the tribunal were curtailed until more recent years.[35] This general delegated approach was, however, replicated in New South Wales (NSW) and Western Australia in 1975, South Australia (SA) in 1990, the ACT in 1995, the NT in 2001, Queensland in 2013 and Tasmania in 2014. Despite this general move towards systematisation, standardisation and independent oversight of decision-making concerning individual resources, the allocation of legislative party resources continued to be subject to substantially lesser levels of oversight and transparency.

Although office-holders qualifying for access to legislative party tools-of-trade resources tend to be identified in the entitlements handbooks produced by individual parliaments, such texts stop short of setting

---

33   The Commonwealth Remuneration Tribunal was established through the *Remuneration Tribunal Act 1973*; the NSW Remuneration Tribunals were established under the *Statutory and Other Offices Remuneration Act 1975*; Western Australia's Salaries and Allowances Tribunal was established through the *Salaries and Allowances Act 1975*; the Remuneration Tribunal of South Australia through the *Remuneration Act 1990*; and the Queensland Independent Remuneration Tribunal was established through the *Queensland Independent Remuneration Tribunal Act 2013*. Kerr Report.

34   Cathy Madden and Deirdre McKeown (2013) *Parliamentary Remuneration and Entitlements*, Canberra: Parliament of Australia.

35   Jones, 'One Step at a Time'.

out the extent of resources that are to be provided. Determinations of this nature are instead left to the premier or prime minister of the jurisdiction in question. This is the case, for example, in relation to resources provided to legislative parties in the Commonwealth Parliament, where 'convention'[36] dictates that, subject to his or her discretion, the prime minister may allocate one additional staff member to minor parties consisting of fewer than five serving members. Each leader of a minor party holding parliamentary party status—that is, those meeting or exceeding the five serving member threshold—is provided with a substantially more generous complement of staff. The Greens, for example, were allocated 13 positions in 2010. Additional staffing for the opposition is greater again, conventionally set at 21 per cent of the allocation for the government. In 2010 this meant 420 additional positions for the government and 88 for the opposition.[37] In announcing the 2010 allocation of additional staff, the Special Minister of State argued:

> It is obvious that the current political environment is a challenging one. It is important the Government, Opposition, Minor Parties and independents are able to access advice and prepare and facilitate negotiated outcomes to serve the Parliament and the people in an efficient and effective way.[38]

These additional staff positions are provided in a bloc to the Leader of the Opposition or the leader of a minor party, who can then reallocate them at his or her discretion.

State-level parliaments operate under similar arrangements. The Leader of the Opposition in the Queensland State Parliament, for example, receives tools-of-trade resources subject to an application to and approval by the State premier. In this case, levels of staffing and resources are not established or set, but rather are subject to negotiation and interpretation. Importantly, the Leader of the Opposition must make a specific request for the number of staff they require and the premier may then grant or deny that request. This of course opens up

---

36   Tony Abbott MP (2013) Official press conference, 17 September, Brunei, available at: pm.gov.au/media/2013-10-10/press-conference-brunei.

37   The number of personal positions allocated to the government had reached 467.9 in 2007, but had been cut back by the incoming Labor Government.

38   Gary Gray, AO, MP (2010) 'Media Release: Ministerial and Parliamentary Staffing to Increase', 28 September, Canberra, available at: parlinfo.aph.gov.au/parlInfo/search/display/display.w3p;query%3DId%3A%22media%2Fpressrel%2F328953%22.

the practice of bargaining, which is an important aspect of this form of allowance, the full extent to which it plays a part becoming most apparent when we look to the fringes of legislative party resource provision—namely, the process by which parties that qualify for reduced resources, or none at all, attempt to acquire them.

Discretion and bargaining in the allocation of tools of trade

An example of bargaining in relation to tools-of-trade resources can be found in the prominent agreements made by the Australian Labor Party (ALP) when trying to form the government of the 43rd Parliament in 2010. One concession made to crossbench MPs holding the balance of power was to provide them with additional personal staff in exchange for pledges of support on matters of 'confidence and supply'.[39] This resulted in the lower house Greens MP Andrew Bandt and Independents Tony Windsor, Rob Oakeshott, Andrew Wilkie and Bob Katter each being allocated a personal staff of two in addition to the standard four electorate staff.[40] In contrast, Senators John Madigan and Nick Xenophon (a minor party Senator and Independent Senator, respectively), who did not factor in the Senate balance of power, received only one personal staffing position each in the 43rd Parliament. The 44th Parliament saw a reversal of this situation when the Independents and The Greens no longer held the balance of power in the House of Representatives. Subsequently, their personal staff allowances were reduced to one each, while the crossbench Senators, who now held the balance of power, were each allocated two personal staff positions (see Chapter 1, Table 1.3).

A further example can be seen in Clive Palmer's formal request on 4 June 2014 that the Palmer United Party (PUP) be designated as a parliamentary party and for staffing numbers to be provided in line with those received by The Greens. Palmer argued:

---

39   Julia Gillard MP (2010) 'Letter Confirming Acceptance of Agreement to Support ALP Government', Canberra, available at: tonywindsor.com.au/releases/AgreementToFormGovt.pdf.
40   'The Australian Labor Party and the Independent Members (Mr Tony Windsor and Mr Rob Oakeshott) ("the parties")—Agreement', 7 September 2010, available at: resources.news.com.au/files/2010/09/07/1225915/542989-final-agreement-with-the-independents.pdf.

> If we don't get any resources you can well imagine it will take longer
> for the three people to do their job and maybe you'll only get one bill
> through a year.[41]

With three incoming Senators and a seat in the House of
Representatives, the PUP was one seat short of eligibility for
parliamentary party status. This remained the case despite efforts
to have the party's voting pact with Senator Ricky Muir of the
Motoring Enthusiast Party acknowledged to make up the shortfall.[42]
While receiving a degree of publicity at the time, the attempt to gain
parliamentary party status was ultimately a fruitless endeavour, which
may be explained by the PUP's reduced bargaining position within a
record 18-strong Senate crossbench.

Although Palmer's prediction of a one bill per annum work rate may
have somewhat exaggerated the level of obstruction caused by the
under-resourcing of the PUP, members do require adequate staffing to
ensure they have sufficient capacity to give due consideration to the
full range of legislation and other business before either house.

Family First Senator Bob Day and Independent Senators Nick Xenophon
and John Madigan also concurred with the need for increased staffing
when asked to comment on Palmer's request, although they differed
on how this might be achieved.[43] While Madigan and Xenophon
indicated a need for increased individual staffing allowances, Senator
Day suggested that a 'crossbench secretariat' could be a workable
solution.[44] Nevertheless, there was uniformity in the calls made for
increased resources, and this perhaps indicates the need for some form
of review aimed at assessing the adequacy of resources provided to
these crossbench members and those in comparable situations.

This situation has not changed significantly over the past two decades.
In 1996, Bob Brown expressed similar sentiments when The Greens
had two Senators and fell below the parliamentary party threshold.

41   Bob Brown speaking on *The Senate: What Goes Around Comes Around* (5 May 1996),
ABC Radio, Canberra, available at: abc.net.au/radionational/programs/backgroundbriefing/the-
senate-what-goes-around-comes-around/3563852#transcript.
42   Lenore Taylor (2014) 'Clive Palmer Fights for Parliamentary Resources Boom but Still
No Reply', *The Guardian*, 24 April.
43   John Madigan was a member of the Democratic Labour Party until he resigned to become
an Independent in September 2013.
44   Taylor, 'Clive Palmer Fights for Parliamentary Resources Boom but Still No Reply'.

This was in contrast with the Australian Democrats, who had seven members and designated parliamentary party status. Speaking of the negotiations surrounding the formation of the Howard Government in 1996, Senator Brown stated:

> I expected to have a staff establishment which would be equal to the job ... we have to deal with the full range of legislative initiatives coming into the Senate, same as the House of Reps ... and you need the wherewithal to know what the legislation is that you're dealing with, otherwise you vote No. And it doesn't get through, and the load can build up.[45]

Brown also, however, highlighted the difficulty the current resource allocation regime creates for minor parties and Independents:

> People are normally shy about talking about the need for staffing the job that they're doing because it leads so easily to media condemnation or scurrying about with the view that here's somebody who's trying to increase their own bailiwick.[46]

The latter point, in particular, highlights the problematic nature of the power dynamic that this discretionary mode of allocation creates. Larger parties are automatically allocated relatively large levels of resources, which means this form of resource access is rarely spoken of. However, Independents and minor party actors, who must negotiate to achieve modest increases in the resources available to them, must weigh up the benefits against the potentially negative publicity that can accompany such requests. Those placed in the position of having to raise their heads above the parapet to advocate for additional party resources do so at the risk of bearing the brunt of 'public disquiet' concerning political entitlements and state subvention of politics.[47] Disquiet of this nature can reach fever pitch at times of financial hardship or when scandals emerge concerning the misuse of parliamentary allowances, and this can create a reluctance to press the issue.

On the other hand, failing to do so can also result in negative public relations outcomes. That is because additional staff allow parliamentarians to deal more effectively with the substantial

---

45   Brown, in *The Senate*.
46   ibid.
47   Timothy John Abey (Chair), Nicole Mary Wells and Barbara Deegan (2014) *Report of the Parliamentary Salaries and Allowances Tribunal Inquiring into Basic Salary, Allowances and Benefits Provided to Members of the Tasmanian Parliament*, Hobart: Parliament of Tasmania, p. 2.

workloads that come their way. This alone can impact positively on a legislator's reputation among fellow parliamentarians and, vitally, among the press gallery. However, the effect can go further. A hugely important part of any parliamentarian's job is to communicate what they have achieved in office to their electorate. Publicity of this sort, however, rarely arises spontaneously and is generally the product of long hours spent courting members of the press, distributing press releases and publicity materials, cultivating an online presence and, vitally, working with constituents on issues of importance. Additional staffing provides breathing space for this work and, by extension, has the potential to bolster the re-election prospects of members down the line.

Issues arising from the discretionary allocation of resources

There is a place for discretion in the allocation of resources, particularly when it comes to how they are deployed within parties. For example, when allocated additional personal staff under this scheme, the leader of a party may, at their discretion, redeploy them to party colleagues. This is important as it ensures that parties have relative freedom to decide how to make the best use of the collective resources available to them. Intraparty distribution aside, however, the wisdom of making the overall allocation of such resources a matter of discretion is questionable.

One downside is that discretionary authority of this sort may be used to pressure minor parliamentary actors into lending support to government or it may have the effect of marginalising those of little relevance to the government formation process. Those refusing, or unable, to engage in bargaining have the potential to be left at a substantial disadvantage compared with parliamentary colleagues who automatically qualify for party-based tools-of-trade resources or broker deals of their own. While this is simply an extension of the political dynamics that arise from the electoral process—and it may be argued that those choosing not to trade support for resources have only themselves to blame—the use of taxpayer-funded resources for such political purposes is problematic.

It is, first, not consistent with the spirit of resource allocation as originally intended: a mechanism to promote the principles of equal franchise, equal mandate and equal access to democratic politics by ensuring that each vote and member is regarded with equal value, and parliamentarians are provided with equal tools with which to do the job. The track record of tools-of-trade resources being used as rewards for those lending support to government demonstrates how something as seemingly innocuous as staffing, office space and ICT can become politicised. And it appears that the discretionary basis of allocations has contributed to this shift away from the principle of uniform access towards a more politically motivated form of provision. This goes against the spirit of the public subvention of politics, the ultimate purpose of which is to level the playing field.

This mode of allocation also calls into question the neutrality of parliamentary institutions. Where differential levels of resources are provided on the basis of affiliation and bargaining power, as distinct from an objective assessment of need, the institutions of parliament can be seen as encouraging certain forms of affiliation and behaviour while discouraging others. When considered in this light, these institutions may more accurately be classified as incentive structures, as they reward behaviour consistent with the preferences of the decision-makers determining resource allocations. What makes this problematic is that taxpayer-funded resources provided to support the operation of parliament are appropriated and used for political ends. Parallels can be drawn between this situation and that of the earlier example of the Liberal Speaker of the House of Representatives, Bronwyn Bishop, using her parliamentary travel entitlements to attend a Liberal Party fundraiser. This time, however, the entitlements are not the only things being used for political purposes, but the very institutional structures through which they are allocated. Yet, to date, little attention has been paid to the prominent role of discretion and bargaining in the resource allocation mechanism.

The way tools-of-trade resources are allocated presents a barrier to achieving greater levels of transparency in the area of parliamentary resource and allowance provision more generally. This is not simply due to the lack of standards and guidelines to be referred to when identifying the levels of resources allocated to different groupings— although these issues do make identifying levels of resource access rather difficult. A worrying by-product of this mechanism is that it appears to curtail discussion surrounding this form of resource support and the mode by which allocations are made. There is a reticence among those who stand to benefit most from a change to the regime to speak of these resources, as indicated by Bob Brown's statements on the matter. For one thing, doing so has the potential to damage current or future levels of resource access as members criticising the system are effectively biting the hand that feeds them. This could sully political relationships and close off resource access into the future. Fear of reprisal from the public for raising the issue is also a real concern—again, highlighted by Brown. In this respect, Tucker has it right. There is a highly negative attitude among the public towards providing even the most modest supports for politicians. The very idea of individuals presenting themselves to their premier and asking 'please sir, I'd like some more' is a risk that must be weighed against the potential benefits of the additional resources and, of course, the risk of having the request rejected. Politically speaking, this places Independents and smaller parties at a strategic disadvantage to their peers who belong to larger parties.

Conclusions

In the Australian context, the extent to which the prime minister or premier has power to allocate parliamentary resources creates a level of uncertainty for recipients. Access to resources is a moveable feast, particularly for those who must negotiate with government to gain staffing allocations. This can result in increased resources for individual parliamentarians and legislative parties that enter into positive relationships with the government or in reduced resources for those reluctant to lend such support or with little bargaining power. As such, while access to these resources in part turns on electorally determined factors such as party strength, the needs of the government play a key role. This, in turn, creates a level of uncertainty felt most acutely by those most dependent on the discretion of government for receipt of these allowances—that is, those parties hovering around the threshold of parliamentary party status and Independents.

This power dynamic illustrates how parliamentary resources may be allocated by the prime minister to achieve political ends, by virtue of the lack of formal regulation in this area.[48] Access to resources is governed by the extent to which minor party actors factor in the balance of power and their willingness to trade support to obtain them. This begs the question of whether it is desirable that government be given such freedom to leverage capacity-building resources for political gain. It also brings into question the ability of newly emerging political alternatives to challenge the status quo. Once having achieved parliamentary breakthrough, political actors falling into this category who fail to win enough seats to attain parliamentary party status are faced with the choice of either negotiating with government for additional resources or operating at a disadvantage to those they seek to oppose. By placing minor parties and Independents on a more precarious footing when it comes to resource provision, the principle of equal representation is undermined.

One way of addressing this issue—in addition to limiting discretion and standardising entitlements in this area—may be to reconsider the link between resource entitlements and the criteria used to determine whether a party acquires parliamentary party status. While it aids procedural clarity to set out what does and does not constitute a parliamentary party, the necessity of applying the same criteria in determining who qualifies for additional tools-of-trade resources is questionable. Precedent exists in other jurisdictions for disaggregating the two and this may be a useful line of inquiry in the Australian context. For example, Irish political parties seeking parliamentary group status must have a minimum of five members elected to the Dáil Éireann (lower house).[49] Having attained this status, these groups are entitled to procedural privileges such as a guaranteed portion of all speaking time, priority questions to ministers, a place at leaders' questions and a role in determining the items discussed during private members' time.[50] Lack of group status does not, however, disqualify minor parties or Independents from resources

---

48   Senator Evans speaking at the Senate Finance and Public Administration Legislation Committee (13 February 2006), Parliament of Australia, Canberra.

49   Prior to a 2016 reform, this qualification was set at seven.

50   *Standing Orders of Dáil Éireann Relative to Public Business* (2011), Dublin: Oireachtas Éireann.

such as the monetary PAA.[51] Each party with a minimum of one member elected to either the lower or the upper house is entitled to an automatic complement of party staff, office space, equipment and financial allowance proportionate to its number. Moreover, allocations are made using a defined mathematical formula that takes account of party strength rather than the negotiating position of parliamentary actors.[52] While the Irish system is by no means perfect and efforts at reform were ongoing at the time of writing, its practice of divorcing a certain level of resource access from parliamentary group status may be worth considering in the Australian context given the issues highlighted here.

Another aspect of this scheme that would benefit from further review is the effect the allocations mechanism has on the behaviour and re-election prospects of legislators.[53] It is anticipated that if such an effect is present it is likely to manifest both directly and indirectly, although further investigation would be helpful in confirming or rebutting this. In a direct sense, those parliamentarians belonging to legislative parties qualifying for such rewards may be better equipped to make use of policymaking and participation opportunities. Moreover, when it comes to election time, these members have increased levels of resources available to drive their campaigns. As a result, the indirect effect is that these members may be perceived as more capable, effective and organised than Independents or those aligned to minor parties, who either do not benefit from such resources or receive reduced levels. This has the potential to generate a positive feedback loop whereby such perceived superiority leads to improved electoral performance, which in turn leads to larger resource allocations. Admittedly, quantifying this indirect effect would be challenging in light of the multitude of variables that contributes to electoral outcomes. There is, however, an established literature that highlights the electoral advantage that accompanies incumbency[54] and

---

51 Although it must be noted that reduced allocations are made only to Independents—a grievance for that category of parliamentarian.
52 *Oireachtas (Ministerial and Parliamentary Offices) (Secretarial Facilities) Regulations 2013* (No. 2 of 2013), Ireland.
53 Simon Hix (1998) 'Elections, Parties and Institutional Design: A Comparative Perspective on European Union Democracy', *West European Politics* 21(3): 19–52.
54 Joel W. Johnson (2012) 'Campaign Spending in Proportional Electoral Systems: Incumbents Versus Challengers Revisited', *Comparative Political Studies* 46(8): 968–93.

also the advantages of appearing to come from outside the political class. As such, this issue may merit consideration within the context of these areas of scholarship.

Finally, an overt dependence on informal 'convention' as the guiding hand in parliamentary party resource allocation creates a barrier to transparency. This is compounded by the lack of formal review and appeal mechanisms, which in turn creates difficulties in measuring the extent of resource access among parliamentarians and in identifying allocation patterns both within and across parliamentary terms. Those parliamentarians operating outside parties with recognised parliamentary party status appear to experience significant uncertainty regarding the levels of access to parliamentary resources and the extent to which they may fluctuate from parliamentary term to parliamentary term. Granted, uncertainty is part of parliamentary life in that each election brings with it the prospect of seat loss and resulting job losses for staff. Yet this uncertainty is compounded for those whose access to key resources is precarious by virtue of their party affiliation. Whether they are liked or loathed, as long as Independents and minor parties win election to parliament through free and fair elections, an argument can be made for their entitlement to equal levels of resource access relative to their parliamentary colleagues. Unfortunately, the present system does not guarantee this and, as such, it merits examination and reform. It is therefore hoped that by shedding a little light on the issue, this chapter may prompt policymakers to consider a review of these practices so they may be brought into line with other forms of resource allocation. It is anticipated that this would go some way to addressing the need for transparency, certainty and consistency in this area of parliamentary life.

5

Putting the cartel before the house? Public funding of parties in Queensland

Graeme Orr

In the cartel thesis of party behaviour, parliamentary parties have incentives to forget their political rivalry and cooperate on electoral reforms. This is especially so between the major parties in majoritarian electoral systems like those in Australia. In the political finance realm, the hypothesis is that the dominant parties will seek to featherbed themselves and minimise competition from alternative players. The cartel idea is not that these motivations necessarily override all principles or competitive instincts or that they are universal irrespective of conditions,[1] but that cartel-like behaviour can be *expected*. A prime example is the maintenance of majoritarian voting systems themselves.

This chapter presents a subnational case study to examine why public funding is adopted and the strength of the cartel thesis in explaining the political and legislative dynamics of its evolution. Political finance laws at the subnational level in Australia have been a source of innovation in recent years, despite the law barely evolving in over 30

1   Richard S. Katz and Peter Mair (2012) 'Parties, Interest Groups and Cartels: A Comment', *Party Politics* 18(1): 107.

years at the national level.[2] This chapter considers the curious case of the State of Queensland. Queensland, it must be acknowledged, presents a somewhat special case in lacking an upper house.[3] With a unicameral parliament, and not needing to consult let alone negotiate with other parties in the design of the legislation, governments can legislate with impunity.

Party regulation in Queensland presents a fairly naked example of incumbency advantage with aspects of cartel behaviour. Queensland has veered from mimicking the Commonwealth's light-touch political finance regulation to highly regulated and back to light regulation in barely one electoral cycle (2011–14). In each of these instances of reform, first an Australian Labor Party (ALP), then a Liberal National Party (LNP) government, has driven through public funding provisions whose generosity has suggested rent-seeking.[4] The LNP reforms also included egregious elements discriminating against minor parties and Independents, suggesting duopolistic behaviour. Yet such cartelism is not inevitable, as is revealed when the Queensland approach is compared with contemporaneous reforms in other States. This reinforces Ekaterina Rashkova and Ingrid van Biezen's insight that while governing parties may have cartelistic or featherbedding motivations in adopting public funding, that is certainly not its necessary effect.[5]

Public funding of political parties

Public funding of parties has returned to the forefront of debate about institutional reform and the law of politics in Australia. Ostensibly, this has been driven by party finance scandals centred on New South

---

2   Graeme Orr (2016) 'Political Finance Law in Australia: Innovation and Enervation', *Election Law Journal* 16(1): 58–70.
3   See Nicholas Aroney, Scott Prasser and J. R. Nethercote (eds) (2008) *Restraining Elective Dictatorship: The Upper House Solution*, Perth: UWA Press.
4   On rent-seeking, see Ingrid van Biezen and Petr Kopecký (2007) 'The State and the Parties: Public Funding, Public Regulation and Rent-Seeking in Contemporary Democracies', *Party Politics* 13(2): 235.
5   See footnote 69, this chapter.

Wales (NSW),[6] which triggered proposals to ban private donations in favour of full public funding of parties. Indeed both ALP and Liberal Party leaders, in NSW at least, have backed full public funding, at least of elections, as have other conservative leaders.[7] Full public funding, however, has not attracted the support of experts and is unlikely to eventuate for a mix of practical and constitutional reasons.[8]

Nonetheless, this turn towards embracing *more* public funding represents a pivot away from traditional cynicism concerning taxpayer support. Such cynicism permeated public and media debate in earlier decades. In some cases, it succeeded in blocking moves to introduce public funding (as was the case, until recently, in Western Australia); in other cases, it succeeded in blocking proposals to increase funding (for instance, the Commonwealth Government withdrew a Bill to increase funding in May 2013, when the Opposition reneged on its support in the face of public unease). It is timely, then, to consider the origins, rationales and nature of public funding of parties.

There is not space here to detail the different funding regimes across Australia; this has been done elsewhere and is discussed in Chapter 1 of this volume.[9] Public funding, aka state subsidies or subventions, has taken a number of guises in Australia. These various methods have been justified on the basis of injecting 'clean' money into the political system. But each method has also involved elements of rewarding the stronger—whether it be the electorally successful or the parties most able to attract donors. The predominant guise for public funding has been direct grants to parties in the form of post-election payments.

---

6   NSW Independent Commission Against Corruption (ICAC) (2014–15) *NSW Public Officials and Members of Parliament—Allegations Concerning Corrupt Conduct involving Australian Water Holdings Pty Ltd (Operation Credo) and Allegations Concerning Soliciting, Receiving and Concealing Payments (Operation Spicer)*, Sydney: ICAC, available at: icac.nsw.gov.au/investigations/current-investigations/investigationdetail/203.

7   Premier Baird (Liberal) endorsed the idea, previously floated by Premier Iemma (ALP) and supported in principle by Opposition Leader Robertson (ALP): Geoff Winestock and Scott Parker (2014) 'Baird Announces Donations Crackdown but Not Until 2015', *Australian Financial Review*, 28 May: 6. In 2015, both the LNP Opposition Leader in Queensland and the Country Liberal Party Chief Minister of the Northern Territory embraced the idea as well.

8   Department of Premier and Cabinet, Panel of Experts ['Schott Inquiry'] (December 2014) *Political Donations: Final Report. Volume 1*, Sydney: NSW Government, Ch. 4. See also George Williams (2014) 'Public Funding of Elections is Costly and Simply Unfair', *Sydney Morning Herald*, 3 June: 18; and Joo-Cheong Tham (2014) 'Don't Ban Political Donors', *Australian Financial Review*, 7 May: 43.

9   See Joo-Cheong Tham (2010) *Money and Politics: The Democracy We Can't Afford*, Sydney: UNSW Press, Ch. 5; and Orr, 'Political Finance Law in Australia', pp. 61–2, Appendix.

This has typically been available on a 'dollars per vote' basis, subject to a minimum vote share. As we will see, other models include reimbursement on a sliding scale of actual campaign expenditure and annual 'administration' funding throughout the parliamentary cycle, depending on the party's success in having Members of Parliament (MPs) elected.

Other forms of taxpayer support for parties are not tied to electioneering. One involves income tax deductions for donations—a federal rule that treats registered parties as quasi-charities to encourage smaller-scale donations as a form of political participation.[10] The other involves extra staff and allowances to MPs and parliamentary caucuses, as well as Commonwealth funding of party think tanks and international activity.[11] These supports are directed to the parliamentary wing of the party, rather than its administrative wing, and exist ostensibly to enhance legislative and constituency work. But they are relevant to party organisations as their benefit bleeds back to the party as a whole and its electoral advocacy.

The dawn of public funding in Australia

For 20 years, Queensland law has formally allocated some taxpayer funding to State political parties or candidates. From 1994 until 2011, those laws were simple and stable. They borrowed directly from the Commonwealth model—begun in 1983 but which itself drew from the pioneering NSW system of 1981.[12] A party or candidate that achieved 4 per cent of the vote in a seat qualified for payment for those votes. That model was based on the idea of partial funding of electoral campaigns.

---

10   There is partisan contention about the level of taxation relief and its application to corporate as opposed to individual donors. Deductibility applies to the first $1,500 per annum and corporate donors are included.

11   On the latter type of funding, see Chapter 1, this volume.

12   Ernest Chaples (1981) 'Public Campaign Finance: New South Wales Bites the Bullet', *Australian Quarterly* 53(1): 4. The NSW scheme was capped so no party could receive more than 50 per cent of the funding, however electorally successful. It later expanded to include annual funding to defray parties' administrative costs.

Money thus can be 'earned' for every first preference vote received. For Commonwealth elections, the funding rate has grown more generous over time, as shown in Figure 5.1. The first Commonwealth public funding regime was tied to the basic postal rate—90 cents per elector per election, or three stamps' worth[13]—as if campaigning was still paper-based, as in the United Kingdom.

But since the major cost of Australian electioneering has long been broadcast advertising, the level of public funding was unsurprisingly ratcheted up. The biggest increase came in the 1990s, when funding for a Senate vote was raised to equal that for a House of Representatives vote. This not only increased the overall pool of funds, it also helped minor parties, as they do better at Senate than House elections and they tend not to attract business donors. Similarly, Queensland public funding rates over time rose from $1 to well over $2 per vote (remembering that in unicameral Queensland, electors have a single vote and there are no upper house campaigns to fund). After each triennial State poll, moneys were thus paid to defray electioneering expenditure. Unlike national elections, Queensland persevered with a 'reimbursement' requirement that calls for receipts of actual expenditure.[14]

Queensland's adoption of public funding in 1994 stemmed from the recommendation of the independent Electoral and Administrative Review Commission.[15] This followed a major anticorruption Royal Commission report, which included concerns about 'the possibility of improper favour being shown or being seen to have been shown by the government to political donors'.[16] A longstanding conservative Coalition Government was found to have presided over corruption in the police force. There was also evidence of businessmen making cash donations directly to the premier and to the secretary of the National Party, both to assist the governing party and to influence factional battles within it. After the fall of that Coalition Government,

13   I. C. Harris (1984) 'The Australian Joint Select Committee on Electoral Reform', *The Table* 52: 52.
14   This avoided occasional windfall profits.
15   Electoral and Administrative Review Commission (EARC) (1992) *Investigation of Public Registration of Political Donations, Public Funding of Election Campaigns and Related Issues*, Brisbane: EARC.
16   G. E. 'Tony' Fitzgerald QC ['Fitzgerald Inquiry'] (1989) *Commission of Inquiry into Possible Illegal Activities and Associated Police Misconduct, 1989: Report*, Brisbane: Queensland Government.

the new ALP administration supported public funding,[17] while the Liberal and National parties at the time opposed it as an 'attack on the fundamental freedom of the individual'[18] and a 'pollie tax'.[19] In this, the conservative parties were repeating their position on the introduction of Commonwealth public funding: they opposed it on principle, but would share in it once enacted.[20]

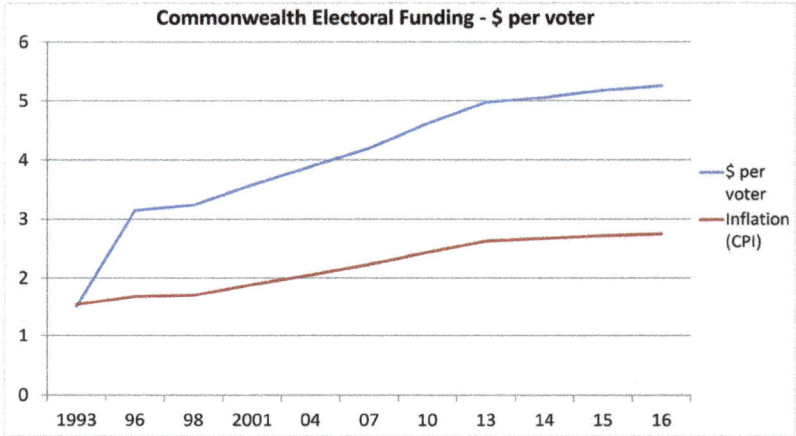

Figure 5.1 Growth in public funding rate (Commonwealth elections)
Source: Australian Electoral Commission.

Public funding's three rationales: Resourcing parties, dampening demand for private money and political equality

A pragmatic intention of public funding was to ensure parties were adequately resourced. Public funding was introduced in Queensland only because a short-lived nationwide ban on paid broadcast election

---

17   Parliamentary Committee on Electoral and Administrative Review (PCEAR) (1993) *Investigation of Public Registration of Political Donations, Public Funding of Election Campaigns and Related Issues*, Report No. 20, November, Brisbane: Queensland Parliament.
18   ibid., para. 3.12. That said, the Opposition was more concerned to champion the rights of union members to not indirectly fund the ALP than it was to oppose public funding (paras 3.13–19).
19   Denver Beanland (Liberal), *Queensland Parliamentary Debates*, 24 November 1994, p. 10,809.
20   Joint Select Committee on Electoral Reform (JSCER) (1983) *First Report*, September, Canberra: Parliament of Australia, paras 9.11–9.17.

advertising did not survive constitutional challenge.[21] The loss of that ban—a measure meant to dampen the cost of electioneering—was said to justify public funding by helping to bridge the cost of campaigning and sources of finance. This bears out Anika Gauja's insight that, around the world, public funding has been 'introduced, in part, as a mechanism to ensure parties' survival in electoral democracies characterized by increasing campaign costs and declining party memberships'.[22] It is also consonant with Zim Nwokora's observation that parties—understood as ongoing entities as opposed to temporary legislative majorities—seek institutional measures that give them organisational security and predictability.[23] Ideally, public resourcing of parties contributes to their institutional strength, and is not simply a crutch for the major parties. It can assist in maintaining a viable opposition party through lean years, as well as helping minor parties build capacity and hence sustain interparty competitiveness.

Along with public funding, the contemporaneous introduction of mandatory disclosure of larger donations and loans in Queensland was also expected to dampen the 'supply' of private funds.[24] The focus of reform was thus on the revenue side of party activities within a free 'market' for political money. Debate about capping electoral expenditure or donations would not emerge seriously until the late 2000s. This was despite caps on expenditure having been imposed on Australian candidates for nearly a century until the 1970s,[25] being part of the opt-in system of public funding of US presidential campaigns and applied to Canadian parties since 1974.

Public funding was initially understood as a quid pro quo for the obligation to disclose donations and loans (although such disclosure applied to all parties, including small parties who would not benefit from public funding). Disclosure, conversely, was seen as an 'essential

21   EARC, *Investigation of Public Registration of Political Donations*, para. 4.83.
22   Anika Gauja (2010) *Political Parties and Elections: Legislating for Representative Democracy*, Farnham: Ashgate, p. 162.
23   Zim Nwokora (2014) 'The Distinctive Politics of Campaign Finance Reform', *Party Politics* 20(6): 918.
24   EARC, *Investigation of Public Registration of Political Donations*, p. 111.
25   Deborah Cass and Sonia Burrows (2000) 'Commonwealth Regulation of Campaign Finance: Public Funding, Disclosure and Expenditure Limits', *Sydney Law Review* 22(4): 477, 484–5 and 491–2.

corollary' of public funding:[26] the shining of sunlight on to private money in tandem with the injection of 'clean', no-strings-attached public money. Unlike disclosure, public funding makes almost no organisational demands on party organisations. In that sense, it poses no immediate questions for the freedom of political association.

Public funding, however, does indirectly risk corrosion of the internal vitality of parties as forums for political participation. Echoing Nwokora's observation that party administrators have a strong interest in the financial security of their party as an entity, reliance on external sources of funding—whether it be overly generous public funding or corporate largesse—may exacerbate the atrophying of parties' grassroots connections (a risk raised by the professionalisation of party administration and centralisation of policy control in parliamentary leaderships). It is difficult, however, to measure the organisational effects of parties becoming overly reliant on public funding. In the absence of full public funding year in and year out, and given the reputational and financial costs of hiring 'supporters', Australian parties still need members to leaflet households during campaigns and at polling stations. Constituency campaigns can also benefit from mobilising members as local fundraisers. If nothing else, if public funding were generous enough to wean parties from overreliance on institutional donors, it should also shore up the influence of individual party members as opposed to outside donors.

Aside from helping secure party resources, the more noble aims of public funding relate to political integrity and equality. In (over)selling the introduction of public funding of parties at the Commonwealth level, Minister Beazley claimed its cost was 'a small insurance to pay against the possibility of corruption' and that it 'ensures that different parties offering themselves for election have an equal opportunity to present their policies to the electorate'.[27] Ideally, public funding inhibits demand for large-scale private donations and can create a more level playing field.[28] In Australia as a whole, it has not worked well on the integrity measure, because of a lack of expenditure caps to inhibit growth in electioneering expenditure or donation caps generally.

---

26 Kim Beazley (ALP), *House of Representatives Parliamentary Debates*, 2 November 1983, p. 2215.

27 ibid.

28 EARC stressed the rationale of levelling the playing field: EARC, *Investigation of Public Registration of Political Donations*, paras 4.9, 4.15.

Parties therefore still seek large donations, with the attendant risk and perception of the buying of influence. Public funding, however, has worked somewhat better in tempering the inequality between incumbents and outsiders, and between larger and smaller parties.

Political equality in the Queensland party context

Commentators such as Tham have criticised existing means of public funding as 'both ineffectual and unfair'.[29] The 'unfairness' criticism may be overstated. Fairness must also consider citizen concerns about taxpayers' money being directed into partisan politics. Election funding per vote is at least simple for citizens to comprehend, and fair in the sense that dollars follow their first-preference voting choices[30] (what US reformers call 'voting with vouchers' or 'voting with dollars').[31] Opposition parties, which attract fewer business donations than governments,[32] can 'bank' on a certain level of funding, and the more popular minor parties and Independents are also catered for.[33]

While not amounting to affirmative action in favour of smaller parties—with the exception of microparties struggling to achieve the threshold to qualify for any funding—public funding in Australia has tended to be highly proportional to electoral support. After the 2009 election, for instance, the Queensland ALP and LNP each received almost 44 per cent of public funding (on approximately 42 per cent of the vote each), the Queensland Greens received almost 7.5 per cent of public funding (on just over 8 per cent of the vote) and Independents collectively did better than their combined vote share (as there are numerous locally popular Independents).

---

29   Tham, *Money and Politics*, p. 127.
30   JSCER, *First Report*, para. 9.27.
31   Bruce Ackerman and Ian Ayres (2002) *Voting with Dollars: A New Paradigm for Campaign Finance*, New Haven, Conn.: Yale University Press; Rick Hasen (1996) 'Clipping Coupons for Democracy: An Egalitarian/Public Choice Defense of Campaign Finance Vouchers', *California Law Review* 84(1): 1–59.
32   Iain McMenamin (2013) *If Money Talks, What Does it Say? Corruption and Business Financing of Political Parties*, Oxford: Oxford University Press, pp. 81–2.
33   On the importance of public funding for The Greens and Australian Democrats, see Joo-Cheong Tham and David Grove (2004) 'Public Funding and Expenditure Regulation of Australian Political Parties: Some Reflections', *Federal Law Review* 32(3): 397–401.

Such rewards are particularly important given Queensland's electoral system is otherwise stacked against smaller parties seeking to grow organically. There is a majoritarian voting system and no upper house. The Queensland Greens and Australian Democrats have never held a seat at State level, and minor party MPs have mostly come from groups splintering from established, especially conservative, parties.[34]

As Figure 5.2 shows, the Queensland Greens, despite having relatively robust grassroots, receive between 65 and 80 per cent of their revenue from public funding in years when it is available (typically after a State or Commonwealth election). This suggests even greater reliance on public funding than in the early 2000s when, Australia-wide, The Greens and the Australian Democrats drew between 25 and 40 per cent of their revenue from public funding.[35] As smaller parties consolidate, their share of public funding improves because their vote share reaches the threshold in more seats, but, unless they acquire the balance of power and attune their ideology to that of corporate or union donors, they cannot attract big donations.[36]

While Queensland's electoral system is harsh on minor parties, its sociodemography is kinder on Independents, who often flourish in Queensland's decentralised regions. State-level examples such as the Independent MPs for Nambour and Gladstone have held their seats for over 15 years and increased their majorities in the process. Independents elected to regional Queensland seats at the federal level—Pauline Hanson (Ipswich), Bob Katter (north-western Queensland) and Clive Palmer (Sunshine Coast)—have even leveraged their status to found national political movements. Public funding was framed in Queensland, as it was nationally, with the parties insisting on controlling the funding through direct payments to them, rather than to the candidates who at least notionally 'earned' it. But Independent candidates were nonetheless entitled to funding on an equal basis.

---

34   The Queensland Labor Party and even North Queensland Labor Party in the 1950s and One Nation (which splintered into a City–Country Alliance) in the late 1990s. Today's Katter's Australian Party and Palmer United Party are named after founders who served with the old National Party and each has relied on poaching LNP MPs.

35   Marian Sawer, Norman Abjorensen and Phil Larkin (2009) *Australia: The State of Democracy*, Sydney: The Federation Press, p. 113; and Tham and Grove, 'Public Funding and Expenditure Regulation of Australian Political Parties'.

36   There are exceptions, such as philanthropist-entrepreneur Graeme Wood's record, one-off $1.6 million gift to The Australian Greens in 2010.

% Income from Public Funding (Commonwealth or State)

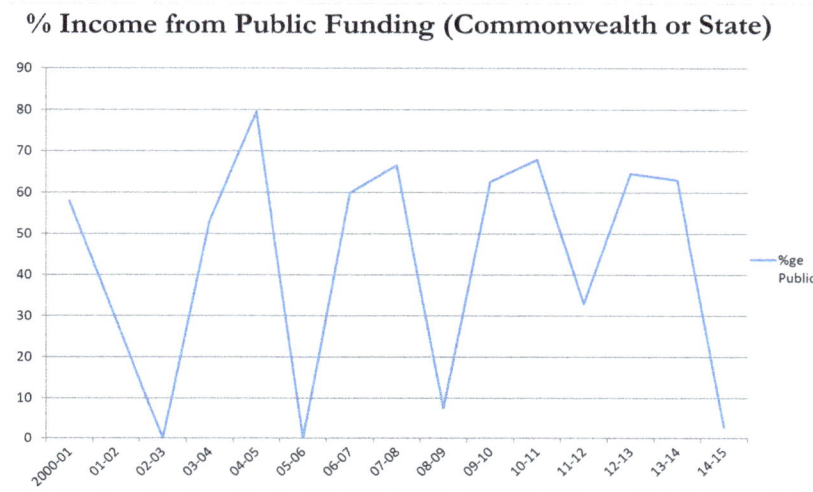

Figure 5.2 Queensland Greens' income from public funding
Sources: Australian Electoral Commission and Electoral Commission Queensland.

Sweeter carrots, sharper sticks: The 2011 Queensland ALP reforms

By 2011, after the best part of two decades in power and under Australia's first elected female premier, the Queensland ALP Government was coming to an end. It faced an election no later than March 2012, with opinion polls predicting a shellacking. (That wipe-out came to pass. The party won just seven of 89 seats and garnered under 27 per cent of the primary vote.) It had encountered criticism, including from former corruption-fighting Royal Commissioner Tony Fitzgerald, about a slippage in ethics and integrity in government, including the purchase of political access.[37] Premier Bligh responded with a discussion paper, *Integrity and Accountability in Queensland*, in August 2009. Besides a self-imposed ban on ministers selling access by attending fundraising functions,[38] the paper suggested limiting

---

37   Tony Fitzgerald QC (2009) Introductory Address: Inaugural Griffith University: Tony Fitzgerald Lecture, available at: griffith.edu.au/__data/assets/pdf_file/0020/156125/Tony-Fitzgerald---Arthurs-introduction---Griffith-lecture-web.pdf.

38   See Brian Costar (2014) Selling Access to Elected Officials: Beyond Regulation?, Paper presented to the Academy of the Social Sciences in Australia Workshop: The Legal Regulation of Political Parties in Australia, University of Sydney.

electioneering expenditure and briefly flagged an intention to cap donations, explicitly implying a compensatory increase in public funding.[39]

What ensued was a long period of brainstorming and policymaking within the government, and some public discussion, before the release of a White Paper, *Reforming Queensland's Electoral System*, in December 2011.[40] The White Paper outlined a legislative model that appeared in a Bill several months later. The model revolved around:

a. tightening disclosure (which the ALP had already made more regular)
b. capping donations to parties to $5,000 per annum from a single source (at least for campaign as opposed to administrative purposes)
c. capping electioneering expenditure for parties and interest groups
d. dramatically increasing public funding.

NSW had, a year earlier, moved to cap donations and election expenses, as did the Australian Capital Territory (ACT) in 2012.[41] Queensland's reforms erected a first in Australian political history: an eastern State wall of comprehensive political finance schemes.[42] Queensland borrowed significantly from the NSW regime at the time, particularly (as the next paragraph explains) the idea of guaranteeing a percentage of election campaign costs. A Queensland innovation, however, was to cap only donations that were fed into a State or local government campaign account. State law, for constitutional reasons, cannot regulate donations to Commonwealth election campaigns. NSW, however, had gone further, and capped donations that funded party administration, not just campaigning. The Queensland exception was a way around two sticking points. Union contributions were one, and they remained uncapped insofar as they supported ALP administration rather than campaigning. The other was the fact that, at the time, a billionaire by the name of Clive Palmer was helping bankroll the LNP (as noted above, Palmer has since founded his own party and became a federal MP).

---

39 Queensland Government (2009) *Integrity and Accountability in Queensland*, August, Brisbane: Queensland Government, pp. 14–15.
40 *Election Funding and Disclosures Amendment Act 2010* (NSW).
41 *Electoral Amendment Act 2012* (ACT).
42 National laws remain light-touch: Graeme Orr (2010) *The Law of Politics: Elections, Parties and Money in Australia*, Sydney: The Federation Press, pp. 239–40, 256–8.

In the 2011 reform, public funding was sweetened indeed, especially from the perspective of Queensland's major parties. A sliding scale for reimbursement of certain campaign expenditures replaced funding per vote. The scale was generous: up to 75 per cent of the capped expenditure limit for centralised party spending and up to 52.5 per cent of the limit for candidate-level expenditure.[43] As only the major parties normally ever approach those caps, the system would reinforce their financial and hence campaign dominance. Yet smaller parties could benefit over their previous position, provided they could attract well-off donors or guarantors. Hence the system was potentially more competitive than one based purely on vote share. Katter's Australian Party, a populist agrarian party, benefited when it received almost $1.4 million in 2012—over 9 per cent of the total public funding, which was less than its vote share of 11.5 per cent but $850,000 more than it would have received under the dollars-per-vote scheme.

The new model also permitted 'advance payments' of public funding of up to 50 per cent of previous electoral entitlements.[44] This formed a particular benefit to the established parties and MPs, helping them rely on public funding rather than having to raise sizeable donations or loans upfront.

In another borrowing from NSW, biannual funding of parties' administrative activities was introduced. The Queensland minister sought to justify the significant increases in overall funding in familiar terms, appealing to resourcing ('it is expensive to have an election and it is expensive to have a democracy') and integrity (campaigning 'costs money—money which can come from either wealthy benefactors with special strings attached or public funding').[45]

The Opposition and crossbenchers were not consulted in this policymaking process.[46] The government consulted only the Electoral Commission. The timing of the White Paper, released on Christmas Eve, was not auspicious for debate. Public submissions closed in mid-

---

43   *Electoral Accountability Amendment Act 2011* (Qld), introducing new sections 177DA–DB to the *Electoral Act 1992* (Qld).

44   ibid., introducing new section 177DC to the *Electoral Act 1992* (Qld).

45   Paul Lucas (ALP), *Queensland Parliamentary Debates*, 11 May 2011, p. 1416.

46   Jarrod Bleijie (LNP), *Queensland Parliamentary Debates*, 11 May 2011, p. 1413 ('This bill is a beast of the Labor Party that we had no input into and the Independents had no input into').

February. The poor timing was exacerbated by floods that devastated most of the State in late January. Only nine public submissions were received, and none was published.

The ALP's reform Bill was tabled in parliament for a month. Yet despite its complexity (it contained 90 pages of new political finance law alone), it was not subject to any committee scrutiny. The government then pushed the Bill through, subject to a series of intricate amendments, in a single afternoon/evening's debate.

The conservative Opposition objected to the Bill as a whole. It argued that an increase in public funding was not justified (especially as the State rebuilt after the floods) and that the Bill had been hastily drafted. It specifically objected to party funding on a reimbursement scale, arguing that minor parties might disproportionately benefit[47]— an argument that assumed minor parties could bankroll sizeable campaigns in the first place. For their part, the Queensland Greens objected to the Bill as a windfall for the major parties. The new stream of administrative funding was available only to parties with MPs or to Independent MPs. Even so, the five Independent MPs voted against the Bill. In 2011–12, the new stream of administrative funding added $4.16 million in public funding,[48] most of it to the two major parties.

While the caps in the Bill conformed to social-democratic principles, there was widespread suspicion that the enhanced public funding and its generous sliding scale were a boondoggle for an ALP government facing electoral oblivion. As that wipe-out came to pass, the ALP still received $6 million in public funding—over five times the amount it would have received under the funding-per-vote system. It received 40 per cent of total public funding on not quite 27 per cent of the vote. The LNP received over 44 per cent of the funding on not quite 50 per cent of the vote. In all, $15.14 million was paid out for that election.[49] The minor parties did less well in their relative share of funding, but the rising tide of funding meant that, in absolute terms, all parties and candidates were better off.

47   ibid., p. 1423.
48   Electoral Commission Queensland (ECQ) (2012) *2011–12 Annual Report*, Brisbane: ECQ, p. 12.
49   Electoral Commission Queensland (ECQ) (2013) *2012–13 Annual Report*, Brisbane: ECQ, p. 6.

No quid pro quo: The 2014 Queensland LNP reforms

On assuming power with an Australian record seat share of nearly 88 per cent, the newly elected conservative government moved quickly to repeal the regular administrative funding of parties. It did so before the end of 2012, as a cost-saving measure to address what it said were 'outrageous' payments to political parties. On 3 January 2013, it released the *Electoral Reform Discussion Paper*.[50] The paper read like a bland issues paper, without indicating the government's thinking on reform. Approximately two months were allowed for public submission. Unlike its predecessor, at least the new government published all 254 of the submissions.

In July 2013, the LNP Government played some of its hand. Its *Electoral Reform: Queensland Electoral Review Outcomes* paper recommended a complete revamp of the Queensland political funding landscape[51]—for the second time in three years. Consistent with libertarian philosophy, the government proposed abandoning limits on political donations and electoral expenditure. It toyed with more regular disclosure of donations, but soon reversed this position, citing timorous legal advice that States could not demand more information from their political parties than the national laws required. (Timorous, because there is no difficulty in complying with a Commonwealth disclosure system and a more revealing State disclosure system. In fact, constitutional principle requires that each level of government retains some autonomy over its own electoral system because that system is integral to its existence as a body politic.)[52]

On public funding, the sliding scale of reimbursement of party electioneering expenditure was returned to the traditional dollars-per-vote model. Just as the sliding scale had insulated the ALP through its calamitous loss of support in the 2012 election, undoing it would pose difficulties for the ALP until its vote share was repaired.

---

50   Department of Justice and Attorney-General (2013) *Electoral Reform Discussion Paper*, January, Brisbane: Queensland Government.
51   Department of Justice and Attorney-General (2013) *Electoral Reform: Queensland Electoral Review Outcomes*, July, Brisbane: Queensland Government.
52   *ACTV v Commonwealth* (1992) 177 Commonwealth Law Reports, pp. 163–4. See also *Local Government Association (Qld) v Queensland* [2001] QCA 517, paras 47, 69–70.

The government also proposed raising the vote share threshold to earn public funding to 10 per cent. This measure was guaranteed to nobble the three significant minor parties in Queensland: the Queensland Greens, Katter's Australian Party and (to a lesser extent, since its founder was a billionaire) the emerging Palmer United Party. When it was introduced in late November 2013, the Bill went further in discriminating against the minor parties by providing that Independents receive post-election funding at *half* the rate of the parties—$1.45 compared with $2.90 per vote. If anything, Independents' campaigns may need higher rather than lower funding, as they lack the economies of scale and expertise of party campaigns.

The Bill also proposed reintroducing funding of the parties in non-election years, just a year after it had been abolished. This policy reversal had not been canvassed in the public consultations. It was to be denied not only to parties without MPs, but also to Independent MPs. The measure was dressed up as 'policy development funding'. Unlike the NSW or the former Queensland schemes for administrative funding, there was no limit on a single party dominating the fund. In fact, during the life of the then parliament, the LNP would receive the majority of funds (as this new layer of funding was to be based on vote share in the previous election). Also unlike the NSW or former Queensland schemes, there were no strings attached: this funding can be squirrelled away for electioneering.

Most remarkably of all, in an Australian first, the amount of funding would be set neither by parliament nor by an index, but by the Attorney-General from time to time. To the government's credit, it seemed genuine in wishing to significantly reduce the total amount of party funding, from a potential $23 million over a three-year electoral cycle under the ALP's short-lived scheme. How much that is reduced will, however, depend on the parsimony of each attorney-general. In addition, the free market in donations was made retrospective to the tabling of the Bill, and the raising of disclosure levels was also made retrospective to the previous financial year. The major parties, and especially the incumbent government, could begin building war chests for the 2015 election—an election in which campaign expenditure would once again be unlimited.

The Bill was scrutinised by a committee dominated, given the makeup of parliament, by government MPs (five to two). The committee consulted over the Christmas–New Year period and received 180 submissions. It held a brief public hearing (one morning, on a day devoted to numerous, unrelated Bills) and delivered a report that was split on party lines.[53] However, on one point, government members rebelled, calling for the threshold to earn electoral funding to be raised not to 10 per cent but to 6 per cent. The government agreed to that softening of the negative impact of the funding reform on minor parties and Independents.

Outside the government, responses to the new political funding proposals were largely negative.[54] Yet the ALP Opposition voted *with* the LNP Government in favour of discriminating against Independents in the post-election and annual 'policy development' funding schemes, and in not attaching conditions to the use of public funding.[55] The ALP also supported backdating the funding laws to the previous financial year.[56] On neither matter did the ALP or the government seek to justify its position to parliament. The ALP did, however, express opposition to raising the threshold to earn post-election funding to 6 per cent, arguing it was unfair on smaller players.[57]

In contrast, all the crossbenchers—a group collectively larger than the official ALP Opposition—vociferously opposed the enhanced public funding measures. The disparate treatment of Independents and moves to reduce election funding of minor parties were said to be 'offensive in the extreme' and reason to be 'disgusted'.[58] Annual 'policy development' payments favouring the major parties were a 'joke', 'disgusting' and a criteria-free 'slush fund'.[59] The funding

---

53   Legal Affairs and Community Safety Committee (2014) *Electoral Reform Amendment Bill*, Report No. 56, February, Brisbane: Parliament of Queensland.

54   Supporting a free market in donations and expenditure, but tight disclosure of both, see: Anthony Gray (2014) 'Political Finance Regulation is a Field Strewn with Pitfalls', *The Courier-Mail*, 19 May: 20.

55   *Queensland Parliamentary Debates*, 22 May 2014, pp. 1858–61.

56   ibid, p. 1870.

57   Annastacia Palaszczuk (ALP), *Queensland Parliamentary Debates*, 21 May 2014, pp. 1738–9; and 22 May 2014, p. 1858.

58   Liz Cunningham (Independent) and Shane Knuth (Katter's Australian Party), *Queensland Parliamentary Debates*, 22 May 2014, pp. 1833–4 and p. 1842, respectively.

59   Ray Hopper (Katter's Australian Party), Alex Douglas (Palmer United Party) and Peter Wellington (Independent), *Queensland Parliamentary Debates*, 22 May 2014, p. 1813, pp. 1840–1 and p. 1861, respectively.

scheme overall was said to 'target minor parties ... that want to grow organically' and undermine the important role of Independents.[60] These voices represented two minor parties (Katter's Australian Party and the Palmer United Party) and a brace of regional Independents. The Greens, though they represented around 7 per cent of Queensland voters, lacked a parliamentary voice; they also opposed the new law. One government MP spoke against and abstained from voting for the laws, arguing that true liberalism required better disclosure and capping of donations. A day later, he resigned from parliament, citing the electoral finance laws as one reason he could not continue serving under the LNP.[61]

In comparison with the 2012 election, the amount of election funding paid in 2015 reduced considerably, to $10.75 million. Of this, the two major parties received 86.23 per cent of the public funding, in fairly equal shares. The total amount of public funding was reduced, as promised; however, the minor parties suffered in two ways, due to the reduction in overall payments and because of the raising of the threshold to 6 per cent of the primary vote.[62]

Public funding: Cleaning up parties or parties cleaning up?

Philosophical leanings or principled ideological accounts of the public interest are far from irrelevant to questions about the law governing politics. They help ground debates about reform along fairly predictable lines: social-democratic parties tend to hew to egalitarian approaches and conservative parties tend to favour libertarian or free-market approaches. In Nwokora's account of the drivers motivating political finance law specifically, principled approaches are subject less to brute cartelism and more to a nuanced and sometimes dichotomous party self-interest.[63] This dichotomy is not a distinction between parties of

---

60   Robbie Katter (Katter's Australian Party), *Queensland Parliamentary Debates*, 22 May 2014, pp. 1847–8.
61   Chris Davis (LNP), *Queensland Parliamentary Debates*, 22 May 2014, p. 1846. He had previously been sacked as an assistant minister for commenting against government policy.
62   The minor parties and Independents received just 13.77 per cent of public funding, despite collectively securing 21.21 per cent of the vote. Electoral Commission Queensland, Funding and Disclosure Director, Email to author, 12 April 2016.
63   Nwokora, 'The Distinctive Politics of Campaign Finance Reform', pp. 918–29.

the left and right as such, but a contrast between the interests of the party machine—in securing long-term organisational security and minimising the financial risks of inevitable periods out of power—and those of the parliamentary caucus and their leaders to secure shorter-term incumbency benefits and electioneering advantage.

Electoral reform, of course, rarely happens without aligning with governing party self-interest, since governments are invariably in control of what passes through the lower house. Exceptions can occur in hung parliaments (as when the ACT Legislative Assembly imposed restrictions on government advertising in 2009).[64] High-profile scandals also occasionally act as fillips to reform, forcing parties to act against their philosophical leanings and even self-interest. This can happen cataclysmically, as in Queensland after the governmental meltdown following the 1988 royal commission into corruption, or in an unfolding response to a series of corrosive revelations, as in NSW over recent years.

What insight into these various theories does the Queensland case study lend us? The initial period, until 1994, saw Queensland lagging behind the Commonwealth and NSW in not providing public funding for parties. This was explicable in terms of incumbency self-interest as well as the 'open-for-business' mentality of the long-term National Party–dominated government. The quasi-revolution of 1988 did not immediately see the ALP use its majority to adopt public funding (unlike the ALP governments of 1981 in NSW and 1983 nationally). The Queensland ALP was well funded by a still numerically strong trade union movement and an investment fund; it was also pledged to honour the independent reform process.

But by 1994 pressures were building in the cost of campaigning, to the point that the ALP was happy to introduce public funding. The then conservative Opposition rejected it in principle, but did not fight for a 'right' to opt out of such funding. An implicit cartel-ish force can be seen at work here: the major party machines understood the security that public funding would bring, while their legislative wings appreciated the campaign support at a time when minor parties were rare in Queensland.

---

64   *Government Agencies (Campaign Advertising) Act 2009* (ACT).

In the significant but short-lived ALP reforms of 2011, a very obvious case of abuse of incumbency can be diagnosed. It manifested in a massive ramping up of public funding via a reimbursement of campaign costs and in the introduction of regular funding for party administration. This suited both the ALP's administrative wing and the about-to-be-ousted parliamentary team (which faced a rout and reliance on declining levels of union money at a time when corporate largesse was flooding back to an LNP that was on the verge of power). The 2011 reforms were also couched as egalitarian measures to limit campaign expenditure and the size of campaign donations, befitting social-democratic principles. But these came belatedly, after a long term in government. And even then, an exception was carved out for donations for party administrative purposes, to reassure the party machines. The LNP Opposition objected to the reforms, but once again happily shared in the money.

Back in power in 2012, the LNP Government moved quickly to undo administrative funding of parties, consistent with its fiscal conservatism. Yet within a year, it was restoring that regular pipeline of funding, and in a discriminatory form that breached the rule of law in two ways. One was by blatantly discriminating against Independent MPs and parties like the Queensland Greens; the other was by leaving the amount of administrative funding to fluctuate on the whim of a minister. The LNP also moved to deprive minor parties of post-election funding, by increasing the threshold by 150 per cent (from achieving 4 per cent to 10 per cent of the vote share)—an unprecedented move in Australia. Although it took its own backbench advice to reduce the increase to 50 per cent (from achieving 4 per cent to 6 per cent of the vote share), it insisted on halving the rate at which Independents earn such funding—a discrimination also unprecedented in Australia.

The conservative government and ALP Opposition split on predictable ideological lines on the question of caps on donations and party expenditure; however, the ALP Opposition supported the extra lines of public funding and did not oppose the discrimination against Independents. While the 2013–14 reforms were less hasty than the 2011 reforms, and the consultation process was better (it could hardly have been worse), in both cases the governing party acted in the certainty of a sizeable majority. In each instance, the Independents and minor parties opposed the reforms—even though the 2011 reforms, by increasing public funding, stood to benefit them.

By 2015, the ALP had returned to power and a further review of the system was planned. It moved quickly to reinstate biannual disclosure of donations above $1,000, and promised a broader review of the State's political finance system. The more moderate conservative Opposition leader (perhaps fearing a dearth of donations while in Opposition) surprised many by announcing his support for full public funding of parties' election campaigns.[65] Perhaps these moves can lead to a lasting compromise and a stable model, but in the process Queensland will have embarked on three major overhauls of its party finance regime in barely five years. With a unicameral parliament, giddying legislative pendulums are, of course, far from unheard of.

In South Australia (SA), by contrast, across 2013, an ALP government expected to face defeat (a defeat that did not eventuate). Yet it combined with both its Liberal Opposition and The Greens, a key player in the upper house, to negotiate multipartisan political finance reform for the first time in modern Australia. The result was an opt-in public funding and expenditure limit system, with continuous donation disclosure but no donation caps.[66] Tellingly, the public funding scheme, based on dollars per vote, was actually tilted towards, rather than against, newer and smaller players, with a higher value per vote allocated for the first 10 per cent of the votes received by parties without MPs.

Like Queensland, the Territories in Australia also have unicameral legislatures. The Northern Territory, partly due to its small demographics and budget, has never offered public funding. (With a small number of voters and a limited media market, its campaigns are cheaper and more localised.) Befitting its status as Australia's most social-democratic and bureaucratic jurisdiction, however, the ACT minority ALP Government enacted a detailed campaign finance regime in 2012, with Greens support. This included a $10,000 donation cap, limits on campaign expenditure and relatively continuous disclosure of donations. The regime was built on an existing public funding scheme based on votes received. Yet within fewer than three years, the ACT ALP Government (still with minority status, but acting cartelistically with the Liberal Opposition's support) loosened

---

65   Australian Associated Press (AAP) (2015) 'LNP to Consider Full Public Funding of Elections', *Brisbane Times* [Online], 29 May.
66   *Electoral (Funding, Expenditure and Disclosure) Amendment Act 2013* (SA), taking effect from mid-2015. Aside from the lack of donation caps, the system resembles the much-vaunted New York City campaign finance model.

the system by abolishing donation caps and reducing the frequency of disclosure.[67] Remarkably, the public funding rate was quadrupled from $2 to $8 per vote—a perverse move given the abandonment of donation caps.

The multipartisan approach in SA and the process in NSW that has been driven by ongoing political scandals stand in contrast. The NSW process has not been entirely free of self-serving incumbent behaviour. The outgoing ALP Government imposed donation caps that did not apply to union affiliation fees; the incoming Liberal Government sought to crack down on contributions by unions (but fell foul of the High Court).[68] Nonetheless, driven by principle as well as by media and public pressure, parties in NSW have coalesced in agreeing on the desirability of a tightly regulated political finance system, overcoming conservative instincts towards libertarianism in political finance. The cartel aspects of Queensland's approach to public funding in recent years—putting the interests of the major parties before those of the broader interest of 'the house' or electoral balance—are thus not inevitable.

Ultimately, however, as the overall ramping up of public funding in Queensland and NSW's push for full public funding of campaign costs and even party overheads reveal, 'clean' public money can also be a way for parties to 'clean up'. This is not to say public funding is an evil. At least in the NSW model, with caps on donations and expenditure, the party finance system as a whole can seek to balance integrity, resourcing and equality aims. But while providing some stability for those minor parties that achieve significant popular support, thereby compensating for their difficulties in attracting sizeable benefactors, public funding in Australia (with the possible exception of the new SA system) has tended to reinscribe the privileged position of the major parties.

Reinscribing a privileged position, however, is not the same as cartelism. While rising levels of public funding may be a sign of professionalised parties becoming more dependent on state resources, public funding has overall been of significant assistance to minor

---

67   Disclosure was monthly and weekly in an election year; it is now quarterly, with weekly disclosure retained only in the three months before an election.

68   *Unions NSW v NSW* [2013] HCA 58.

parties in Queensland. Indeed, the State remains a fertile jurisdiction for the emergence of new parties. Paradoxically, smaller and newer parties may be more 'cartelised'—in the sense of *dependent* on public funding—than the major parties, but happily so. This reinforces Rashkova and van Biezen's finding that public funding, though it may stem from cartel or featherbedding behaviour, does not adversely affect the permeability of the party system to new entrants and competition.[69]

The drivers of political finance systems and their regulation are a mix of principles (liberal or social-democratic ideology), self-interest (both party machine and parliamentarians) and events (scandals and legislative curiosity and borrowings). The Queensland example has exhibited all of these factors, aside from obvious scandals. Cartel behaviour has manifested itself in amendments that short-changed minor parties and Independents and in featherbedding of public funding when it suited the major parties. Yet the story is as much one of normative rivalry between libertarian and collectivist positions, and of attempts by incumbents to balance their parliamentary interest in an incumbency advantage with their party machine's interest in the stability that enhanced public funding can bring.

69   Ekaterina Rashkova and Ingrid van Biezen (2014) 'Deterring New Party Entry? The Impact of State Regulation on the Permeability of Party Systems', *Party Politics* 20(6): 890–903.

6

More regulated, more level? Assessing the impact of spending and donation caps on Australian State elections

Jennifer Rayner

To level the playing field and stand up for a truly democratic electoral system in Australia … it's time to cap election spending and political donations.

— Christine Milne[1]

It is acknowledged in both scholarly research and popular commentary that the Labor and Liberal parties enjoy a range of advantages over their minor party counterparts. In particular, these major parties possess financial, organisational and human resources that provide them with a distinct advantage during election campaigns and, it is often argued, skew the electoral playing field heavily in their favour. Consequently, calls to cap the amounts that political parties can spend and receive when campaigning for a federal election are a mainstay of Australian political discourse. The unconstrained way in which parties can raise and spend money has variously been referred to as

---

1   Press conference, 29 May 2013.

'a risk for democracy and fairness',[2] a source of 'unfair advantage' for the established major players[3] and a 'corrupting influence' that links electoral success to the size of a party's advertising expenditure rather than the strength of its policies and arguments.[4]

Central to this debate is the analogy of the 'playing field' on which political parties—as electoral opponents—should ideally compete on an even footing. It is suggested that money in politics tilts the electoral playing field in favour of a small handful of actors, and that greater regulation and restriction of campaign financing (including caps on donations and spending) are therefore needed to level out this field again. Although this chapter acknowledges there are several normative propositions that underlie the notion of the level playing field, it does not engage in a debate about the appropriateness of this analogy. Instead, the fundamental question addressed in this chapter is: do spending and donation caps actually achieve their desired outcome of fostering more equal electoral competition or 'levelling the playing field' between political actors?

Proponents of these reforms rarely provide any specific evidence to back up their calls for change, and international research on this question offers a decidedly equivocal view.[5] Taking this debate forward through original empirical research, the chapter assesses the impact of campaign finance caps in the Australian electoral context. In recent years, both New South Wales (NSW) and Queensland have introduced such caps for State elections, providing excellent contemporaneous case studies for exploring the impact of increased financial regulation on party behaviour.[6]

---

2   Brenton Holmes (2014) 'Money in Electoral Politics: No Small Risk for Democracy and Fairness', *FlagPost: Information and Research from the Parliamentary Library*, Canberra: Parliament of Australia, available at: aph.gov.au/About_Parliament/Parliamentary_Departments/Parliamentary_Library/FlagPost/2014/April/MoneyInPolitics.

3   Marian Sawer (2013) 'The State of Australian Democracy', *The Conversation*, 3 September, available at: theconversation.com/election-2013-essays-the-state-of-australian-democracy-17530.

4   Lee Rhiannon (2011) *Dissenting Report: Joint Standing Committee on Electoral Matters Inquiry into the Funding of Political Parties and Election Campaigns*, Canberra: Parliament of Australia.

5   See, for example, Kevin Milligan and Marie Rekkas (2008) 'Campaign Spending Limits, Incumbent Spending, and Election Outcomes', *The Canadian Journal of Economics* 41(4): 1351–74; Ron Johnston and Charles Pattie (2008) 'Money and Votes: A New Zealand Example', *Political Geography* 27(1): 113–33.

6   See Table 1.2 in this volume for a comparison of characteristics of the State and Territory regulatory regimes and the dates of their introduction.

Utilising published party disclosures on campaign donations and spending, the chapter begins by analysing debates concerning the significance of money in elections. It then establishes how much of a financial disparity existed between big and small parties before the reforms were introduced and examines what, if anything, the caps have done to close that gap. The focus here is the system of private funding of parties, which, as Graeme Orr highlights in his chapter, sits alongside public funding in Australia. The analysis shows that while the introduction of donations and expenditure caps has created greater financial parity between the two major political parties, it has done little to reduce the discrepancy between major and minor parties' financial positions.

The significance of money in politics

Before analysing the two Australian case studies, it is worth unpacking some of the ideas that underpin calls for campaign finance reform and the idea of the level playing field. Although the primary focus of the chapter is on the intersection of money and electoral competition, there are numerous other reasons for regulating and restricting political finance. These include curbing undue influence by outside groups and minimising the volume of advertising and the associated focus on media presentation over policy development and community engagement.

In terms of electoral competition, the most significant idea underpinning calls for caps is that money provides a competitive advantage when campaigning for elected office. If money did not provide such an advantage, it would not matter if some parties earn and spend more of it than others. The question of just *how much* money matters—and whom it advantages the most—has frequently been explored in the international literature on elections and campaigning. The broad consensus is that although the party or candidate with the deepest pockets does not always win, there is generally a positive relationship between spending and electoral performance. For example, research by Johnston and colleagues over two decades in the United Kingdom consistently found that—net of other factors—increased spending translated to increased vote share on election day.[7] Research in countries as diverse as Canada,[8] Ireland,[9] Korea[10] and the United States[11] has reached similar, although not always so consistent, conclusions. In Australia, the more limited reporting requirements for campaign spending have made it difficult to replicate this kind of detailed empirical research. However, in the 1990s, Forrest conducted a series of studies that drew on NSW data to explore the relationship between spending and outcomes at elections in that State. He concluded that money appeared to deliver similar electoral benefits to those seen internationally, although the size of that benefit varied in connection with the level of political volatility at any given election.[12]

Interviews with over 60 Australian major and minor party representatives conducted as part of my doctoral research revealed a strong consensus that money matters a great deal when it comes to designing and delivering election campaigns.[13] Interviewees reported that money is a crucial determinant of how widely, frequently and effectively a party can convey its campaign messages to voters, how many seats it can run in, the strength of on-the-ground campaigning

7   Ron Johnston and Charles Pattie (1997) 'Where's the Difference? Decomposing the Impact of Local Election Campaigns in Great Britain', *Electoral Studies* 16: 165–74; Charles Pattie, Ron Johnston and Ed Fieldhouse (1995) 'Winning the Local Vote: The Effectiveness of Constituency Campaign Spending in Great Britain, 1983–1992', *American Political Science Review* 89: 969–83; Ron Johnston (1987) *Money and Votes: Constituency Campaign Spending and Election Results*, London: Croom Helm.

8   Ken Carty and Munroe Eagles (1999) 'Do Local Campaigns Matter? Campaign Spending, the Local Canvass and Party Support in Canada', *Electoral Studies* 18: 69–87; Munroe Eagles (1993) 'Money and Votes in Canada: Campaign Spending and Parliamentary Election Outcomes, 1984–1988', *Canadian Public Policy* 19: 432–49.

9   Ken Benoit and Michael Marsh (2003) 'For a Few Euros More: Campaign Spending Effects in the Irish Local Elections of 1999', *Party Politics* 9(5): 561–82.

10   Myungsoon Shin, Youngjae Jin, Donald Gross and Kihong Eom (2005) 'Money Matters in Party-centred Politics: Campaign Spending in Korean Congressional Elections', *Electoral Studies* 24(1): 85–101.

11   Robert Erikson and Thomas Palfrey (2000) 'Equilibria in Campaign Spending Games: Theory and Data', *American Political Science Review* 94: 595–609; Alan Gerber (1998) 'Estimating the Effect of Campaign Spending on Senate Election Outcomes Using Instrumental Variables', *American Political Science Review* 92(2): 401–11; Donald Green and Johnathan Krasno (1990) 'Rebuttal to Jacobson's "New Evidence for Old Arguments"', *American Journal of Political Science* 34: 363–72.

12   James Forrest, Ron Johnston and Charles Pattie (1999) 'The Effectiveness of Constituency Campaign Spending in Australian State Elections during Times of Electoral Volatility: The New South Wales Case, 1988–95', *Environment and Planning* 31(1999): 1119–28; James Forrest (1997) 'The Effects of Local Campaign Spending on the Geography of the Flow-of-the-Vote at the 1991 New South Wales State Election', *Australian Geographer* 28(2): 229–40.

13   Jennifer Rayner (2014) Beyond Winning: Party Goals and Campaign Strategy in Australian Elections, Doctoral thesis, Canberra: The Australian National University.

within these and how much professional help it can access to guide its strategising and implementation. Furthermore, money was a frequently cited factor when these representatives sought to explain why their parties had or had not carried out particular campaign activities.[14] Importantly, however, many of the interviewees reflected that a sizeable budget is generally not sufficient to get an underperforming candidate elected or make up for a lack of resonant message. So while parties do not see money as everything, they clearly see it as a very important factor driving the delivery of their campaigns.

Disparities in campaign budgets

A second idea underlying the discussion about caps and the level playing field is that there is an asymmetry to campaign budgets that provides some Australian parties with an advantage over others. To what extent is this really the case?

Examining the dollar amounts declared for the past three federal election years indicates that there are major disparities in the amounts earned and spent by Australian parties.

This gulf in party budgets would not come as a surprise to most observers of politics. Importantly, however, Table 6.1 indicates that there is not just a division between wealthy major parties and poor minor ones. Rather, Australia's system is better conceptualised as a three-tiered one, with the Labor and Liberal parties representing a top tier in which budgets are counted in tens of millions. The entry of the Palmer United Party (PUP) into the federal political arena in 2013, backed by billionaire Clive Palmer, was a significant development. Formed just six months before the federal election, PUP was able to field candidates in all 150 House of Representatives seats and to raise and spend as much money as the established major parties. Beneath Labor, Liberal and PUP sit parties such as The Greens and The Nationals, with budgets that hover between $2 million and $5 million. Newer parties such as Family First also appear to be progressing rapidly towards this bracket. Finally, far beneath these two tiers sit the rest of the minor parties, with budgets that are counted in hundreds of thousands of dollars, and sometimes even less.

14   ibid.

Table 6.1 Australian party finances, 2007, 2010 and 2013

Party	2007		2010		2013	
	Declared donations	Declared spending	Declared donations	Declared spending	Declared donations	Declared spending
Australian Labor Party	$61,765,260	$60,850,361	$37,056,055	$36,021,598	$40,138,087	$33,556,742
Liberal Party of Australia	$34,662,036	$35,590,845	$36,337,983	$35,963,094	$43,012,140	$45,593,018
Palmer United Party	n/a	n/a	n/a	n/a	$28,827,604	$28,822,742
Australian Greens	$1,965,185	$1,996,044	$4,556,529	$4,507,818	$6,346,373	$6,076,383
The Nationals	$1,809,362	$2,168,372	$1,094,375	$1,338,919	$1,731,952	$2,052,337
Citizens Electoral Council of Australia	$1,800,281	$1,807,643	$1,854,684	$1,863,766	$2,090,891	$2,035,943
Family First	$152,313	$8,105	$1,368,021	$1,366,002	$1,113,588	$1,194,882
Socialist Alliance	$102,787	$100,998	$110,209	$112,337	$89,234	$98,979
Australian Democrats	$62,802	$91,705	$116,246	$137,294	$107,003	$143,320
One Nation	$9,760	$40,982	$61,451	$115,478	$23,308	$48,424

n/a not applicable

Note: Table shows only amounts declared by federal parties and does not include additional amounts earned and spent by State party branches.

Source: Original returns submitted to the Australian Electoral Commission, accessed 28 April 2014 and 2 August 2015.

If we consider the figures for the three Australian States that require detailed campaign reporting, similar disparities are apparent in terms of party finances.

Table 6.2 Australian State party finances, State elections, 2011–13

Party	Election	Declared donations	Declared spending
Liberal Party of Australia	Western Australia 2013	$11,381,300*	$5,141,459
Australian Labor Party	Western Australia 2013	$5,819,500*	$2,756,512
The Greens	Western Australia 2013	$1,305,589*	$446,090
The Nationals	Western Australia 2013	$1,533,867*	$323,692
Australian Christians	Western Australia 2013	$466,217*	$60,460
Liberal National Party	Queensland 2012	$16,860,534	$7,154,900
Australian Labor Party	Queensland 2012	$10,753,968	$7,118,139
Katter's Australian Party	Queensland 2012	$2,098,379	$1,180,719
The Greens	Queensland 2012	$484,464	$748,054
One Nation	Queensland 2012	$29,772	$40,637
Liberal Party of Australia	New South Wales 2011	$9,824,074	$11,376,435
Australian Labor Party	New South Wales 2011	$3,760,765	$11,105,679
The Nationals	New South Wales 2011	$2,311,510	$2,993,694
The Greens	New South Wales 2011	$339,040	$1,686,502
Christian Democratic Party	New South Wales 2011	$504,540	$308,477
Family First	New South Wales 2011	$25,687	$37,965
Socialist Alliance	New South Wales 2011	$22,221	$9,662

* Includes donations made in the reporting period encompassing the 2013 federal election.

Sources: Original campaign returns submitted to the WA Electoral Commission, Electoral Commission Queensland and NSW Election Funding Authority, accessed 20 January 2014.

The three-tiered division of wealth observed at the federal level also appears to be in place within Australia's State parties, although the overall scale of spending is smaller. So if money provides the kind of electoral advantage that international and local research suggests it does, it is clear from these figures that the major parties enjoy a considerable advantage over all other political contenders. Only a political party backed by considerable personal wealth, such as PUP, can rival the major parties in terms of fundraising and spending. Importantly, however, we can see that larger minor parties such as The Greens and The Nationals that have a history of parliamentary representation also enjoy a distinct advantage over most other parties entering the electoral arena.

A more level playing field for whom?

Another issue often unaddressed in the discussion about donation and spending caps is which political actors are actually supposed to benefit from the levelling that these reforms initiate. Much of the international literature on campaign financing focuses on inequalities between incumbents and challengers, because research in contexts such as the United States and Canada has consistently found that incumbents enjoy a financial—and therefore electoral—advantage.[15] However, in Australia's party-dominated system, incumbency does not convey the same advantages in and of itself, because campaign funds are primarily controlled by party head office. Popular incumbents may raise some of their own money and enjoy non-financial advantages such as higher public visibility,[16] but the competition in terms of spending and donations primarily happens at the party level.

---

15 See, for example, Jamie Carson, Erik Engstrom and Jason Roberts (2007) 'Candidate Quality, Personal Vote and the Incumbency Advantage in Congress', *American Political Science Review* 101(2): 289–301; Stephen Ansolabehere and James Snyder (2002) 'The Incumbency Advantage in US Elections: An Analysis of State and Federal Offices, 1942–2000', *Election Law Journal* 1(3): 315–38; Brian Gaines (1998) 'The Impersonal Vote? Constituency Service and Incumbency Advantage in British Elections, 1950–92', *Legislative Studies Quarterly* 23(2): 167–95; Gary King (1991) 'Constituency Service and Incumbency Advantage', *British Journal of Political Science* 21(1): 119–28.

16 Markus Prior (2006) 'The Incumbent in the Living Room: The Rise of Television and the Incumbency Advantage in US House Elections', *Journal of Politics* 68(3): 657–73.

In that case, are we concerned about equalising the contest between the two major parties, such that we end the supposed 'arms race' of campaign spending? Or are we interested in levelling the field between major and minor parties, such that The Greens, Family First and other non-governing parties can compete more effectively against Labor and the Liberals?

In introducing the NSW legislation capping spending and donations in 2010, then Premier Kristina Keneally stated:

> These reforms are ... directed at reducing the advantages of money in dominating political debate. They provide for a more level playing field for candidates seeking election, as well as for third parties who wish to participate in political debate. These reforms are about putting a limit on the political arms race, under which those with the most money have the loudest voice and can simply drown out the voices of all others. The reforms will help to give voters a better opportunity to be *fully and fairly informed of the policies of all political parties, candidates and interested third parties.*[17]

Similarly, when tabling Queensland's Electoral Reform and Accountability Amendment Bill in 2011, then Attorney-General Paul Lucas said: 'The bill will introduce a cap on donations for use in state campaigns to ensure *equitable access to the political process for all participants.*'[18]

These statements suggest that the goal of Australia's two existing schemes is to create a playing field that is even for all who choose to enter it. This is clearly an unrealistic ambition, given the major disparities among Australian parties in terms of both their capacity to raise money and their broader institutional, knowledge and organisational resources. But nor is it necessarily desirable that niche or special interest parties should compete on a level footing with parties of government with substantial public support when campaigning in elections.

---

17   Kristina Keneally (2010) 'Second Reading Speech', Election Funding and Disclosures Amendment Bill 2010, 28 October. Emphasis added.
18   Paul Lucas (2011) 'Second Reading Speech', Electoral Reform and Accountability Amendment Bill 2011, 7 April. Emphasis added.

Instead, I would simply suggest that when seeking to determine whether spending and donation caps 'work', it would be setting the bar too high to expect them to create a completely level playing field for all political parties. In the following discussion, then, the benchmark for success will be the extent to which the NSW and Queensland caps have narrowed the financial gulf between major and minor parties, rather than their capacity to close this altogether.

The Australian experience

Having discussed why capping donations and spending is seen as a way to level the electoral playing field, and having identified how we might determine the success or failure of such caps, we can now turn our attention to the two Australian case studies. The following section briefly outlines the key features of the NSW and Queensland schemes, and then explores what impact their introduction has had on party budgets.

Table 6.3 summarises the relevant restrictions on campaign donations and spending that were introduced in NSW in 2010 and Queensland in 2011. Norton, as well as Tham and Anderson, provide more in-depth discussions of the legal and definitional nuances of these laws, as well as the context of their introduction.[19] For the purpose of this discussion, I am primarily concerned with the headline figures regulating the amounts that parties and candidates may receive and spend. As noted at the beginning of this chapter, the legislative changes introduced in 2010 and 2011—and their consequent impact on political donations and expenditure in the 2011 (NSW) and 2012 (Queensland) State elections—have specifically been chosen because of the unique contemporaneous and comparable data that reform period provides. The 2011 and 2012 State elections and the legislative regimes under which they were fought therefore offer a rare and valuable window through which to examine the impact of caps across two different States.

---

19   Andrew Norton (2011) *Democracy and Money: The Dangers of Campaign Finance Reform*, CIS Policy Monograph 119, Sydney: Centre for Independent Studies; Joo-Cheong Tham and Malcolm Anderson (2011) *How Effective are the New South Wales Election Spending Limits in Preventing Election 'Arms Races'? A Preliminary Inquiry*, Melbourne: Democratic Audit of Australia.

Table 6.3 NSW and Queensland caps introduced in 2010 and 2011

	New South Wales	Queensland
Party spending allowed	$100,000 x number of Legislative Assembly seats contested—parties contesting more than 10 seats $50,000 cap also applies within this for electoral communication in any single electorate $1,050,000—parties running for the Legislative Council and 10 or fewer Legislative Assembly seats	$80,000 x number of electorates contested
Candidate spending allowed	$100,000—additional to party cap	$50,000—additional to party cap
Third-party spending allowed	$1,050,000	$500,000—subject to $75,000 cap in any single electorate
Maximum donation allowed#	$5,000 for a registered party or group $2,000 for a sitting MP, candidate or third-party campaigner $2,000 for a party that is not registered	$5,000 for a registered party or group $2,000 for a sitting MP, candidate or third-party campaigner
Reporting threshold	$1,000	$1,000
Restricted donors	Donations from property developers, gambling and liquor industry businesses and tobacco industry businesses are prohibited	None

Donation caps apply to the receiving party rather than the donor. That is, a donor may donate more than these amounts and it is up to the receiving party to either return the funds or place them in a separate account for other purposes (for example, a federal campaign account).

Notes: Caps applying for 2011 State election—amounts are indexed to inflation and increase on 1 July each year. Caps applying for the 2012 State election—amounts are indexed to inflation and increase on 1 July each year.

Sources: NSW Election Funding Authority (2014) *Caps on Political Donations*, Sydney: Election Funding Authority; Electoral Commission Queensland (ECQ) (2014) *Funding and Disclosure: Queensland State*, Brisbane: ECQ.

While the NSW scheme remains largely in place (pending reforms subsequent to the Premier's Expert Panel on Political Finance, instigated in light of campaign financing irregularities revealed by the Independent Commission Against Corruption),[20] the Newman Government scrapped Queensland's caps in 2013 and brought that State back into line with the federal campaign financing laws (see Graeme Orr, this volume).[21] In 2015 a new Labor Government brought the threshold for disclosure of donations back down to $1,000, but to date (October 2016) has not restored donation or expenditure caps.

As Table 6.3 indicates, the two schemes operated along broadly similar lines, although there are some important differences. Each set a maximum amount that parties may spend per electorate (indexed annually), adding up to an overall cap for spending across the State. Each also capped the total amount that parties and candidates may receive from any single donor and set a reasonably low threshold for disclosing these donations.[22] Importantly, however, the two schemes differed in how they managed spending within any individual electorate. In Queensland at the 2012 State election, parties could spend up to the $80,000 cap in any single seat. In NSW, however, an additional cap of $50,000 applied for materials promoting an individual candidate within any single seat, which meant that the parties had to allocate the other half of their $100,000 cap to Statewide campaigning. Furthermore, the Queensland scheme allowed candidates to spend a further $50,000 on top of their party's general spending, while the NSW scheme was more generous in setting a $100,000 additional cap for candidates. The net result of these rules is that for the 2011 NSW State election, the most a party and candidate combined could spend

---

20   Kerry Schott, Andrew Tink and John Watkins (2014) *Political Donations Final Report. Volumes 1 and* 2, Sydney: NSW Department of Premier and Cabinet, available at: dpc.nsw.gov. au/announcements/panel_of_experts_-_political_donations; Mike Baird (2014) 'Statement: ICAC', Media statement, 28 April, available at: members.nsw.liberal.org.au/news/state-news/ mike-baird-statement-icac; John Robertson (2014) 'NSW Labor Calls for an End to Campaign Donations to Restore Confidence in Politics and Government', Media statement, 5 May.
21   The Queensland Parliament passed the Electoral Reform Amendment Bill 2013 on 22 May 2014. In addition to scrapping spending and donation caps, the Bill also introduced Australia's first voter identification laws, requiring Queensland voters to provide one of several forms of photographic and non-photographic identification when voting in State elections. The Bill also increased the threshold for parties receiving public funding, meaning that parties must now earn 6 per cent of first-preference votes before being eligible to receive reimbursement for their campaign expenses. The Queensland Opposition and community groups vigorously opposed all of these changes on the grounds that they would diminish transparency, disenfranchise voters and further entrench the electoral dominance of the major parties. However, with a 69-seat majority in Queensland's unicameral Parliament, there was little to prevent the Liberal National Party (LNP) Government from passing the Bill unamended.
22   By comparison, the current (October 2016) federal disclosure threshold is $13,200.

in any single electorate was $150,000, while in Queensland in 2012 the maximum was $130,000. These figures have since increased in line with indexation arrangements established in the legislation.

Case study 1: Queensland

Turning our attention first to Queensland as the more recent of the two schemes, Figure 6.1 shows the campaign spending for the parties that contested all three of the State elections between 2006 and 2012.[23] For the 2006 and 2009 elections, there were no restrictions on the amount that parties could spend. The spending caps discussed in Table 6.3 then came into effect in 2011 and applied for the duration of the 2012 election campaign.

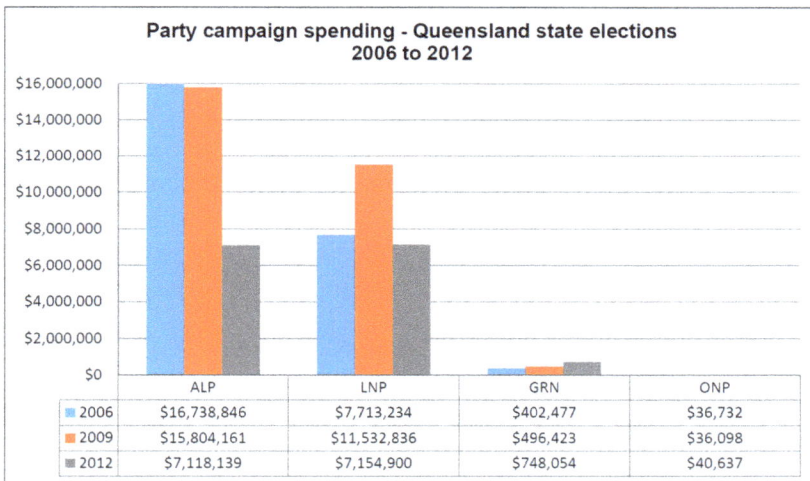

Party campaign spending - Queensland state elections 2006 to 2012

	ALP	LNP	GRN	ONP
2006	$16,738,846	$7,713,234	$402,477	$36,732
2009	$15,804,161	$11,532,836	$496,423	$36,098
2012	$7,118,139	$7,154,900	$748,054	$40,637

Figure 6.1 Queensland campaign spending, 2006–12

Sources: Spending figures for 2009 and 2012 calculated from original returns submitted to Electoral Commission Queensland; spending figures for 2006 calculated from original returns submitted to the Australian Electoral Commission.

Note: ALP = Australian Labor Party; LNP = Liberal National Party; GRN = The Greens; ONP = One Nation.

---

23   The Liberal and National parties contested the 2006 election as separate entities, but formally merged to form the Liberal National Party before the 2009 election. For the sake of consistency, the 2006 LNP figure is an aggregate of the individual Liberal and National parties' spending.

What is immediately striking from the data in Figure 6.1 is how dramatically major party spending has diverged over the past three elections, as the Australian Labor Party (ALP) significantly outspent the Liberal National Party (LNP) at each of the two elections before the caps were introduced. The 'arms race' thesis of campaign spending contends that major party budgets should generally mirror each other and increase with each electoral contest, but recent research by Anderson and Tham suggests that the kind of variance observed here may actually be more common. They point out that parties in and out of government have different capacities to attract donor funds and also differ in their incentives to spend up big depending on whether the election is likely to be closely fought or very one-sided. This leads to considerable variation in spending between parties from election to election.[24]

For the 2012 election, the maximum allowable spend for a party running candidates in all 89 Queensland electorates was $7.12 million. The fact that both the ALP and the LNP spent this amount almost to the dollar (despite a past history of spending more) would appear to indicate that the caps had a constraining effect on their spending. This observation is strengthened if we compare the amount the parties spent with the amount they received in donations; this information is presented as two separate figures because the difference between the major and minor parties is so great as to make graphing on a single scale difficult.

Figures 6.2 and 6.3 indicate that prior to the introduction of the caps, Queensland's major parties spent approximately the same amount as they received in donations, while the minor parties fluctuated between spending substantially more and substantially less than they received. However, after the introduction of the caps, no party could spend more than $7.1 million regardless of how much money it had accumulated. Because of this, we see a larger gap between the amounts the ALP and the LNP received and the amounts they spent: $3.6 million in Labor's case and $9.7 million for the LNP. Importantly, too, we see that despite the LNP receiving over $6 million more in donations than the ALP, that party spent just $36,000 more on its election campaign. Given the close relationship between spending and donations at the previous

---

24   Malcolm Anderson and Joo-Cheong Tham (2014) 'Dynamics of Electoral Expenditure and the "Arms Race" Thesis: The Case of New South Wales', *Australian Journal of Political Science* 49(1): 84–101.

two elections, it seems likely that this spending gap would have been significantly larger if the LNP had been free to spend more of the money it received in donations. For the two minor parties, we see no particular change after the introduction of the caps, beyond noting that the gap between donations received and amount spent increased in the opposite direction—dramatically so in the case of The Greens.

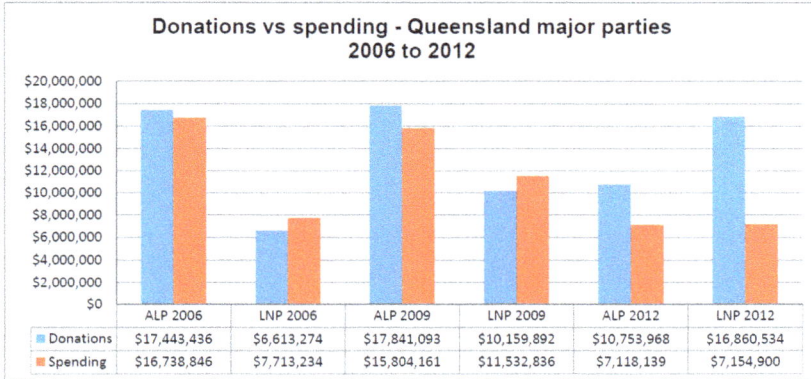

Donations vs spending - Queensland major parties 2006 to 2012

	ALP 2006	LNP 2006	ALP 2009	LNP 2009	ALP 2012	LNP 2012
Donations	$17,443,436	$6,613,274	$17,841,093	$10,159,892	$10,753,968	$16,860,534
Spending	$16,738,846	$7,713,234	$15,804,161	$11,532,836	$7,118,139	$7,154,900

Figure 6.2 Queensland major party donations relative to spending, 2006–12

Sources: Spending and donation figures for 2009 and 2012 calculated from original returns submitted to Electoral Commission Queensland; spending and donation figures for 2006 calculated from original returns submitted to the Australian Electoral Commission.

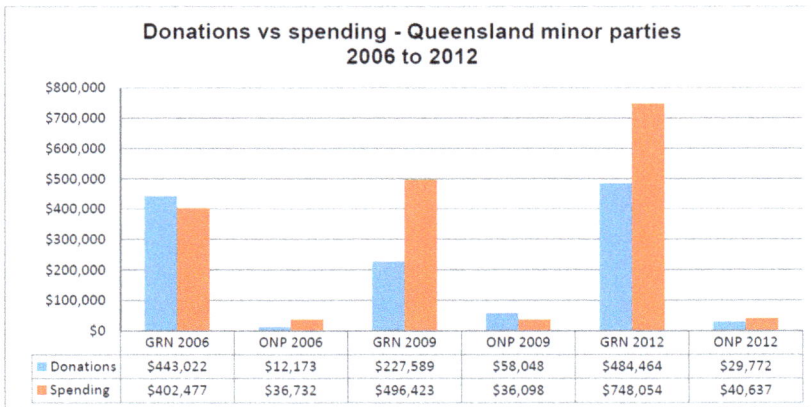

Donations vs spending - Queensland minor parties 2006 to 2012

	GRN 2006	ONP 2006	GRN 2009	ONP 2009	GRN 2012	ONP 2012
Donations	$443,022	$12,173	$227,589	$58,048	$484,464	$29,772
Spending	$402,477	$36,732	$496,423	$36,098	$748,054	$40,637

Figure 6.3 Queensland minor party donations relative to spending, 2006–12

Sources: Spending and donation figures for 2009 and 2012 calculated from original returns submitted to Electoral Commission Queensland; spending and donation figures for 2006 calculated from original returns submitted to the Australian Electoral Commission.

To give a clearer sense of these trends in constant terms, Table 6.4 details the donations and money spent per enrolled voter in each of these three election years. Anderson and Tham opted to adjust all dollar figures to 2011 terms in their analysis,[25] but since we are primarily interested in the relationship between party budgets and the capacity to campaign effectively, the amounts spent and received per voter make for a more valuable point of comparison here.

Table 6.4 Queensland party funds: Dollars per voter

	2006		2009		2012	
Size of roll	2,484,479		2,660,940		2,746,844	
	Received	Spent	Received	Spent	Received	Spent
Australian Labor Party	$7.020	$6.730	$6.700	$5.940	$3.910	$2.590
Liberal National Party	$2.660	$3.100	$3.810	$4.330	$6.130	$2.600
The Greens	$0.180	$0.160	$0.080	$0.190	$0.180	$0.270
One Nation	$0.004	$0.014	$0.021	$0.013	$0.010	$0.014

Sources: Figures for 2009 and 2012 calculated from original returns submitted to Electoral Commission Queensland; figures for 2006 calculated from original returns submitted to the Australian Electoral Commission.

Three things are evident from the data in Table 6.4. First, the introduction of caps appears to have significantly reduced financial disparities between the two major parties in Queensland—at least on the spending side. The ALP and the LNP went from spending vastly different amounts on their campaigns to having budgets that were almost identical, as is evident from their respective spending per voter. The caps do not appear to have had the same impact on donations, as the LNP received one-and-a-half times the amount of money donated to the ALP even with restrictions on how much any one person or company could donate. However, this disparity in donations was ultimately of little benefit to the LNP, as the party was prohibited from spending it on the state campaign. This is in contrast with the previous two elections, where the ALP received significantly more in donations and was therefore able to spend far more on its re-election efforts.

Second, the introduction of caps has somewhat narrowed the financial gulf between the two major parties and their minor counterparts, but again only on the spending side. Table 6.5 illustrates this trend by detailing the money received and spent by the major parties for every $1 of minor party funding.

---

25   ibid.

Table 6.5 Ratios of major and minor party finances: Queensland*

	2009				2012			
	Donations		Spending		Donations		Spending	
	ALP	LNP	ALP	LNP	ALP	LNP	ALP	LNP
The Greens	78:1	44:1	31:1	23:1	22:1	39:1	9:1	9.5:1
One Nation	307:1	175:1	437:1	319:1	361:1	566:1	175:1	176:1

* Ratio of dollars received and spent by the major parties relative to every dollar of minor party funding (all minor parties aggregated).

Interestingly, the spending ratio of The Greens to One Nation (ONP) dollars actually increased between 2009 and 2012, at 13:1 and 18:1, respectively. However, this appears to have had little to do with the introduction of the caps and more to do with the fact that The Greens' campaign budget increased significantly while One Nation's remained almost static. Again, the fact that the major parties received many millions of dollars more in donations than the minor parties was ultimately of little benefit at the 2012 election, as both were prohibited from spending more than $7.12 million regardless of how much money they had accumulated.

The third point evident from these data is that minor parties do not spend or receive anything like the amount of money that major parties do, regardless of what campaign finance rules are in place. While the ratio of minor to major party spending fell in 2012, The Greens were still spending just 18 cents per voter compared with approximately $2.60 each for the two major parties, while One Nation spent slightly more than 1 cent per voter.[26] As a consequence, the volume, reach and professionalism of their campaigns varied significantly.[27] Interviews with representatives of both minor parties suggest that the caps were of little consequence to them, as they rarely came within distance of hitting them. For example, The Greens reportedly reached the $80,000 party cap in just one seat, Mount Coot-tha, while One Nation's single largest spend was just under $30,000, in the seat of Beaudesert. Importantly, however, The Greens were still outspent in Mount Coot-tha, as the ALP's sitting Member of Parliament (MP), Treasurer Andrew Fraser, was able to spend a further $44,847 from

26   The One Nation dollar-per-voter figure is somewhat less comparable because the party did not run candidates in all seats.
27   Rayner, Beyond Winning.

his individual cap on top of his party's $80,000 cap. Similarly, LNP candidate Saxon Rice spent $48,171 in addition to her party's full spend. In contrast, The Greens' candidate, Adam Stone, was able to muster only an additional $1,823 to top up his party's spending.[28] So while the ratio by which Queensland's minor parties are outspent may have fallen fairly sharply after the introduction of spending caps, in practical terms they were still at a significant financial disadvantage in 2012 compared with the two major parties.[29]

Where these caps do appear to have had more of an impact is in levelling the field *between* the two major parties. Specifically, the spending caps cancelled out the impact of differing fundraising capacities, because the parties could not spend more than the capped amount regardless of how much they raised. At the 2012 election, the ALP would have been at a significant disadvantage compared with the LNP if the spending caps had not been in place, because the government's predicted loss meant that it failed to attract donations on the same scale as the Opposition. The volume of donations Labor received easily exceeded the new cap, however, and so the party was able to closely match the LNP's spending despite having less money on hand overall. It seems unlikely that this is the kind of levelling proponents of finance caps have in mind when advocating for their introduction, but the Queensland case suggests that this may actually be the most direct effect of such reforms.

Case study 2: New South Wales

Turning our attention to NSW, the data suggest similar trends and patterns to those seen in Queensland—that is, spending and donation caps go some way towards narrowing the gulf between major and minor party budgets, but do far more to equalise the contest between the two major parties.

---

28 All candidate figures are sourced from original campaign returns submitted to Electoral Commission Queensland, available at: www.ecq.qld.gov.au/candidates-and-parties/funding-and-disclosure/disclosure-returns.

29 Whether or not this disparity is desirable reflects broader debates about different types of party democracy, electoral competition and the appropriate ratio of resources to electoral support.

Figure 6.4 provides a side-by-side comparison of spending for a selection of major and minor parties contesting both Legislative Assembly and Legislative Council elections between 2003 and 2011, while Figures 6.5 and 6.6 provide the details on spending relative to donations.

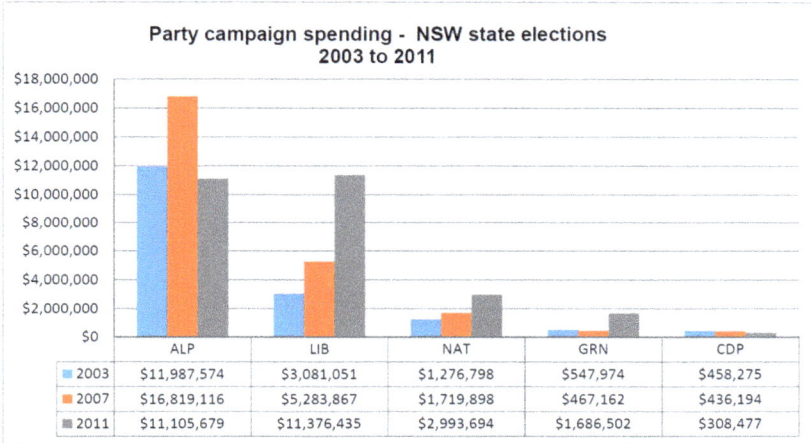

Party campaign spending - NSW state elections 2003 to 2011

	ALP	LIB	NAT	GRN	CDP
2003	$11,987,574	$3,081,051	$1,276,798	$547,974	$458,275
2007	$16,819,116	$5,283,867	$1,719,898	$467,162	$436,194
2011	$11,105,679	$11,376,435	$2,993,694	$1,686,502	$308,477

Figure 6.4 NSW campaign spending, 2003–11
Source: All spending figures from the NSW Election Funding Authority.

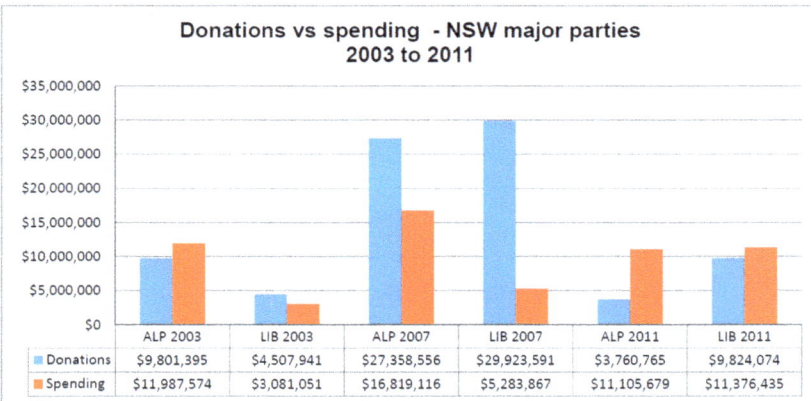

Donations vs spending - NSW major parties 2003 to 2011

	ALP 2003	LIB 2003	ALP 2007	LIB 2007	ALP 2011	LIB 2011
Donations	$9,801,395	$4,507,941	$27,358,556	$29,923,591	$3,760,765	$9,824,074
Spending	$11,987,574	$3,081,051	$16,819,116	$5,283,867	$11,105,679	$11,376,435

Figure 6.5 NSW major party donations relative to spending, 2003–11
Source: All spending figures from the NSW Election Funding Authority.

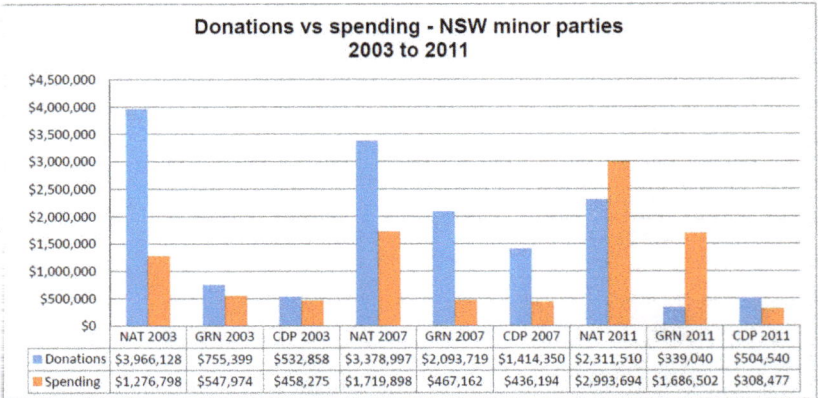

Figure 6.6 NSW minor party donations relative to spending, 2003–11
Source: All spending figures from the NSW Election Funding Authority.

These figures again demonstrate significant variation in party budgets in 2003 and 2007—both among the major parties and between them and the minor ones. The gap in spending between the Labor and Liberal parties is then almost entirely erased in 2011 after the introduction of the caps, but there continues to be a significant gulf between these two parties' budgets and the amounts spent by the three minor parties. This is clearly reflected in Table 6.6, which again highlights the dollar figures earned and spent per enrolled voter in each election year.

Table 6.6 NSW party funds: Dollars per voter

	2003		2007		2011	
Size of roll	4,272,104		4,374,029		4,635,810	
	Received	Spent	Received	Spent	Received	Spent
Australian Labor Party	$2.29	$2.81	$6.25	$3.85	$0.81	$2.40
Liberal Party	$1.05	$0.72	$6.84	$1.21	$2.11	$2.45
The Nationals	$0.92	$0.30	$0.77	$0.39	$0.50	$0.65
The Greens	$0.18	$0.13	$0.47	$0.11	$0.07	$0.36
Christian Democratic Party	$0.12	$0.11	$0.32	$0.10	$0.11	$0.07

Source: Figures calculated from spending data from the NSW Election Funding Authority.

It is interesting to note that for the 2011 election, all parties except the Christian Democratic Party (CDP) spent more than they received in donations—sometimes significantly so. This suggests that: a) the parties had been stockpiling funds from previous years in anticipation of the new finance regime; and b) the prohibition on accepting money from certain categories of donor resulted in a serious hit to party fundraising capacities, particularly for the major parties.[30] Having said that, it is not possible to make a direct comparison between the donations received in 2007 and those in 2011 because the former was also a federal election year, so donations to all parties dramatically exceeded their spending on the NSW campaign.

Table 6.6 shows that, as in Queensland, in NSW there were major differences in the amounts spent and received per voter between major and minor parties—both before and after the introduction of the caps. However, the picture becomes more complicated if we consider the ratios of funding, as detailed in Table 6.7. In this instance, we have opted to compare 2003 and 2011, because of the donations anomaly in 2007.

Table 6.7 Ratios of major and minor party finances: NSW*

	2003				2011			
	Donations		Spending		Donations		Spending	
	ALP	LIB	ALP	LIB	ALP	LIB	ALP	LIB
The Nationals	2:1	1.2:1	9:1	3:1	2:1	4:1	4:1	4:1
The Greens	13:1	6:1	22:1	6:1	11:1	29:1	7:1	7:1
Christian Democratic Party	18:1	8:1	26:1	7:1	7:1	19:1	36:1	36:1

* Ratio of dollars received and spent by the major parties relative to every dollar of minor party funding (all minor parties aggregated).

Source: Calculated from spending and donations data from the NSW Election Funding Authority.

Table 6.7 indicates that the financial gap between major and minor parties in NSW was already significantly smaller than that in Queensland before the introduction of caps. In fact, the ratio of major to minor party finances in NSW before the caps were introduced was

---

30 Of course, given the details emerging from the Independent Commission Against Corruption's ongoing inquiries, it is possible further donations were simply channelled through other avenues that were not declared to the Election Funding Authority.

lower than comparable ratios achieved in Queensland after regulatory reform. This suggests that NSW minor parties were playing on a more even field than their Queensland counterparts even before legislative attempts to level this. Interestingly, Table 6.7 also shows that after the introduction of the NSW caps, the minor party ratios became more varied in comparison with those for the major parties. The general trend appears to be that the financial gap between the ALP and the minor parties shrank, while it increased for the Liberal Party. However, it is difficult to determine how much of this is due to the impact of the caps and how much relates to the variable patterns of party spending at the previous elections. Further data will be needed from the 2015 election and beyond to definitively address this point.

In terms of assessing the effectiveness of the NSW caps, the data presented here are somewhat more ambiguous about their impact than is the case for Queensland. As in that State, in NSW it seems clear that major parties raised and spent substantially more money than their minor counterparts before the spending and donations caps were introduced, and continued to do so after they were put in place. Also in common with Queensland, in NSW the most significant narrowing of financial gaps took place between the two major parties, as the difference in their campaign budgets shifted from millions of dollars to just a few hundred thousand. There continued to be a significant gulf in the volume of donations received by these two parties, although in 2011 the Liberals had the upper hand rather than Labor. This reversal probably has more to do with the political environment than the caps themselves, although, again, further data will be needed to confirm this.

While this analysis suggests that donation and spending caps do not provide a substantial benefit to minor parties at a Statewide level, NSW offers one case that suggests that they *may* do so at the individual electorate level. For example, at the 2011 election, the seat of Balmain was among the most high profile, as Labor Minister Verity Firth was challenged by popular local Greens Mayor, Jamie Parker. The NSW Greens had never previously managed to place a member into the State's Legislative Assembly, but were ultimately successful in doing so in Balmain after Parker secured 50.1 per cent of the vote on preferences. In an interview conducted after the election, Parker suggested that the caps were a significant factor in the result, because they prevented him from being 'smashed financially' by Firth and the ALP.[31] Both parties reportedly spent the maximum amount allowed in central spending and the individual candidate returns show that Parker then spent $79,337 from his personal cap while Firth spent $100,281.[32] Parker reflected that in previous elections in which he had been involved, the ALP had been able to deluge electorates in direct mail, television advertising and other campaign materials when the result was expected to be closely run. In 2011, however, the spending cap prevented Firth and Labor from spending more than $150,000 to hold on to the seat, so The Greens were able to come within $20,000 of matching their spending.[33] Importantly, however, this would not have been the case if Parker had struggled to raise additional funds for his individual spending, as was generally the case with The Greens candidates in Queensland. The fact that he was able to raise almost $80,000 may reflect his impressive personal characteristics or it may simply have been a result of the strong anti-Labor sentiment then prevalent in NSW. However, in 2015—a State election characterised by an arguably less volatile political environment—Parker retained the seat of Balmain, polling 37 per cent of the primary vote to Firth's 31 per cent share.

While it is impossible to draw any conclusions about the broader effectiveness of caps from this single instance, the Balmain experience suggests that it would be worth looking at competition in individual electorates to gain further insights into how far these go towards creating a level playing field between major and minor parties. This would be a much larger research undertaking than examining party spending, as it would involve analysing the individual returns for every candidate contesting each State seat over a series of elections. For that reason, I have not included such analysis here; the contribution is simply to highlight the Balmain case as one that may point to a trend worth exploring through future research.

---

31   Author interview.
32   All candidate figures sourced from original campaign returns submitted to the NSW Election Funding Authority, available at: elections.nsw.gov.au/fd/disclosure/view_disclosures.
33   Author interview.

Conclusion: Do spending and donation caps help to level the field?

In light of the above discussion about patterns in party financing before and after the introduction of tighter regulations in Queensland and NSW, could we say that spending and donation caps help to create a more level electoral playing field in terms of equalising the amount of money political parties are able to raise and spend?

The answer would appear to be a resounding 'yes', *if* we specifically consider competition between the two major parties. Both the Queensland and the NSW cases suggest that capping spending effectively levelled past differences between Labor and the Liberals/LNP by cancelling out the impact of their divergent fundraising capacities. Because neither party could spend more than a fixed amount, the past advantage enjoyed by the party receiving more donations was effectively erased. This was particularly evident in Queensland, where the LNP managed to raise over $16 million in spite of the donation caps, but was unable to put this bounty to work because of the $7.1 million total spending cap. This suggests that in terms of levelling the playing field, it is the spending side that matters far more than capping donations.

If we consider competition between the major and minor parties, however, the answer changes from an emphatic 'yes' to a more pessimistic 'not really'. On the donations side, the introduction of caps seems to have done little to reduce the incredibly high ratio of major party dollars received compared with minor party ones and, in a number of cases, this actually increased after the caps were put in place. On the expenditure side, there was a marked reduction in the ratio of major party to minor party dollars spent in Queensland, but no clear pattern was apparent in NSW. Furthermore, the dollar-per-voter figures provided in Tables 6.4 and 6.6 clearly demonstrate that even where the *ratio* of spending has shrunk, the vast differences in the *dollar figures* involved mean that minor parties remain at a serious and stark disadvantage. Given that caps do appear to restrain major party spending to the maximum amount allowed by the regulatory scheme, this issue could be addressed by significantly lowering the value of the caps. For example, at the 2014 New Zealand national election parties were subject to a total cap of just under $3 million while individual candidate spending was capped at just $25,700,[34] so there is some international precedent for setting the bar much lower than is currently the case in the two Australian schemes. However, given that the caps are set by parliaments that are dominated by the two major parties, it seems unlikely that we would ever see them drop these so low as to truly equalise the contest for their minor party competitors.

Finally, if we consider the case of Balmain, this suggests that spending and donation caps possibly do 'a bit' to equalise competition between major parties and those in the second tier of party wealth *in specific electorates*. By preventing major parties from bringing their superior resources to bear in any single seat, the spending caps may prevent the voices of minor party candidates from being drowned out, and therefore increase their chances of election. Importantly, however, the comparison between The Greens' experiences in Queensland and in NSW suggests that candidates need to be able to match their major party counterparts' individual spending *as well as* matching them in the party spending to secure any meaningful advantage. By logical extension, this would seem to mean that only 'major minor' parties such as The Greens or The Nationals are likely to benefit from this levelling, as it seems highly unlikely that any of the 'minor minor' parties in the third tier of wealth would be able to scale such a financial obstacle.

Overall, then, the financial cap schemes examined in Queensland and NSW do not appear to create the kind of level field on which proponents of a federal scheme might wish to play. Having said that, there are many good reasons why caps may still be beneficial, including limiting opportunities for outside groups to influence political outcomes through large donations; reducing the volume of advertising and promotional clutter associated with elections; and freeing up parties to focus more of their time on policy development and community engagement rather than fundraising. In all of these areas, there may well be a case to be made for the effectiveness of spending and donation caps. However, this discussion has specifically

---

34   *New Zealand Electoral Act 1993*, Part 6A, s. 205C and s. 206C.

focused on whether increased financial regulation can make electoral competition—in terms of the money parties raise and spend—more even. The evidence presented here from two recent Australian case studies is by no means definitive, but does suggest that in the form in which they have been applied to date, spending and donation caps do little to level out Australia's skewed political pitch.

7

Dilemmas of party regulation: Hands-on courts versus hands-off legislators?

Anika Gauja

As chapters in this book have highlighted, the legal regulation of political parties is problematic for two important reasons. The first is that it is very difficult to demarcate between political parties as private associations and as public entities. While at first glance this distinction might seem overly technical, the regulatory implications are extremely significant. In Chapter 1 of this volume, Marian Sawer and I discussed the fact that, in Australia, only relatively recently has the law acknowledged political parties to be anything more than voluntary associations, similar in status to social and sports clubs. There has not been anything like the degree of regulation and requirements for internal democracy imposed on trade unions. This has had important consequences for voters—for example, in the area of campaign financing. For most of the twentieth century, party finance was effectively unregulated, causing significant concerns about the role of money in electoral politics and the fairness of the electoral contest, through, for example, a lack of transparency in political donations and differential rates of party spending.

Apart from the effects on voters of suspicion over party financing, the 'private' status of political parties has also affected party members. In the absence of laws regulating internal governance structures, party members have witnessed the rise of practices such as 'branch-stacking' and have been limited in their ability to hold party elites to account. Internal dispute-resolution processes have often been unsatisfactory. The absence of any substantial legal regulation of the financial and internal affairs of political parties has been portrayed by many as a 'double standard'; they see a disconnect between the importance of political parties in modern systems of representative government and their status at law. Concern over this disconnect has prompted calls for increased regulation.[1]

The second factor complicating regulation is that political parties are not only the subjects of party law, but also those responsible for formulating it in government. The potential for conflicts of interest to arise and for partisan or incumbent interests to be privileged in the exercise of lawmaking is a real danger. Michael Kang argues:

> [P]arty leaders and their allies have every incentive to foster a regulatory environment that benefits them. Party regulation, as a result, often represents politically motivated modification of the legal landscape to the calculated advantage of certain party actors and to the disadvantage of others.[2]

Although referring to the United States, Kang's observations might equally apply to the Australian context (see, for example, Graeme Orr's chapter on political finance reforms in Queensland). As former senator Ricky Muir, who represented the Motoring Enthusiast Party, said, electoral reform proposals tend to be for the benefit of the major parties and to the detriment of minor parties, despite the constructive role played by the latter in legislative review.[3]

---

1   Anika Gauja (2010) *Political Parties and Elections: Legislating for Representative Democracy*, Farnham: Ashgate; Scott Bennett (2002) *Australia's Political Parties: More Regulation?*, Parliamentary Library Research Paper No. 21 2001–02, Canberra: Parliament of Australia; Teresa Somes (1996) 'The Legal Status of Political Parties', in Marian Simms (ed.) *The Paradox of Parties: Australian Political Parties in the 1990s*, Sydney: Allen & Unwin.
2   Michael Kang (2005) 'The Hydraulics and Politics of Party Regulation', *Iowa Law Review* 91: 160.
3   Lenore Taylor (2015), 'Turnbull Government Faces Battle to Change Voting Rules for Senate', *The Guardian*, 22 September.

Despite these complications, the trend internationally is for the growth of party regulation, driven on the one hand by the belief that political parties are important democratic actors, and on the other by the belief that their activities should be correspondingly monitored.[4] In Germany, the legal position of parties is so strongly articulated in the country's Basic Law that they are regarded as 'institutions of constitutional law'.[5] Parties also feature prominently in the constitutions of Portugal and Spain and, as Ingrid van Biezen and others have shown, party regulation has expanded across Europe following the collapse of the Soviet Union (see Table 1.1). Political parties in the United States are some of the most comprehensively regulated in the world, despite constitutional freedoms of speech and association that could conceivably be used as a shield to protect them from interference by the state. As I have shown, the impact of First Amendment rights on attempts to regulate the activities of political parties continues to produce a constant source of tension in American jurisprudence.[6]

The partisan nature of regulation and the ambivalent distinction between the public and private activities of political parties raise two important questions: Should political parties be regulated at all? If so, who should regulate them? In this chapter, I engage with both of these questions by comparing how parties are regulated by legislation with how the courts have adjudicated their internal activities. This approach acknowledges that party regulation comprises more than the constitutions, legislation and international standard-setting discussed in Chapter 1; it also includes a body of diverse case law. The comparison of the regulatory approaches taken by partisan actors (parliaments) and non-partisan actors (courts) reveals the varying attitudes of these actors to the appropriate role and function of political parties in society.

---

4   See, for example, Ingrid van Biezen and Daniela Romee Piccio (2013) 'Shaping Intra-party Democracy: On the Legal Regulation of Internal Party Organizations', in William Cross and Richard Katz (eds) *The Challenges of Intra-party Democracy*, Oxford: Oxford University Press, pp. 27–48; John Keane (2009) *The Life and Death of Democracy*, London: Simon & Schuster. Regulation in this sense both consolidates and provides a check on power.
5   Wolfgang Müller and Ulrich Sieberer (2006) 'Party Law', in Richard Katz and William Crotty (eds) *Handbook of Party Politics*, London: Sage, p. 439.
6   Gauja, *Political Parties and Elections*.

The chapter is structured in five parts. The first discusses the distinction between the 'public' activities of political parties and their status as 'private' voluntary associations at law. I show how these public activities have been used to justify regulatory intervention. The second section outlines the particular importance of party organisations as sites of contestation—and arenas in which the debate between public and private is at its most controversial. The third section outlines how in Australia legislative regulations touch on (or steer clear of) the internal activities of political parties. The fourth section contrasts this legislative approach with that taken by the courts in the adjudication of intraparty disputes. The final section reviews some of the recommendations offered by two recent reports from New South Wales (NSW) touching on the internal governance structures of political parties.

Autonomy versus regulatory democracy

The issue of autonomy of civil society organisations (such as parties, unions and charities) is particularly important as the state/civil society distinction goes to the fundamental question of whether or not state regulation is desirable, the extent to which the state and the public law should intervene in the activities of these organisations and which of these activities they should regulate.

If we categorise parties as 'public' institutions, receiving public resources and performing public functions such as legislative recruitment, regulating both their internal activities and the way in which they compete for political power may be desirable. The aim of such regulation might be more democratic forms of institutional governance (intraparty democracy) or more representative parliaments (for example, through requiring gender or minority group quotas in candidate selection contests).

Political parties are the exception in terms of the lack of regulation of internal governance; other non-governmental organisations performing public functions are extensively regulated. Historically, the regulation of the internal affairs of Australian unions—justified on the basis of their economic importance—far surpassed that found in Canada, the United States and the United Kingdom. In 1973, amendments to the *Conciliation and Arbitration Act 1904* gave financial members the right to vote directly in elections for office-bearers and in plebiscites concerning union rules and policy. Unless exempted, all elections for office in trade unions or employer organisations must be conducted by the Australian Electoral Commission (AEC).[7] Voluntary organisations, including those with significant representative functions, must comply with internal governance standards to be registered with the Australian Charities and Not-for-profits Commission; in 2016 over 1,000 lost their charitable status for failure to lodge annual reports, hence losing access to tax benefits and deductible gift status. Cooperatives must comply with the democratic governance provisions enshrined in cooperatives legislation, including democratic member control and one member, one vote.

Highlighting this regulatory disjuncture, Gary Johns has argued:

> The major political parties have legislated to ensure the scrutiny of the democratic process in the key voluntary associations in industrial relations. They have done so, it appears, to enhance the confidence of the community and members in the conduct of ballots. There can be few more important ballots than those which determine who is to carry the party label of a major Australian party … Why then would the parties not do the same for themselves?[8]

If the issue of autonomy is seen as central, however, and political parties are seen as having special claims to such autonomy in the interests of political pluralism, state regulation may be seen as an undesirable intrusion on these independent political entities and an unnecessary interference with the political expression of citizens.

As outlined in Chapter 1, the relationship between parties and the state has gained a great deal of prominence in recent years, particularly since the publication of Richard Katz and Peter Mair's 'cartel party' thesis. Katz and Mair argue that as the membership of political parties declines, parties rely more and more heavily on extracting the resources of the state to sustain their electoral and organisational activities. Since its publication in 1995, it remains the most-cited article in the journal *Party Politics*. The cartel thesis sits alongside a more generalist political science scholarship that sees political parties

---

7   Steve O'Neill (2011) *Trade Union Membership Standards for Not for Profit Regulation: Standards Too High?*, Parliamentary Library Research Paper No. 11 2010–11, Canberra: Parliament of Australia.
8   Gary Johns (2001) 'Desirability of Regulating Political Parties', *Agenda* 8(4): 298, 300.

becoming, more and more, organs of the state and less organs of civil society.[9] However, the idea of a movement from private to public is not necessarily synonymous with the proposition that political parties are, or are becoming, agents of the state. Gary Johns argues that some political parties may choose to register, contest elections and become 'public' entities, but may never achieve office and/or receive state support. Conversely, political parties may achieve parliamentary representation and/or receive state support, yet remain private organisations in their internal affairs, closed to external scrutiny.[10] This perspective assumes that the public/private distinction is based on the extent to which a political party is regulated by public law or receives legal recognition, rather than being an 'organic' reflection of the place and function of political parties in a modern representative democracy.

Party organisations as a contested space

Where a political party performs functions that are clearly of a public nature, such as legislative recruitment, there is a compelling argument for regulation to establish the rules of the game and to maintain a fair contest between participants (see Orr and Rayner, this volume). However, the application of this logic to the internal workings of political parties is far more controversial. Australian political parties have generally been very reluctant to expose their internal operations to the scrutiny of the law. The constitution and rules of the Australian Labor Party (ALP) state, for example:

> It is intended that the National Constitution and everything done in connection with it, all arrangements relating to it (whether express or implied) and any agreement or business entered into or payment made or under the National Constitution, will not bring about any legal relationship, rights, duties or outcome of any kind, or be enforceable by law, or be the subject of legal proceedings. Instead

9   Richard Katz and Peter Mair (1995) 'Changing Models of Party Organization and Party Democracy: The Emergence of the Cartel Party', *Party Politics* 1(1): 5–28; Richard Katz and Peter Mair (2009) 'The Cartel Party Thesis: A Restatement', *Perspectives on Politics* 7(4): 753–66. See, for example, Leon Epstein (1986) *Political Parties in the American Mold*, Madison, WI: University of Wisconsin Press, p. 157; Ingrid van Biezen (2004) 'Political Parties as Public Utilities', *Party Politics* 10(6): 701–22, at p. 705.
10   Gary Johns (1999) 'Political Parties: From Private to Public', *Commonwealth and Comparative Politics* 37(2): 89–113, at p. 90.

all such arrangements, agreements and business are only binding in honour … it is further expressly intended that all disputes within the Party, or between one member and another that relate to the Party be resolved in accordance with the National Constitution and the rules of the state branches and not through legal proceedings.[11]

While the preference of parties is clear, scholars disagree on whether the regulation of intraparty affairs is desirable in the first instance, what form it ought to take and what activities or functions it should encompass. Calls for the increased regulation of political parties to ensure they operate according to the principles of internal party democracy are in part a by-product of, and closely linked to, perceptions that political parties are failing in their democratic function. Empirical evidence from across the advanced industrial democracies suggests that party membership is in steady decline, electoral turnout and campaign participation are dropping and partisan attachments have significantly weakened.[12] Consequently, intraparty democracy (supported by legal regulation) has gained interest in recent years:

because of its apparent potential to promote a 'virtuous cycle' linking ordinary citizens to government, benefiting the parties that adopt it, and more generally contributing to the stability and legitimacy of the democracies in which these parties compete for power.[13]

The implication is that parties should be operating as 'schools for democracy', providing space for public deliberation and training for citizens to engage with each other as democratic equals, like cooperatives.

This view echoes some of the sentiments expressed by the Rudd ALP Government's 2009 *Electoral Reform Green Paper: Strengthening Australia's Democracy*, which put forward the proposal that 'political

---

11 Australian Labor Party (ALP) (2015) *National Constitution and Rules*, Canberra: ALP, as adopted 26 July 2015, Part A, 2(a)–(c).

12 Peter Mair and Ingrid van Biezen (2001) 'Party Membership in Twenty European Democracies', *Party Politics* 7: 5–21; Susan Scarrow (2000) 'Parties without Members? Party Organization in a Changing Electoral Environment', in Russel Dalton and Martin Wattenberg (eds) *Parties without Partisans*, Oxford: Oxford University Press; Mark Franklin (2004) *Voter Turnout and the Dynamics of Electoral Competition*, New York: Cambridge University Press; Martin Wattenberg (2003) *Where Have All the Voters Gone?*, Cambridge, Mass.: Harvard University Press.

13 Susan Scarrow (2005) *Implementing Intra-party Democracy*, Washington, DC: National Democratic Institute, p. 3. See also William Cross and Richard Katz (eds) (2013) *The Challenges of Intra-party Democracy*, Oxford: Oxford University Press.

parties should be required to conduct themselves democratically, responsibly and professionally' to 'foster a civic culture'.[14] More recently, the 'Panel of Experts' appointed by the NSW Premier Mike Baird to review political finance in that State recommended that 'public funding should be conditional on good governance practices and assurance that the public funds are expended and accounted for appropriately'. Noting that there are 'currently very few legislated governance standards or requirements on parties who receive public funds', a situation 'exacerbated by the fact that the major parties are unincorporated (or voluntary) associations similar to community groups and sporting clubs', the panel said regulatory reform was a necessary and 'important step towards restoring community trust in politicians, parties and government'.[15]

A similar perspective is advocated by Ewing, who links taxpayer funding with the condition that parties' internal practices conform to socially acceptable principles, invoking the idea of state-sanctioned obligation. Ewing has argued that political parties should adopt democratic practices not simply as a matter of principle, but also in exchange for the provision of public funding. In what he terms a 'charter of members' rights', political parties should facilitate democratic procedures for policymaking, leadership selection and 'open and inclusive procedures' for the selection of parliamentary candidates.[16]

However, there is a danger in prescribing particular organisational forms for political parties, particularly when they invoke a model of the 'mass party' with its extensive, bottom-up membership participation—a model that has been defunct for many years and that scholars now suggest may never have existed. Imposing internal models of democracy on parties seems to ignore the fact that desirable democratic outcomes (such as the representation of women in legislatures) may not be achieved through more democratic (inclusive) intraparty procedures. While these two things may go together in some post-materialist parties, it is not always the case in older parties.

---

14   Australian Government (2009) *Electoral Reform Green Paper: Strengthening Australia's Democracy*, Canberra: Government of Australia, p. 116.
15   Kerry Schott, Andrew Tink and John Watkins (Panel of Experts) (2014) *Political Donations Final Report. Volume 1*, Sydney: NSW Department of Premier and Cabinet, p. 7.
16   Keith Ewing (2007) *The Cost of Democracy: Party Funding in Modern British Politics*, Oxford: Hart Publishing, pp. 247–8.

And some would argue that parties organised in a democratic fashion are 'not well armed for the struggles of politics' and are placed at a distinct disadvantage compared with those structured along 'authoritarian and autocratic lines'.[17]

The debate over the extent of the regulation of parties' internal activities reflects the differing emphases on parties as participatory and as electoral organisations. If the primary purpose of parties is to contest elections then democratising internal activities such as candidate selection might be a hindrance to their competitiveness. There might be reliance on general elections rather than regulation to 'punish' parties with undemocratic or unpopular internal arrangements, if the voters are aware of these and wish to do so. Conversely, if political parties are seen as sites for citizen participation in politics then there is a more compelling argument for regulating their internal activities. Such regulation might seek to enforce democratic process and outcomes (for example, the participation of members or gender quotas).

The scope of legislative regulation: How do political parties police themselves?

Contributors to this volume have already outlined the main aspects of Australian party regulation, so I shall only discuss here its general scope and intent. As discussed by Sarah John in her chapter, as well as in Chapter 1 by Marian Sawer and myself, the primary legislative recognition of political parties in Australia occurred with the passing of amendments to the *Commonwealth Electoral Act* in 1983, which allowed for the formal registration of political parties to contest federal elections. What is particularly interesting to note is that this and subsequent legislation (and associated regulation) were driven not only by the desire to introduce ballot labels—for example, in jurisdictions such as NSW—but also and more so by the introduction of public funding of elections.

---

17   Maurice Duverger (1954) *Political Parties*, London: Methuen, p. 134; see also Joseph Schumpeter (1942) *Capitalism, Socialism and Democracy*, London: Allen & Unwin.

In the late 1960s and early 1970s, political campaigning in Australia began changing significantly.[18] Having adopted techniques such as opinion polling and paid television advertising, both major parties had difficulty meeting the rising cost of campaigning. To meet the financial shortfall, the Hawke Government introduced public funding for election campaigns in 1984—something introduced in NSW for State elections three years earlier (see Table 1.2). The major parties publicly advocated this funding on the basis that it would lessen reliance on corporate donors.[19] According to the Report of the Joint Select Committee on Electoral Reform (JSCER), the rationale of the scheme was to:

> assist parties in financial difficulties; to lessen corruption; to avoid excessive reliance upon 'special interests' and institutional sources of finance; to equalise opportunities between the parties, and; to stimulate political education and research.[20]

The compliance provisions associated with party registration and public funding in Australia have been well documented in previous studies and in Norm Kelly's chapter in this volume. At the federal level, parties registered for the receipt of public funding under the *Commonwealth Electoral Act 1918* (Cth) must be established on the basis of a written constitution, have a minimum of 500 financial members or one Member of Parliament (MP) and are required to submit an annual disclosure of the sources of party funding. The benefits of registration include the use of the party name beside individual candidates on ballot papers, public funding provided that the party's endorsed candidates poll at least 4 per cent of the primary vote and a copy of the electoral roll containing the postal contact details of all enrolled electors, which parties can make use of for campaigning purposes.

Although registered political parties require a formal written constitution under the provisions of the *Commonwealth Electoral Act*, the structure and content of the party constitution are essentially regarded as internal matters for individual political parties to

---

18   Sally Young (2004) *The Persuaders: Inside the Hidden Machine of Political Advertising*, Melbourne: Pluto Press; also see Stephen Mills (2014) *The Professionals: Strategy, Money and the Rise of the Political Campaigner in Australia*, Melbourne: Black Inc.

19   Gauja, *Political Parties and Elections*, pp. 145–7.

20   Joint Select Committee on Electoral Reform (JSCER) (1983) *First Report*, Canberra: Parliament of the Commonwealth of Australia, pp. 153–4. See also Graeme Orr (2003) 'The Currency of Democracy: Campaign Finance Law in Australia', *UNSW Law Journal* 26(1): 1–31.

determine. The Act requires only that the aims of the party (one of which must be the endorsement of candidates to contest federal elections) be enumerated, in addition to the terms and conditions of party membership (for example, the procedures for accepting or terminating membership). It is important to note that like the aims of the party, the Act requires only that the terms and conditions of party membership be formally codified in the party's constitution and does not impose any requirements as to their actual content. Although recommended by the AEC, the current regulatory regime does not require political parties to formulate rules for the appointment of office-bearers within the party organisation or to detail procedures for amending the party's constitution. Nor does the Act require the party to submit any details of its structure.

Turning to candidate selection, although the *Electoral Act* defines political parties as organisations whose objective or activity is to promote the election to parliament of 'candidates endorsed by it', there is no mention of how political parties should choose their candidates for parliamentary office. Only in Queensland does statute provide that candidate selection processes must take place according to the general principles of free and democratic elections.[21] The upshot is that Australian political parties, while passing legislation that confers significant financial benefits on their organisations, have done little to expose their internal operations to public regulation and scrutiny.

Judicial developments in party regulation

To look only at statute law, however, obscures the fact that the courts are also an important source of regulation of political parties. Despite the lack of overt legislative regulation, party members have increasingly sought to challenge candidate selection outcomes and processes in the Australian courts. This has led to a substantial body of case law on whether intraparty affairs (such as candidate selection) are justiciable and, if so, how these affairs should be conducted.

For most of the twentieth century, political parties were characterised at common law as 'voluntary associations'. The case of *Cameron v Hogan* (1934) 51 CLR 358 (hereinafter *Cameron*), heard one-quarter

---

21   *Electoral Act 1992* (Qld), s. 73A.

cf a century after the consolidation of the party system in Australia, placed the internal affairs of political parties largely beyond the reach of the law. However, this situation changed in the latter half of the twentieth century when the courts began contemplating the public role and importance of parties. The historical progression highlights the symbiotic relationship between judicial and legislative developments in the regulation of political parties. Both are closely related—with the former using the legislative and constitutional recognition of parties as a justification for judicial intervention in what was once considered the 'domestic concern' of the parties.[22]

Numerous scholars have charted the evolution of political parties in Australian jurisprudence from voluntary associations to public utilities.[23] In this section, I focus on how this changing status has impacted on the way in which the courts have resolved intraparty disputes, in effect creating a body of law that de facto regulates the internal organisation of contemporary parties. Using a series of cases as illustrative examples, I discuss how courts have addressed some of the challenges posed by the public/private distinction—in particular, how they have reconciled parties' associational freedoms with their very public roles in representative electoral systems. This section of the chapter also examines the extent to which courts have responded to the 'threat' of partisan lawmaking and been willing to intervene when legislation clearly reflects partisan interests or favours the incumbent(s).

The rights of members versus non-members

The way in which political parties have been recognised and categorised as voluntary associations has important implications for the rights and powers of the membership. For example, as noted above, the High Court of Australia's decision in *Cameron* gave Australian political parties the status of voluntary associations.[24] The consequence of this categorisation was that a member of a voluntary association could enforce the rules or constitution of that association only if, under those rules, the member had a right of

---

22   Justice Starke, *Cameron v Hogan* (1934) 51 CLR 358, at 376.
23   Graeme Orr (2010) *The Law of Politics: Elections, Parties and Money in Australia*, Sydney: The Federation Press; Gauja, *Political Parties and Elections*.
24   (1934) 51 CLR 358.

a civil or a proprietary nature. This narrow construction severely limited the membership's ability to mount an action where the party constitution had been breached.

The practical and political implications of this judicial approach to political parties are that decision-making within parties must be exercised according to the rules and constitution of the party. There is no legal requirement that decisions of the party be made democratically—indeed, it is entirely possible to have an autocratic party organisation—but they must be made fairly and according to the principles of natural justice. Questions of procedural fairness and natural justice arose in the Australian case *Baker v Liberal Party of Australia (SA Division)*, which concerned the admission of members to the South Australian (SA) branch of the Liberal Party of Australia.[25] The party had rejected the membership applications of some 500 applicants lodged by an association called the Combined Shooters and Firearms Council of South Australia. Baker was one such applicant. The Liberal Party perceived the 500 applications that included that of Baker as constituting a potential takeover threat and a compromise to its independence. The party claimed that the SA State Executive had the power, under the party's constitution, to reject an application for membership without giving reason.

Justice Bollen of the SA Supreme Court accepted the argument that the party could reject a membership application without giving reasons, provided that the application was considered. The court also rejected the argument that the plaintiff had a legitimate expectation that she would become a member if she complied with the procedure for application.[26] The court agreed with the Liberal Party's submission that the principles of natural justice that relate to the reasonableness or fairness of the decision do not apply in the case of an application for membership to a voluntary association. As admission had not yet occurred, no legal relationship existed between the parties and hence there was no proprietary interest to protect. However, the situation would have been different had Baker been a member of the party:

---

25 (1997) 68 SASR 366; Anika Gauja (2006) 'From Hogan to Hanson: The Regulation and Changing Legal Status of Australian Political Parties', *Public Law Review* 17: 282–99, at p. 297.
26 Justice Bollen at 374.

'of course it would have all been different had the plaintiff been admitted to membership and then had her membership purportedly cancelled, that is, been dismissed or struck off'.[27]

While in this instance the principles of natural justice were beyond the reach of an applicant to a political party, the decision in *Baker* illustrates the close relationship between the principles employed in the adjudication of intraparty disputes and the requirement of procedural fairness applicable to governmental bodies in the realm of administrative law. Caroline Morris has observed a similar trend in the developing case law of the UK courts.[28] The decision also raises the issue of the differential status of party members and non-members. In an era in which political parties are opening up their organisations to increased participation from non-members through initiatives such as community preselections and supporters' networks, the decision in *Baker* brings into question whether those who participate in what were once seen as intraparty decisions, but who are not members, will have the same legal rights to challenge and enforce party processes as those who are financial members of the organisation.

Candidate selection

An example of a high-profile and influential case concerning candidate selection in Australia is *Clarke v Australian Labor Party (SA Branch) (1999)*.[29] In this case, a member of the SA State Legislature (and prospective candidate) sought to challenge 2,000 new memberships introduced into the party prior to his selection contest to influence the outcome of the party vote. Clarke argued that the validation of these memberships by a special convention of the party did not conform to the party's constitutional process. The Supreme Court of South Australia held that the dispute was justiciable due to the 'statutory recognition by the South Australian Parliament of political parties' in the provisions of the *Electoral Act 1985* (SA).[30]

---

27   ibid., at 375.
28   Caroline Morris (2008) 'Conceptualising Candidate Selection in the Courts: Where to After *Watt v. Ashan?*', *Public Law* (2008): 415–29.
29   (1999) 74 SASR 109.
30   *Clarke v Australian Labor Party (SA Branch)* (1999) 74 SASR 109, per Justice Mulligan at para. 65.

In assessing the constitutional validity of the memberships and the party's validation of them, Justice Mulligan looked to the objectives and rationale of the party as expressed in official party documents. Resolutions of the 1955 and 1979 conferences of the party were analysed to illustrate that 'the Party is a democratic socialist party and, in effect, that its objectives are to be achieved by the democratic process'.[31] It was against these identified democratic values that the court determined the constitutional validity of the party's exercise of power in the resolution of Clarke's dispute:

> The manner of obtaining membership is clear. The fee must be paid to the Sub-Branch which must consider the application for membership at a general meeting. This construction of the Rules also accords with the democratic nature of the party … It provides a safeguard against a group of persons whose interests and motives were contrary to those of the Sub-Branch and the party suddenly joining by merely paying a fee and filling out a form.[32]

Justice Mulligan also criticised the internal dispute-resolution mechanisms of the party, noting that, in some instances, the plaintiff's claim was 'not resolved' by the party or the response was 'limited'. The court regarded the way in which the party's executive had dealt with the dispute as unsatisfactory and noted that the complaint should have been referred to the party's disputes tribunal and resolved by process of conciliation.[33] The special convention to amend the rules and constitution of the party was not regarded as an adequate internal dispute-resolution mechanism, despite the defendant's contention that the plaintiff could have attended the meeting to argue his case against the proposed amendments.

The significance of the *Clarke* decision lies not only in its approval of the justiciability of intraparty disputes concerning candidate selection, but also in the way in which the court interpreted the ALP's rules and constitution in light of democratic principles—namely, 'the establishment of an efficient, effective and fair election process'.[34] Far from being exclusively private organisations:

---

31 ibid., para. 47.
32 ibid., para. 111.
33 ibid., paras 94–5.
34 ibid., para. 126.

Certain decisions of a political party's internal process—such as those relating to the selection of candidates for election, for example—are in truth not private matters at all; they are very public, particularly when there are disputes between factions. In such circumstances, a political party may regard it as highly expedient in order to quell faction-fighting that the final decision on the constitutional validity of its internal proceedings be left, not to a domestic tribunal constituted by party members whose impartiality may, however unjustly, be called into question but, rather, to a court whose impartiality is beyond any question.

Judges have called attention to the fact that a modern political party registered under the legislation governing elections is in itself an institution whose internal stability and good governance is important in the democratic process ... Accordingly, there is a public interest in ensuring that a registered political party, which is entitled to funding assistance for electoral expenses from public monies, is administered in accordance with a correct construction of its rules.[35]

This may indicate a trend for the Australian courts to imply and uphold minimum standards of intraparty democracy in party constitutions, particularly when the objective is espoused in the party's constitution and official documents, regardless of the behaviour and management tactics of elected party officials.

Dealing with limited governance arrangements

As we have seen, party registration requirements in Australia are generally quite lax. Although a party must be established on the basis of a written constitution, there are few legislative directives as to what the constitution should actually contain, such as a minimum level of detail for certain intraparty procedures. Hence, a situation can arise where a political party has no, or very few, rules in place to assist a court in resolving any party dispute. This lack of constitutional detail can pose a significant problem for party litigation and the process of adjudicating such cases. How should (or does) a court approach a situation in which the party lacks basic constitutional measures that provide for the processes of internal decision-making?

---

35 *Coleman v Liberal Party of Australia (New South Wales Division) (No. 2)* [2007] 212 FLR 271, at paras 47–8.

Burston v Oldfield presents an example of the NSW Supreme Court's approach to missing constitutional provisions.[36] The case concerned a challenge to the order of candidates on the One Nation NSW ticket for the 2003 NSW Legislative Council election. Two separate meetings of party members claiming to have validly nominated the candidates contested the order of candidates (and hence their potential order of election). The first meeting, that of the State Executive of the party, was held in December 2002. Following dissatisfaction within the party as to the decision of the executive, an alternative meeting of all party members was called for 19 January 2003. Although notice of the meeting was sent to all members, less than the 28 days' notice required by the party constitution was given. Over 70 members attended the meeting, which elected an alternative Legislative Council ticket.

In deciding which of the tickets was valid, One Nation's rules and constitution offered very little assistance to the court. Although it was agreed between the parties that the constitution was valid and binding, it did not contain any provisions relating to the conduct of State Executive meetings, party conferences or special meetings. As Justice Hamilton noted, 'the Political Party was formed and has proceeded in a very informal fashion'; consequently, 'the provisions of the Constitution are exiguous and in some ways more remarkable for what they do not contain than for what they do contain'.[37] To adjudicate the dispute, the court therefore looked instead to the body of incorporated associations law to determine the validity of the meetings and which took precedence.

Burston was decided on the technical question of whether there was a quorum present at the State Executive meeting in December 2002. Applying prior authority of the Australian High Court in interpreting the meaning of a quorum, the Supreme Court held that the State Executive meeting was valid.[38] The special meeting of members, although giving expression to the democratic will of the membership, was not provided for in the party constitution and therefore lacked binding status within the party.[39]

---

36 *Burston v Oldfield* [2003] NSW SC 88; see Gauja 'From Hogan to Hanson', p. 298.
37 *Burston*, at para. 12.
38 ibid., at para. 15.
39 ibid., at para. 16.

Political parties that are formed without adequate governance structures, regardless of the extent to which they can be regarded as 'democratic', present a real problem and are a significant burden for electoral administrators all over the world. For example, the AEC expressed its concern that:

> The 'churning' of party registration at the smaller or emerging end of the spectrum involves the AEC in considerable time and effort in seeking compliance with the administrative requirements of registration. This has involved complex challenges in those situations where parties' administrative arrangements are inadequate to properly deal with internal party management issues. In one case there was contention as to the make up of the party executive arising from procedural deficiencies in the conduct of the national conference at which they were 'elected'. This resulted in an application to voluntarily deregister the party that was questioned on the ground that it did not have the support of the party or its 'executive' generally. It also resulted in a considerable amount of correspondence from members on issues that were not within the scope of the AEC's functions. The AEC has, and wants, no role in internal party management matters. It is for the party, or the Courts, to resolve internal conflicts.[40]

Partisan regulation? The case of Unions NSW

In 2012, the O'Farrell Liberal–National Coalition Government introduced two significant changes to the regulation of political finance in NSW.[41] The first was to restrict the ability to make donations to political parties to individuals on the NSW electoral roll, thereby effectively outlawing donations from corporations, organisations and other entities, as well as individuals not enrolled to vote (for example, permanent residents and those under the age of 18) (section 96D). Previously, bans had applied only to a special class of prohibited donor, which included property developers and businesses involved in the provision of tobacco, liquor and gambling. The second amendment effectively tightened the caps on electoral communications expenditure by requiring that the spending of political parties and 'affiliated organisations' was aggregated for the purpose of meeting

---

40   Australian Electoral Commission (AEC) (2005) *Funding and Disclosure Report Election 2004*, Canberra: AEC, pp. 40–1.
41   *Election Funding, Expenditure and Disclosures Amendment Act 2012* No. 1 (NSW) (hereinafter *EFEDA Act*).

the maximum limit allowed (section 95G(6)). An affiliated organisation was defined as a body authorised by party rules to appoint delegates to a governing body or participate in the selection of candidates.[42]

The legislation was seen as controversial because the restrictive provisions applied disproportionately to the ALP, by virtue of its unique structure and the institutionalised relationship between the party's governance bodies and the union movement. In effect, while the legislative provisions did not specifically single out the ALP, if the party continued to operate according to its existing decision-making processes, it would have been subject to effectively tighter expenditure limits and would not have been able to accept donations from many of the industrial organisations that had historical ties with the movement. The legislation therefore had the potential to significantly affect the internal structure and operation of the party, forcing it to seek alternative means of funding its campaigns and/or restructure its relationship with the union movement.

Unions NSW (the peak body for trade unions in NSW) challenged the constitutional validity of the legislation in the High Court. Unions NSW had a clear interest in the matter as many unions in NSW affiliate with the ALP, sending delegates to its annual conference, participating in the selection of candidates for public and party office, as well as donating to the party organisation. The question for the High Court was whether sections 96D and 96G(6) impermissibly burdened the freedom of political communication as implied in the Australian Constitution.

The court noted that the general purpose of the *Election Funding, Expenditure and Disclosures Act 1981* (NSW)—to regulate political donations and expenditure through a system of donation and expenditure caps and the provision of public funding—was not in dispute. However, the High Court held that neither of the amendments served a legitimate purpose that was connected to the Act, and therefore both section 96D and section 95G(6) were held to be invalid. The majority observed that the terms of section 96D (limiting donations to individual electors) revealed an 'absence of evident purpose and a lack of connection to the scheme' of the Act.[43]

42   ibid., s. 95G(7).
43   *Unions NSW v NSW* [HCA] 58, at para. 52.

The court further found no clear justification for limiting donations in this way, in contrast with other parts of the Act, which quite clearly were directed at integrity and reducing corruption. In ruling that the provision was invalid, the court noted:

> In argument, the identification by the defendant of a relevant purpose for the nature and scope of s 96D's prohibition proved elusive. The defendant pointed to the general purposes of the EFED [*Election Funding, Expenditure and Disclosures*] Act, but was not able to explain how the prohibitions effected by s 96D were connected to them, let alone how the prohibitions could be said to further them.[44]

Section 95G was equally quickly struck down by the court, which did not accept that it served any legitimate purpose in connection with the integrity and anticorruption provisions of the Act. The court queried how affiliation alone might identify an organisation as:

> the same source of funds for the making of electoral communication expenditure. Moreover, it would appear to assume that the objectives of all expenditure made by the party on the one hand and the organisation on the other are coincident.[45]

The court commented that the purpose of the provision was to reduce the amount that a political party affiliated with an industrial organisation may spend at elections, and likewise to limit the amount that may be spent by an affiliated industrial organisation. However, 'what cannot be deduced is how this purpose is connected to the wider anti-corruption purposes of the EFED Act'.[46]

In his reasons, Justice Keane explicitly highlighted the differential effect the legislative amendments had on the ALP. He noted that section 95G treated certain sources of political communication differently to others—for example, third-party campaigners, which may have close ties to a political party and promulgate exactly the same message, are not subject to the aggregation provisions. Ultimately:

> Political communication generated by electoral communication expenditure by organisations affiliated with a party is disfavoured relative to political communication by entities which, though actively supportive of, and indeed entirely ad idem with, a given party,

---

44   ibid., at para. 54.
45   ibid., at para. 63.
46   ibid., at para. 64.

are not affiliated with it. To discriminate between sources of political communication in this way ... is to distort the flow of political communication.[47]

While in this instance the High Court did not hesitate to strike down legislative provisions that, in effect, discriminated against the ALP, it did so without determining whether the provisions were reasonably justified in limiting the implied freedom of political communication. Because of this, it is not clear what types of regulatory provisions relating to the structure and funding of political parties might be deemed legitimate, even if they burden association and communication freedoms of parties. The Australian High Court has also been far more reticent in critiquing the partisan interests at stake than its American and Canadian counterparts.[48]

Conclusion: Where to from here?

While political parties have become subject to increased regulation since the introduction of registration and public funding in the 1980s, these measures predominantly address the public face of parties: how they interact with one another and the electoral system. There is little legislative interference in the internal workings of political parties— for example, how parties select their candidates for public and party office, how they formulate their policies, structure decision-making procedures and administer the party on a daily basis.

With a few exceptions, any directives in this area tend to be the product of the common law and judicial decisions. As this chapter has demonstrated, while the courts were once tentative in extending their reach to what was seen as the private realm of intraparty affairs, they are now more willing to adjudicate intraparty disputes, to enforce a party's rules and procedures, as well as apply common law principles (such as natural justice) to intraparty decisions. This begs the question: Does the current scheme adequately address the challenges of partisanship and the necessity of balancing the autonomy of political parties with

---

47   ibid., at para. 167.
48   See Gauja, *Political Parties and Elections.*

their role in public affairs? Does it ensure that parties' freedoms of association are respected, while facilitating a more transparent and accountable political process?

At the end of 2014, two separate reports into political finance in NSW, published by the Panel of Experts and the Independent Commission Against Corruption (ICAC), recommended that political parties be subject to tighter regulation of their internal governance arrangements. Showing deep scepticism that political parties were capable of adequately regulating themselves, the NSW Panel of Experts expressed concern about the governance arrangements of the major parties as part of its consultation process. The panel noted:

> We produced an Issues Paper that included information and questions about the reform of party governance and the conditions that should be attached to public funding payments. We were disappointed that none of the political parties turned their minds to this issue or suggested options for reform in their submissions. While we were keen to pursue these issues during our consultations and meetings, the focus of the parties was on the funding model for elections.[49]

Given the reluctance of political parties to put forward measures to regulate themselves, the Expert Panel (together with ICAC) suggested that public funding needed to be explicitly linked with good governance and compliance practices. ICAC noted that enacting legislation that would place 'restrictive requirements' on the internal operation of parties would be 'inconsistent with the nature of parties and their role in democracy'. However, it also noted that there:

> is no doubt that the internal party governance arrangements achieved by the current regulatory framework in NSW fall short of what is desirable in terms of holding parties and their senior officers accountable for non-compliance.[50]

Both reports recommended that parties receiving public funding should be required to submit details of their governance standards and accountability processes to the NSW Electoral Commission, and that payment of public funds should be conditional on the commission's

---

49   Panel of Experts, *Political Donations Final Report*, p. 121.
50   Independent Commission Against Corruption (ICAC) (2014) *Election Funding, Expenditure and Disclosure in NSW: Strengthening Accountability and Transparency*, Sydney: ICAC, p. 8.

'approval' of these standards and processes.[51] While the Expert Panel report did not provide detail on what constituted appropriate good governance standards, the ICAC report suggested that the principles of good governance set by the Australian Securities Exchange would be an appropriate model to follow. According to these principles, parties must clearly set out:

- The respective roles and responsibilities of the most senior levels of leadership and management within parties, and how their performance will be monitored and evaluated
- Structuring decision-making at the top level to add value according to the size, composition, skills and commitment of the party
- Promoting ethical and responsible decision-making
- Safeguarding the integrity of financial reporting by having formal and rigorous processes in place that can be independently verified
- Making timely and balanced disclosures in a transparent way
- Respecting the rights of the regulator and the general public to seek accountability
- Establishing and regularly reviewing a risk management framework.[52]

ICAC's report argued that 'because they are principles, the freedom of parties to self-organise is largely preserved'.[53] While financial noncompliance is clearly the target of these recommendations, applying the principles of corporate governance to political parties is controversial. Apart from the capacity of the electoral commission to undertake an oversight role (particularly in light of the AEC's aversion to getting involved in the internal politics of parties—see the previous discussion), the principles assume that decision-making within parties is structured in a hierarchical manner. For example, how might a party with a flat, grassroots organisation (such as The Australian Greens) be able to comply with these provisions?

The ICAC report suggested that compliance need not be onerous; parties in NSW would simply be required to incorporate the principles listed above into their constitutions and rules, and provide details of their leader, party officers, agents and auditors. Rather than

---

51   Panel of Experts, *Political Donations Final Report*, p. 121.
52   ICAC, *Election Funding*, p. 15.
53   ibid., p. 17.

re-engineer party structures, the primary aim of the regulation would be to shift the legal responsibilities for election funding compliance and governance from the party agent to senior party office-holders within the party.[54] The NSW Government has indicated that it accepts these recommendations 'in principle' and will work with political parties and the electoral commission in considering 'how to implement this recommendation'. Yet, by October 2016 there had been no legislative movement in this area. The path to regulatory reform seems strikingly familiar. There is potential that the application of corporate governance principles might be an innovative way forward in navigating and balancing the role of political parties as private associations and public entities (and hence also serve as a model for other Australian jurisdictions). However, the reticence of parties in adopting regulatory reforms that target their internal processes means that change in this area will be gradual, if it happens at all.

---

54   ibid., p. 15.

8

Party rules: The regulatory 'gap'

Anika Gauja and Marian Sawer

As we noted in Chapter 1, the regulation of political parties is relatively new to Australian politics. However, it is now an area of constant change and debate. This is illustrated by the numerous legislative developments taking place at federal and State and Territory levels concerning party financing, registration, ballot access and candidate selection. These developments are analysed in chapters throughout this book and present both opportunities and potential pitfalls for legislators—and even for courts. When courts adopt, review or apply regulations, they are faced with a complex of normative principles as to the appropriate role of political parties in modern representative democracies and their relationship to citizens and the state.

This pattern of development, and the fact that debates over the purpose and effect of regulation are often revisited, suggests a disjuncture between what we seek from party regulation and what is actually achieved. Our contributors have explored this regulatory gap from different perspectives: examining how political parties are viewed and regulated as agents of civil society, as participants in elections and as parliamentary actors. In this conclusion, we consider the nature and causes of this regulatory gap, drawing on evidence presented in the chapters and placing it in an international context.

As the chapters in the book show, there are a number of reasons for the regulatory gap. The first arises because of the tension between different democratic principles and the fact that regulatory regimes may serve competing democratic aims. An example would be regulation that facilitates the formation of a diverse array of political parties and their access to the ballot paper versus regulation that restricts competition to create a more meaningful choice for voters. The second reason for the regulatory gap stems from changing social expectations concerning the role and place of political parties in representative democracy. As we noted in Chapter 1, the popularity of parties as measured by party memberships has declined enormously and citizens place relatively little trust in these political institutions. Attempting to reduce the reliance of political parties on private money so as to remove perceptions of 'undue influence', while overcoming voters' resistance to 'paying' for political parties with their taxes, nicely illustrates the regulatory challenges involved in balancing these expectations. The final reason for the regulatory gap has to do with the partisan nature of lawmaking and the fact that parties control the lawmaking process; democratic ideals will never be met because the interests of parties and individual legislators inevitably get in the way. We argue that it is only by acknowledging the key traits of party regulation that we can begin to develop strategies for closing the regulatory gap.

Regulation as a normative exercise: Balancing competing principles

One of the main areas of agreement among scholars studying party regulation is that the law ought to reflect democratic values that are accepted by the community. In line with such democratic values, any regulatory regime should also be built on the basis of transparency. But what are the democratic values that should be enshrined in party regulation, how can they be expressed/analysed and what are the main areas of agreement/disagreement?

For the most part, the values underlying party regulation have become widely accepted, not only internationally, but also in Australia. They include freedom of political association, freedom of political expression, fair and healthy competition between political parties, broad participation and the right of individuals to choose freely between parties in a pluralist party system. The last principle is spelled out, for example, in the *Inter-American Democratic Charter* adopted by the Organization of American States in 2001, which includes 'a pluralistic system of political parties and organizations' as one of the 'essential elements of representative democracy' (Article 3). The right of individuals to choose freely between political parties appears to entail the existence of a legally acknowledged party system that is not only pluralist but also competitive, with parties able to compete on a level playing field in terms of access to public and private resources and to the media. Pippa Norris has summarised these requirements as the existence in elections of a 'choice of competing parties and candidates, without repression of opposition parties or undue bias in the distribution of campaign resources or media access'.[1] Other requirements of free voter choice—in addition to access to party messages—might include access to information about who is funding the party, requiring transparency about party finances.

One normative framework within which party regulation can be situated is the International Institute for Democracy and Electoral Assistance (International IDEA) state of democracy assessment framework (as used in the Australian Democratic Audit). This framework is based on two basic principles—popular control of government and political equality—that are further distilled into a series of values that can be institutionalised to a greater or lesser degree in democratic systems: participation, authorisation, representation, accountability, transparency, responsiveness and solidarity.[2] Using the normative perspective provided by the quality of democracy framework, we can consider how existing party regulation promotes or detracts from political equality and how equality might be better achieved through different institutional designs. In Chapter 1, we looked at how one aspect of the equality principle—equal opportunity to serve as a political representative—has been incorporated into party regulation internationally by the adoption of legislated candidate

1   Pippa Norris (2004) *Electoral Engineering: Voting Rules and Political Behaviour*, Cambridge: Cambridge University Press, p. 4.
2   Marian Sawer, Norman Abjorensen and Phil Larkin (2009) *Australia: The State of Democracy*, Sydney: The Federation Press, pp. 3–4.

quotas. In Australia, however, there are no constitutional or legislated candidate quotas and the centre-right parties have also been opposed to introducing them at the party level.

The Democratic Audit of Australia spelled out two additional basic principles: those of civil liberties and human rights and the deliberative democracy principle of the quality of public debate and discussion.[3] The reason for spelling out these additional principles, which theoretically should be encompassed by the principles of political equality and popular control of government, was, first, that governments were using electoral majorities based on equal voting rights to justify curtailing parliamentary deliberation, silencing public criticism and infringing civil liberties. Second, insofar as political parties can be seen as sites for political participation rather than simply for electoral competition, there is a strong normative argument that the democratic values surrounding the quality of debate and discussion should also apply to these arenas.

These four principles are reflected in different ways in the work of Australian experts on electoral and party regulation. For example, in a report prepared for the New South Wales (NSW) Electoral Commission, Joo-Cheong Tham argues that political finance legislation should reflect the following principles: protect the integrity of representative government (including preventing corruption); promote fairness in politics; support political parties to discharge their democratic functions; and respect political freedoms (in particular, freedom of political expression and freedom of political association).[4] The liberal values that Orr sees as underlying the law of politics are liberty, equality and integrity and, at the systemic level, the republican ideals of participation and deliberation.[5]

While it is one thing to identify the values that should underpin party regulation from a theoretical standpoint, it is another to implement them through party regulation or even to ensure that the principles

---

3   ibid, pp. 3–4, 13.
4   Joo-Cheong Tham (2012) *Establishing a Sustainable Framework for Election Funding and Spending Laws in New South Wales*, A Report Prepared for the NSW Electoral Commission, Sydney, November, pp. 17–18. See also Joo-Cheong Tham (2003) 'Campaign Finance Reform in Australia: Some Reasons for Reform', in Graeme Orr, Bryan Mercurio and George Williams (eds) (2003) *Realising Democracy: Electoral Law in Australia*, Sydney: The Federation Press, p. 119.
5   Graeme Orr (2010) *The Law of Politics in Australia: Elections, Parties and Money in Australia*, Sydney: The Federation Press, p. 12.

behind particular legislative instruments are transparent. Each of these overarching values carries practical implications and distinct policy prescriptions. The liberty principle suggests caution against overregulation of political parties, which may impinge on freedom of association. The equality principle may suggest provision of free airtime for political broadcasts or the equitable allocation of paid time, as against the advantage provided by wealthy supporters in countries that allow paid political advertising. The integrity principle pushes 'in the direction of transparent party affairs and finances, broad powers for electoral authorities and courts to enforce the law and maintain accountability'.[6] The ideals of participation and deliberation might warrant public support for political parties insofar as their organisation conforms to these values.

What is evident, however, is that some of these principles may conflict. For example, public funding for political parties in the interests of equality, integrity or support for deliberative democracy might run counter to the principle of popular control of government because of public opposition to politicians and political parties having 'their snouts in the trough'. Regulatory measures to encourage participation in party politics by supporting a particular organisational form (for example, the democratic selection of candidates, as currently required by Queensland electoral legislation) could conceivably impede parties' freedom of association. Requirements for parties to have a large number of members could be viewed as restricting the ability of citizens to participate in electoral activities of a party of their choice, rather than as protecting voters from ballot papers the size of a tablecloth. Trying to reconcile competing principles is no easy task, particularly when different members of the community have different views on the desirability of each. The first step, however, is to acknowledge that such conflicts exist. Prioritising some principles over others may be necessary, but this discussion should ideally take place with reference to community attitudes about political parties and their evolving role in modern representative democracies (see below).

Democratic disagreements have often been left to the courts to arbitrate. For example, as shown in the chapters by Jennifer Rayner and Graeme Orr, there is a potential conflict among the principles

---

6   ibid., p. 12.

underpinning campaign finance regulation. Promoting the integrity of elections and a level playing field by capping or banning donations can fall foul of freedoms of political expression—a position that has typically been taken by the US Supreme Court. In contrast, the Canadian Supreme Court has held that some restrictions are needed to ensure equal opportunity for participation in political discourse and to prevent wealthy voices from drowning out others.[7] In the United Kingdom, the House of Lords has upheld the UK prohibition on paid political advertising, arguing that the ban is necessary to maintain a level playing field and to prevent 'well-endowed interests' from using 'the power of the purse to give enhanced prominence to their views'.[8] A majority of European countries, including the United Kingdom, Ireland and the Scandinavian countries, have never allowed paid political advertising, on the grounds of the advantage it gives to deep pockets; instead, they allocate free airtime to political parties in accordance with an equity formula. Money talks, but in most comparable democracies there is regulation to prevent it monopolising the conversation in elections.

As Gauja noted in her chapter, the Australian High Court's decision in *Unions NSW* did little to illuminate the relationship between anticorruption provisions and implied constitutional freedoms. However, its decision in *McCloy v NSW* in late 2015 was unequivocal in balancing the implied freedom of political communication with a constitutional principle of political equality.[9] In this judgement, the High Court upheld the validity of caps on political donations and of legislative measures that prohibited property developers from making political donations and restricted indirect campaign contributions. As outlined in Chapter 1, and covered in more detail

---

[7] For the most recent example of the position taken by the US Supreme Court, see *McCutcheon v FEC* (2014) No. 12-536. For the position adopted by the Canadian Supreme Court on the limiting of third-party advertising, see *Harper v Canada* (2004). Canada has bans on corporate donations and caps on individual donations and candidate, party and third-party expenditure.

[8] The House of Lords. 2008. UKHL 15, 12 March. In 2013, the European Court of Human Rights determined that although the ban was an interference with freedom of expression, it served the legitimate purpose of preserving the impartiality of broadcasting on public interest matters and thereby protecting the democratic process. *Case of Animal Defenders International v The United Kingdom*, available at: hudoc.echr.coe.int/sites/fra/pages/search.aspx?i=001-119244#{"itemid":["001-119244"]}.

[9] *McCloy v New South Wales* [2015] HCA 34. Graeme Orr (2015) 'In McCloy Case, High Court Finally Embraces Political Equality ahead of Political Freedom', *The Conversation*, 8 October, available at: theconversation.com/in-mccloy-case-high-court-finally-embraces-political-equality-ahead-of-political-freedom-48746.

in the chapters by Jennifer Rayner and Graeme Orr, for the past two elections, NSW legislation has restricted donations to political parties to a maximum of $5,000 per annum and donations to individual candidates to $2,000. NSW also prohibits donations from property developers and from alcohol, tobacco and gambling interests.

The case challenging the NSW donation caps and the ban on donations by property developers was brought by a former Newcastle mayor and property developer Jeff McCloy. It stemmed from the ongoing investigation by the NSW Independent Commission Against Corruption (ICAC) into political finance and corruption in NSW and its findings that McCloy made unlawful donations to Liberal Party candidates (indeed, McCloy described himself as a 'walking ATM'). McCloy argued that the provisions of the NSW Act burdened the freedom of political communication by restricting the funds available to political parties and candidates to meet the cost of their political communication activities. He further asserted that the restrictions hampered his ability to gain access, and make representations, to politicians and political parties. McCloy submitted, as donors, he and other property developers were 'entitled to "build and assert political power"'.[10]

The High Court rejected this view. In fact, it strongly asserted that 'guaranteeing the ability of a few to make large political donations in order to secure access to those in power' was antithetical to the underlying constitutional principle of political equality.[11] This moved the Australian High Court much closer to the political equality or fairness positions adopted in jurisdictions such as Canada and the United Kingdom. While the court accepted that the NSW legislation indirectly burdened the freedom of political communication by restricting the funds that were available to political parties and candidates, it declared that these burdens were permissible as they were a legitimate means of pursuing the goal of electoral integrity and removing the risk and perception of corruption and undue influence from NSW politics. The court undertook a balancing exercise to determine whether the restrictions imposed by the law were

10   *McCloy*, at [25].
11   ibid., at [28].

proportionate to its overall aim and, in the process, it paid particular attention to expert reports and evidence of the pervasiveness and impact of political corruption in NSW. It found:

> The provisions do not affect the ability of any person to communicate with another about matters of politics and government nor to seek access to or to influence politicians in ways other than those involving the payment of substantial sums of money … By reducing the funds available to election campaigns there may be some restriction on communication by political parties and candidates to the public. On the other hand, the public interest in removing the risk and perception of corruption is evident. These are provisions which support and enhance equality of access to government, and the system of representative government which the freedom protects. The restriction on the freedom is more than balanced by the benefits sought to be achieved.[12]

The High Court's decision in *McCloy* provides some certainty that political finance regulation—specifically, caps on donations to political parties and the prohibition of donations from property developers and alcohol, gaming and tobacco interests—will not fall foul of the Australian Constitution provided the restrictions are suitable, reasonably necessary and adequate in their balance. Insofar as constitutional uncertainty has acted as a barrier to party finance law reform and harmonisation across the Australian States and Territories, this decision may well provide the necessary clarification to allow other jurisdictions to move in the same direction as NSW. In July 2015, NSW Premier Mike Baird indicated that he would place the issue of national campaign finance reform on the agenda for the next Council of Australian Governments (COAG) meeting.[13] However, no substantive discussion has yet occurred.

In the international arena, perhaps because of such conflicting values over the right of money to speak, there is little agreement on international standards of party regulation and political finance. This is in marked contrast with the extent of soft regulation or

---

12   ibid., at [93].
13   Sean Nicholls (2015) 'Political Leaders Urged to Unite in Overhaul of National Donations Laws', *Sydney Morning Herald*, 28 July.

international standard-setting on the conduct of democratic elections.[14] For example, while it is generally accepted that political parties are one mechanism through which citizens exercise their freedoms of political expression and communication, there is far less agreement when it comes to the level of support that parties should receive from the state or be allowed to receive from private corporations. Transnational bodies such as International IDEA recommend a balance of public and private funding and it is generally argued that it is desirable for the latter to be in the form of small donations encouraged by tax credits— too small to buy policy influence. Digital platforms make this kind of crowd-sourcing relatively easy. Yet, where the balance is to be struck between public and private funding is subject to continuing debate. While acknowledging the competing and often conflicting principles that underpin party regulation is the first step in closing the regulatory gap, reaching agreement on which to emphasise is a more difficult task.

Regulation and the role of political parties in representative democracy

One way to move forward would be to recognise and better integrate community attitudes about the role and place of political parties in representative democracies into the process of adopting party regulation. As we have seen in this book, it is widely agreed that political parties should perform a number of key functions in representative democracies. We can follow Young and Tham in categorising these as the representative function, offering electoral choice through the presentation of policy platforms and leaders that cater to the different preferences of the electorate; an agenda-setting function in stimulating ideas for Australian democracy through policy development and research; a participation function in providing a vehicle for political participation; and last, a governance function

---

14   Anika Gauja (2014) *The Legal Regulation of Political Parties: Is There a Global Normative Standard?*, Working Paper prepared for the Electoral Integrity Project Lunchtime Research Seminar Series, Sydney: University of Sydney; Pippa Norris, Richard W. Frank and Ferran Martinez i Coma (2013) 'Assessing the Quality of Elections', *Journal of Democracy* 24(4): 130.

through elected parliamentarians.[15] The governance function includes both the formation of governments and the holding of governments to account through effective opposition. These functions can also be described, in Kay Lawson's term, as 'linkages', which include campaign, participatory, ideological, representative and policy elements.[16]

However, as we have seen, the extent to which political parties are capable of performing these functions in modern democracies is in doubt. The 2010 Australian Election Study showed that less than one-third of voters had confidence in Australian political parties even though more than two-thirds believed that political parties were essential to make democracy work.[17] Many now believe that political parties are in terminal decline, with young people in particular feeling disengaged from conventional forms of political participation. Scholars point to rapidly declining party memberships, centralisation of party decision-making (reducing their function as conduits for ground-up policy formation), decreasing levels of strong partisanship, increasing distrust in or apathy about parties, policy convergence (perhaps feeding less strong attachment to parties) and the rise of alternative sites for political participation.[18] As mentioned in Chapter 1, in Australia, the online campaigning organisation GetUp! claims more members (over 1 million in 2016) than all the political parties put together. People are much more likely to sign an electronic petition, engage in a consumer boycott or even attend a demonstration than to join a political party. In addition to alternative sites for political participation, there are also alternative vehicles for interest or policy representation. In between elections, citizens are likely to be represented in the policy process by community-based peak bodies, representing their interests as, for example, consumers, pensioners or users of government services.[19] While for some these developments herald the decline of party-based politics, for others, the rise of such

15   Sally Young and Joo-Cheong Tham (2006) *Political Finance in Australia: A Skewed and Secret System*, Report No. 7, Melbourne: Democratic Audit of Australia, p. 2, available at: apo.org.au/research/political-finance-australia-skewed-and-secret-system-0.

16   See Russell J. Dalton, David Farrell and Ian McAllister (2011) *Political Parties and Democratic Linkage: How Parties Organize Democracy*, Oxford: Oxford University Press, pp. 6–9.

17   Aaron Martin (2014) 'The Party is Not Over: Explaining Attitudes towards Political Parties in Australia', *International Journal of Public Opinion Research* 26(1): 1–17.

18   Dalton et al., *Political Parties and Democratic Linkage*, pp. 9–14; Ian Marsh (ed.) (2006) *Political Parties in Transition?*, Sydney: The Federation Press.

19   Marian Sawer and Gianni Zappalà (2001) *Speaking for the People: Representation in Australian Politics*, Melbourne: Melbourne University Press.

diverse forms of participation and critical citizens may in fact be a sign of deeper democratic engagement. Given these trends, do our expectations regarding the regulation of political parties (particularly the extent to which their activities should be supported by the state) need to change?

If political parties are not the preferred or most frequently used form of policy representation or political engagement, why should they be privileged in terms of public funding and support for their political role? Political parties receive a wide range of public benefits as well as tax deductibility for private donations, without the detailed forms of accountability required from other kinds of representative bodies in return for such benefits. Community-based peak bodies, such as the Australian Council of Social Service or Women With Disabilities Australia, play an extremely important representative role in the democratic system, being responsible for speaking on behalf of relevant sections of the community at all times, not just at elections. Such non-governmental organisations also perform other vital democratic functions, creating space for public deliberation and serving as schools of democratic practice. However, the public funding and charitable and deductible gift recipient status of these bodies are never as secure as the equivalent benefits for political parties, even for minor parties outside the party cartel. The perils for non-governmental organisations of advocacy critical of government policy continue, despite High Court confirmation of the compatibility of public advocacy and charitable status (in the Aid/Watch case)[20] and its statutory confirmation in the *Charities Act 2013* (Cth). The Gillard Government also enacted the *Not-for-Profit Sector Freedom to Advocate Act* in 2013 in an attempt to ensure that government funding contracts did not include 'gag' clauses. In 2014, however, the new Abbott Government started removing clauses from Commonwealth funding agreements that guaranteed the right to engage in public advocacy and to criticise government.

One answer to the question of the privileged status of political parties with regard to public resources is that, unlike other non-governmental organisations, political parties combine policy agenda-setting and advocacy with governance functions. The last include, at different

---

20 *Aid/Watch Incorporated v Commissioner of Taxation* [2010] HCA 42.

times, not only contesting elections and being a party of government but also being a party of opposition, undertaking legislative review and executive scrutiny. In other words, the principle has been established that because political parties are needed for healthy electoral competition and parliamentary opposition, they deserve public support. For example, the Australian Department of Foreign Affairs and Trade lists the 'key democratic principles and practices in Australia' as including 'equitably resourced and respected opposition parties'.[21] There has been little of that 'principled commitment to voluntarism', which has been described as underpinning UK reticence to public funding—the idea that 'the taxpayer should not be obliged to fund parties with whom he does not agree'.[22] One can argue that even parties with which one does not agree perform an important function in holding governments to account. Nonetheless, the view that political parties merit support does not extend to licensing the appropriation of state resources provided for another purpose—resources such as parliamentary allowances. Some also find it difficult to accept that public funding can be earned by parties that promote racial division, contrary to official policies to promote racial harmony.

Apart from the issues involved in the funding of political opposition, the governance functions that political parties perform also create significant challenges. The regulation of party funding in Australia relies primarily on disclosure regimes. However, while the level of the disclosure thresholds and their timing/frequency are important subjects of debate, a serious concern is also the *types* of activities that are covered (or not covered) by disclosure provisions. In Australia, significant sums of money can be hidden from public view because they are not classified as 'donations'.[23] This includes the practice of selling access to senior party figures such as ministers and shadow ministers through dinner tickets and paid places at receptions.

Each of the major political parties has, or has had, one or more 'associated entities' that coordinate these fundraising activities on behalf of the party—for example, the Liberal Party's North Sydney Forum, the Millennium Forum and the 500 Club. On the Labor side of

---

21 Department of Foreign Affairs and Trade (DFAT) (2008) *About Australia: Democratic Rights and Freedoms*, Canberra: Government of Australia.
22 Justin Fisher (2009) 'Hayden Phillips and Jack Straw: The Continuation of British Exceptionalism in Party Finance?', *Parliamentary Affairs* 62(2): 306.
23 Sawer et al., *Australia*, p. 141.

politics, these organisations include Progressive Business, the Chifley Forum and Labor Holdings. For example, the NSW Labor Party's Chifley Forum offers members 'the opportunity to connect with senior figures in government, business and the community'. The forum's website claims that by joining as a member, individuals and businesses 'will be invited to attend exclusive events where you can build relationships with current and future Labor leaders'.[24] The activities of the Liberal Party's Free Enterprise Foundation came under scrutiny in ICAC, where it was alleged that the foundation was used to 'launder' political donations from prohibited donors in the lead-up to the 2011 state election.[25] In March 2015, the NSW Electoral Commission decided to withhold $4.4 million in public funding from the Liberal Party on the basis that it failed to disclose the identity of major donors during the 2011 campaign.[26] Until the donors are reported, the Liberal Party will also not be eligible for any future funding under the NSW scheme. In September 2016, following satisfactory disclosure by the party of the relevant donations, the Election Commission released this funding, minus $586,992 (the value of donations deemed to be unlawful).[27]

These types of political contributions fall into what political scientist Iain McMenamin calls 'reciprocal exchanges'.[28] A discrete exchange is 'explicit and simultaneous'; however, a reciprocal exchange involves a degree of uncertainty and the part of each actor is performed separately. Such an exchange might be thought of as relationship building, without any expectation of immediate favours or direct action. These exchanges favour politicians, who cannot 'afford a perception that their political support can be bought', and donors, who may classify them as a tax deductible 'business expense' rather than having to declare them as a political donation.[29] Donation caps or

---

24   NSW Labor (2015) *Chifley Forum*, Sydney: NSW Labor.

25   Kerry Schott, Andrew Tink and John Watkins (2014) *Political Donations Final Report. Volume 1*, Sydney: NSW Department of Premier and Cabinet.

26   NSW Electoral Commission (2016) 'Liberal Party of Australia (NSW Division) Ineligible for Further Public Funding', Statement by Chairperson, NSW Electoral Commission, 23 March, Sydney, available at: elections.nsw.gov.au/about_us/work_of_the_commission/statements_issued_by_the_chair_of_the_commission.

27   NSW Electoral Commission (2016) 'Statement by Chairperson', NSW Electoral Commission, 22 September, Sydney: NSW Electoral Commission, available at: elections.nsw.gov.au/__data/assets/pdf_file/0020/224363/22_September_2016_-_Liberal_Party_of_Australia_NSW_Division.pdf.

28   Iain McMenamin (2013) *If Money Talks, What Does It Say?*, Oxford: Oxford University Press.

29   ibid., p. 12; Sawer et al., *Australia*, p. 141.

bans may limit discrete donations, such as those referred to above in the discussion of the *McCloy* decision, but when this occurs, reciprocal arrangements become more common.

While it is clear that these forums and fundraising organisations trade on the promise of granting access to politicians, whether or not they constitute a type of corrupt and distorting activity is contentious. In 2009, then Queensland Premier Anna Bligh placed a ban on State Labor parliamentarians attending fundraising events with business organisations. Even if the practice of selling access were within the law, Bligh argued, the negative perceptions such fundraising practices created were detrimental for the reputations of both political parties and representative democracy more generally:

> All political parties in Australia engage in these sorts of activities and my concern is the more exclusive they become, the more elite they seem, the more expensive they become, the more that ordinary people start to feel that they don't have the same level of access to their elected representatives as people with a lot of money in their pockets and I don't think that's a good thing for democracy.[30]

Party regulation must therefore reflect these two realities: on the one hand, political parties are privileged political actors, regarded as entitled to public funding despite criticism of government; on the other, they fail to attract citizens to their organisations or to adhere to standards of democratic governance. This failure raises the contentious questions of whether and how the internal organisation of political parties should be resourced and regulated to facilitate democratic participation. Another contentious question is whether regulation should be extended to the 'cash for access' practices referred to above, whereby political parties provide unmediated and unequal access to political power in exchange for money.

---

30 Cited in 'Queensland Premier Anna Bligh Says Political Donations Should be Capped', *News. com.au*, 4 July 2010, available at: news.com.au/national/queensland-premier-anna-bligh-says-political-donations-should-be-capped/story-e6frfkp9-1225887598269. Also see Brian Costar (2011) 'Equality, Liberty and Integrity and the Regulation of Campaign Finance', in Joo-Cheong Tham, Brian Costar and Graeme Orr (eds) *Electoral Democracy: Australian Prospects*, Melbourne: Melbourne University Press.

The partisan nature of party regulation

We have introduced some of the underlying values and current challenges for party regulation in Australia. Scholars generally agree that the legal regulation of political parties should be underpinned by the principles of participation, deliberation, integrity, equality and liberty. However, they also acknowledge a conflict between some of these principles and the policy recommendations that flow from them. Nonetheless, perhaps the most challenging aspect of party regulation is the partisan nature of lawmaking itself, and the inbuilt imperative for legislators—as party representatives—to enact laws that serve their party's interests.

The inability of systems of party regulation to achieve their stated aims or meet democratic ideals occurs both because underlying principles may be in conflict and because the design of electoral systems and the legislation governing their operation is initiated, developed, debated and passed by the parties themselves. Electoral oversight committees of parliament tend to issue both majority and minority reports, along party lines. And although Australian electoral commissions have considerable autonomy in conducting elections, they have no such autonomy with regard to establishing the regulatory framework. So while these electoral management bodies are able to perform functions of party regulation in a neutral way, they lack the independence to establish a framework more in accordance with international standards.[31] Hence, there is an opportunity for governing parties to reinforce pre-existing patterns of dominance or to privilege their own position in the design of regulatory regimes.[32] For example, it is sobering that recent political finance laws, which were held to be unconstitutional by the High Court in the *Unions NSW* decision[33]—in part because of their discriminatory impact on the Australian Labor

---

31 Norm Kelly (2012) *Directions in Australian Electoral Reform: Professionalism and Partisanship in Electoral Management*, Canberra: ANU E Press, p. 153, available at: press.anu.edu.au/titles/directions-in-australian-electoral-reform/. Electoral management bodies have not even been able to eliminate the practice of political parties sending out postal vote applications, despite the otherwise nonpartisan nature of Australian electoral administration.

32 Anika Gauja (2010) *Political Parties and Elections: Legislating for Representative Democracy*, Farnham: Ashgate, p. 7.

33 *Unions NSW v New South Wales* (2013) HCA 58.

Party (ALP)—were legislated by a newly elected Liberal Government. This illustrates how electoral legislation tends to protect incumbency advantage.

As we have seen, incumbency advantage may cover a spectrum from advantaging a governing party, advantaging major parties or advantaging both major and minor parliamentary parties to advantaging all parties and Independents in parliament as against challengers. How such partisan interests are expressed in electoral and parliamentary regulation very much depends on the balance of power within the legislature. On rare occasions, a sitting Independent may call for the reform of incumbency advantage in elections—for example, by stopping parliamentary entitlements the moment an election is called.[34] Australia has been remarkably relaxed about the use of such entitlements for electioneering, including the printing of postal vote applications and how-to-vote cards. In other comparable democracies such as the United States, the United Kingdom and New Zealand, legislators/parliamentarians are not allowed to use their printing and postage entitlements for party-political purposes.[35] While the use of parliamentary allowances for campaign purposes might seem to be a clear-cut incumbency advantage, the allowances may also be used to assist non-sitting candidates from within the same party.

In recent years, studies of party organisation and electoral reform more generally have been concerned with how regulation may serve to protect incumbency advantage, and this has also been noted by legal scholars.[36] In some cases, legislation may blatantly favour both the ideology and the interests of the governing party. However, as noted, regulation may also privilege the interests of all political parties represented in the legislature over new entrants into electoral competition or other political actors. Notwithstanding the content of the law, an equally important aspect of the regulation of political

---

34　Peter Andren MP (2004) *Level Democratic Playing Field: You Must be Joking*, Discussion Paper, November, Melbourne: Democratic Audit of Australia, available at: apo.org.au/files/Resource/andrenpaper.pdf.

35　Australian National Audit Office (ANAO) (2009–10) *Administration of Parliamentarians' Entitlements by the Department of Finance and Deregulation*, Report No. 3, Canberra: ANAO, available at: anao.gov.au/uploads/documents/2009-10_ANAO_Audit_Report_3_.pdf.

36　See, for example, James Bennett (2009) *Stifling Political Competition*, New York: Springer; Colin Feasby (2007) 'Constitutional Questions about Canada's New Political Finance Regime', *Osgoode Hall Law Journal* 45: 513–70; Michael Kang (2005) 'The Hydraulics and Politics of Party Regulation', *Iowa Law Review* 91: 131–87.

parties is the process by which the law is formulated. Opportunities for regulatory reform should encourage consultation and engagement between practitioners, experts and academics (from a range of disciplinary backgrounds, including political scientists, legal scholars and political theorists). Ideally, legislation should be based not simply on bipartisan or even multiparty support, but also on respect for electoral actors beyond the existing parliamentary parties. A good example of such an approach was the establishment of an independent and bipartisan 'Panel of Experts', which examined options for political donation reform in NSW in 2014. Led by Dr Kerry Schott (a high-profile company director), Andrew Tink (a former Liberal Shadow Attorney-General) and John Watkins (a former NSW Labor Deputy Premier), the panel consulted extensively with academics and public interest groups in producing its recommendations for reform.

Final remarks

Throughout this book, we have explored the gap between what is wanted from political party regulation and what is actually achieved. Our authors have done this by looking at several overlapping arenas: the role of parties as agents of civil society; as participants in elections; and as actors in parliamentary politics. The analysis of party regulation in each of these arenas has been underpinned by two broad themes. The first is *the rationale for party regulation* and how it corresponds with the role of parties in democracy and democratic governance. The second is the *politics of party regulation*—how partisan interests, democratic norms and policy diffusion shape regulation. A related consideration is the role of the judiciary and international standard-setting and electoral management bodies in regulating parties.

An important concern is whether the regulation of organisational structures, as agents of civil society, can promote internal democracy and community engagement and, more specifically, whether the regulation of candidate selection processes and legislative recruitment can encourage diversity without sacrificing internal democracy. We have also questioned why political parties should be subject to less regulation of their internal governance than non-governmental organisations that perform vital representative roles in our democratic system and why the public funding of the latter should be so precarious.[37]

Regardless of the regulatory regimes that are introduced, it seems that political parties will be as quick to find loopholes as are large corporations seeking to minimise their taxation. While the interests of shareholders may be the reason given for the latter, for political parties, the interest will always be in maintaining their electoral competitiveness. Ideally, consensus on a central democratic value such as political equality would mean that regulation was unnecessary— parties would agree, for example, that if receiving public money they would refrain from private money. Because this kind of consensus is absent, we do need regulation to prioritise democratic principles such as political equality and to promote a level playing field. However, because the norms underpinning party regulation are contested, often on partisan grounds, we must expect that there will always be a gap between what is desired and what is achieved.

---

37   See further, comparing the light-touch regulation of publicly funded parties with the policing of trade union internal democracy, Graeme Orr (2001) 'Overseeing the Gatekeepers: Should the Preselection of Political Candidates be Regulated', *Public Law Review* 12(2): 89–94.

Appendix: Federally registered political parties, 1984–2016[1]

21st Century Party

A Better Future For Our Children

Abolish Child Support/Family Court Party

Abolish Self Government Coalition

ACT Referendum First Group

Advance Australia Party

Animal Justice Party

Australia First

Australia First Party

Australia First Party (NSW) Incorporated

Australian Antipaedophile Party

Australian Bill of Rights Group

Australian Christian Heritage—Christian Democratic Party

Australian Christians

Australian Conservative Party

Australian Country Party

Australian Cyclists Party

Australian Defence Veterans Party

Australian Democrats

Australian Equality Party (Marriage)

Australian Family Movement

Australian First Nations Political Party

---

1   To 16 May 2016.

Australian Fishing and Lifestyle Party

Australian Greens
    Australian Greens SA
    The Greens NSW
    The Australian Greens—Victoria
    Queensland Greens
    The Greens (WA)

Australian Gruen Party
    The Macarthur Gruen Party

Australian Independents

Australian Labor Party
    Australian Labor Party (Northern Territory) Branch
    Australian Labor Party (NSW Branch)
    Australian Labor Party (Victorian Branch)
    Australian Labor Party (State of Queensland)
    Australian Labor Party (Western Australian Branch)
    Australian Labor Party (South Australian Branch)
    Australian Labor Party (Tasmanian Branch)
    Australian Labor Party (ACT Branch)
    Country Labor Party

Australian Liberty Alliance

Australian Motoring Enthusiast Party

Australian Progressive Alliance

Australian Progressives

Australian Protectionist Party

Australian Recreational Fishers Party

Australian Reform Party

Australian Sex Party

Australian Shooters Party

Australian Sovereignty Party

Australian Sports Party

Australian Stable Population Party

Australian Voice Party

Australian Women's Party

Australians Against Further Immigration

Australians Against Paedophiles Party

Australia's Indigenous Peoples Party

Bank Reform Party

Building Australia Party

Bullet Train for Australia

Call to Australia (Fred Nile) Group
    Call to Australia (Fred Nile) Group—NSW
    Call to Australia (Fred Nile) Group—Vic.
    Call to Australia (Fred Nile) Group—(Qld)
    Call to Australia (Fred Nile) Group—(WA)
    Call to Australia (Fred Nile) Group—(SA)
    Call to Australia (Fred Nile) Group—(Tas)
    Call to Australia (Fred Nile) Group—(ACT)
    Call to Australia (Fred Nile) Group—(NT)
    CTA Child Protection (Elaine Nile) Party

Carers Alliance

Christian Democratic Party (Fred Nile Group)
    Christian Democratic Party (Fred Nile Group)—NSW
    Christian Democratic Party (Fred Nile Group)—Vic
    Christian Democratic Party (Fred Nile Group)—Qld
    Christian Democratic Party (Fred Nile Group)—SA
    Christian Democratic Party (Fred Nile Group)—WA
    Christian Democratic Party (Fred Nile Group)—Tas
    Christian Democratic Party (Fred Nile Group)—ACT
    Christian Democratic Party (Fred Nile Group)—NT

Citizens Electoral Council Australia (NSW)

Citizens' Electoral Councils Group

Citizens' Electoral Councils Of Australia Group
    Citizens Electoral Council Of Australia

City Country Alliance

Climate Change Coalition

Coke in the Bubblers Party

Combined New Australia Party

Common Cause—No Aircraft Noise

Communist Alliance

Communist Party of Australia

Conservative Party of Australia

Conservatives for Climate and Environment Incorporated

Consumer Rights & No Tolls

Country Alliance

Country Liberals (Northern Territory)

CountryMinded

Curtin Labor Alliance

Deadly Serious Party of Australia

Defence and Ex-Services Party of Australia

Democratic Labor Party of Australia

Democratic Socialist Electoral League

Democratic Socialist Party

Derryn Hinch's Justice Party

Drug Law Reform Australia

Ex-Service, Service & Veterans Party

Family First Party

Family Law Reform Party

Future Party

Glenn Lazarus Team

Grey Power

Health Australia Party

Hear Our Voice

Helen Caldicott's—Our Common Future Party

Help End Marijuana Prohibition

Help End Marijuana Prohibition (HEMP) Party

Hope Party Australia

Independent EFF

Irina Dunn Environment Independents

Jacqui Lambie Network

Janet Powell Independents' Network

John Madigan's Manufacturing and Farming Party

Katter's Australian Party

Liberal Democratic Party

Liberal Party of Australia
    Liberal Party of Australia (NSW)
    Liberal Party of Australia (Victorian Division)
    Liberal Party of Australia—Queensland Division
    Liberal National Party of Queensland
    Liberal Party (WA Division) Inc.
    Liberal Party of Australia (SA Division)
    Liberal Party of Australia—Tasmanian Division
    Liberal Party of Australia—ACT Division

Liberals for Forests

Liberty and Democracy Party

Lower Excise Fuel and Beer Party

Mature Australia Party

National Country Party of Australia (WA)

National Party of Australia
    National Party of Australia—NSW
    National Party of Australia—Victoria
    National Party of Australia (Queensland)
    National Party of Australia—(WA)
    National Party of Australia (SA) Inc.
    National Party of Australia—Tasmania
    Young National Party of Australia

Natural Law Party

Natural Medicine Party

New Country Party

Nick Xenophon Group/Team

No Aircraft Noise

No Carbon Tax Climate Sceptics

No Goods and Services Tax Party

Non-Custodial Parents Party (Equal Parenting)

Northern Territory Country Liberal Party

Nuclear Disarmament Party

One Australia Movement

One Australia Party

One Nation

One Nation Western Australia

Online Direct Democracy (Empowering the People!)

Outdoor Recreation Party

Outdoor Recreation Party (Stop The Greens)

Palmer United Party

Pauline Hanson's One Nation
    Pauline Hanson's One Nation (NSW Division)

Pauline's United Australia Party

Pensioner and Citizen Initiated Referendum Alliance

Pensioner Party of Australia

Peter Andren Independent Group

Peter Breen—Reform the Legal System

Phil Cleary—Independent Australia

Pirate Party Australia

Progressive Labour Party

Queensland First

Rebuild Australia Party

Reclaim Australia: Reduce Immigration

Renewable Energy Party

Republican Party of Australia

Rex Connor (Snr) Labor Party

Rise Up Australia Party

Save the ADI Site Party

Science Party

Secular Party of Australia

Senator On-Line (Internet Voting Bills/Issues)

Seniors United NSW

Seniors United Party of Australia

Shooters and Fishers Party

Single Parents Party

Smokers Rights Party

Socialist Alliance

Socialist Equality Party

Socialist Party of Australia

Socialist Workers Party

Stop CSG Party

#Sustainable Australia

Tasmania First Party

Tasmania Senate Team

Tasmanian Independent Senator Brian Harradine Group

Taxi Operators Political Service (Oceania)

The 23 Million

The Aged and Disability Pensioners Party

The Arts Party

The Australian Ethnic Democrats

The Australian Mental Health Party

The Australian Recreation and Fishing Party

The Australian Shooters Party

The Climate Sceptics

The Confederate Action Party of Australia

The Federal Party of Australia

The Fishing Party

The Great Australians

The Greens
    ACT Green Democratic Alliance
    The ACT Greens
    Central Coast Green Party
    Cowper Greens
    Eastern Suburbs Greens
    Green Alliance Senate—New South Wales
    The Greens NSW
    Greens in Lowe
    Illawarra Greens
    Queensland Greens
    Richmond Green Alliance
    Richmond/Clarence Greens
    South Sydney Greens
    Sydney Greens
    Tasmanian Greens
    The Green Party South Australia

> The Greens (WA) Inc.
> The Victorian Green Alliance
> The Australian Greens—Victoria
> The Territory Green Party
> Western Australian Green Party
> Western Suburbs Greens

The Seniors

The Wikileaks Party

Torres United Party

Unite Australia Party

United Tasmania Group

Uniting Australia Party

Unity—Say No To Hanson

Vallentine Peace Group

Voluntary Euthanasia Party

VOTEFLUX.ORG | Upgrade Democracy!

Weekend Trading Party

What Women Want